Joanne —

With my heart-felt
gratitude for your wise
counsel, unflinching support,
and (most of all) enduring
friendship.

Ed

Power, Trade, and War

Power, Trade, and War

Edward D. Mansfield

PRINCETON UNIVERSITY PRESS

PRINCETON, NEW JERSEY

Library of Congress Cataloging-in-Publication Data

Mansfield, Edward D., 1962–
Power, trade, and war / Edward D. Mansfield.
p.   cm.
Includes bibliographical references and index.
ISBN 0-691-03288-2
1. International trade.   2. War—Economic aspects.   3. Power
(Social sciences)   4. International relations.   I. Title.
HF1379.M36   1994   382—dc20   93-13700

This book has been composed in Linotron Sabon

Princeton University Press books are printed on acid-free paper
and meet the guidelines for permanence and durability of the
Committee on Production Guidelines for Book Longevity of the
Council on Library Resources

Printed in the United States of America

1   3   5   7   9   10   8   6   4   2

To Liv

CONTENTS

LIST OF FIGURES

LIST OF TABLES

PREFACE

THIS BOOK examines the relationships among the distribution of power, international trade, and the onset of war. More specifically, a series of new findings are presented concerning: (1) the effects of the distribution of power and international trade on the onset of war; (2) the influence of the distribution of power, war, and international economic factors on the level of international trade; and (3) the factors that account for static and dynamic aspects of the distribution of power. Analyzing these topics is important because they underlie a variety of leading theories of international relations; and empirical tests of these relationships are central to resolving debates concerning the merits of many competing explanations of war, the international political economy, and structural change.

The relationships among power, trade, and war also bear heavily on at least three sets of more general theoretical topics. The first concerns the usefulness of systemic approaches, which have been the subject of considerable controversy among scholars of international relations. But despite the widespread debates concerning these approaches, few empirical analyses have explored the extent to which a systemic approach can be used to explain patterns of international relations. One purpose of this book is to provide such an analysis.

The second set of topics concerns which factors should be emphasized in systemic analyses of international relations. Among systemic approaches, neorealist, neomercantilist, liberal, and interdependence theories are especially influential; and each offers a different set of predictions about the nature and strength of the relationships among power, trade, and war. One reason why each type of theory continues to enjoy substantial popularity is that few empirical attempts have been made to compare the effects of variables emphasized by each of them. While it is clear that disagreements among them do not hinge only on the relationships among power, trade, and war, these relationships are central to the debates among these groups of explanations. A second purpose of this book is to shed new light on the ongoing debates among them.

The third set of topics concerns the nature of the relationships between systemic variables. Of particular importance are the relationships between the distribution of power and both the level of international trade and the incidence of war. Scholars of international relations typically posit that these relationships are monotonic: indeed some of the most influential theories of war and the international political economy are predicated on this argument. In this book I advance a different argument. I maintain that these relationships are nonmonotonic, and that many of the most persistent debates concerning the nature and strength of the effects of the distribution of power have stemmed in part from the lack of attention to the possibility that the distribution of power may have a nonmonotonic influence on trade and war.

Another general purpose of this book is to integrate the study of political conflict and war with the study of the international political economy. Empirical studies of war often give short shrift to economic factors; and studies of the international political economy often ignore the effects of security and war on trade. Yet there is no compelling theoretical reason to exclude variables of this sort in these analyses. In the final analysis, the strength and nature of the relationships between security and economics are empirical issues. One reason why many major issues remain unresolved is that empirical studies of war and trade generally fail to include the effects of both economic and political factors. In this book I attempt to include both and, where it is possible, to compare their effects.

. . .

In the course of writing this book I have accumulated many debts. My largest intellectual debt is owed to Joanne Gowa. She introduced me to many of the issues that this book addresses when I was a graduate student and has commented without complaint and to my great benefit on many drafts of this study. Her insights have improved this book substantially, and I am extremely grateful for her help. I also owe much to the other members of my dissertation committee, Frederick Frey and Avery Goldstein, each of whom helped me to shape many of the ideas in this book.

In addition, I would like to acknowledge the contributions of Marc Busch, William Domke, Robert Jervis, Jacek Kugler, David Lake, Lisa Martin, Brian Pollins, Bruce Russett, Randall Schweller, and David Spiro, each of whom read the entire manuscript and provided many valuable comments and suggestions. I would also like to thank David Baldwin, Jagdish Bhagwati, Thomas Christensen, Youssef Cohen, Eileen Crumm, Edwin Haefele, Stephen Krasner, Charles Kupchan, Jack Levy, Arvid Lukauskas, Timothy McKeown, Helen Milner, Patrick Morgan, Jack Nagel, John O'Rorke, Kenneth Oye, Randolph Siverson, and Jack Snyder for their comments on various portions of this book. The penultimate version of this manuscript was presented at Columbia University's Center for the Social Sciences. I am grateful to the participants in this seminar for their suggestions, and to Harrison White for inviting me to participate in the seminar. I am also indebted to the Columbia University Council on Research in the Humanities and Social Sciences for financial support. It has been my great pleasure to work with Malcolm DeBevoise on this project.

His editorial expertise and many useful suggestions have done much to improve this manuscript. Finally, I would like to thank Salvatore Pitruzzello, Bruce Snyder, and John Albert Snyder for their help preparing the figures in this book.

Portions of this book have appeared elsewhere, and I am grateful to the publishers of these materials for allowing me to use them. Portions of chapter 2 appeared in "The Distribution of Wars Over Time," *World Politics* 41, no. 1 (October 1988), pp. 21–51. Portions of chapter 3 appeared in "The Concentration of Capabilities and the Onset of War," *Journal of Conflict Resolution* 36, no. 1 (March 1992), pp. 3–24. Portions of chapter 5 appeared in "The Concentration of Capabilities and International Trade," *International Organization* 46, no. 3 (Summer 1992), pp. 731–64.

Finally, I owe more than I can gracefully express to my family. My parents, Edwin and Lucile Mansfield, have been a constant source of support, encouragement, and strength. The impending arrival of my daughter, Katherine Cecile Hamilton Mansfield, spurred the penultimate version of this book to its conclusion. My greatest debt is to my wife, Liv Holemans Mansfield. She has endured this project with extraordinary patience and grace. Without her support and understanding, this book could not have been completed. My greatest personal satisfaction in completing this book is dedicating it to her.

Power, Trade, and War

Chapter 1

INTRODUCTION

THE PURPOSE of this book is to examine the relationships among power, trade, and war. The specific questions that are addressed in this study have a long and rich tradition in the field of international relations. To what extent does the distribution of power influence the onset of war and patterns of international trade? If variations in the distribution of power account for patterns of war and trade, is it possible to explain why these variations occur? Do patterns of international trade help to explain the conditions under which wars begin; and is the effect of trade more or less salient than that of the distribution of power in this regard? To what extent does war impact patterns of international trade? Are political factors more or less important determinants of war and commerce than economic factors?

These questions continue to occupy the attention of scholars because, despite the enormous amount of attention that they have received, answers to them remain elusive. Moreover, they are important because they bear on a host of theoretical issues that are fundamental to the study of international relations. In particular, since these questions form the basis of many long-standing debates concerning the causes of war and the factors that influence international trade, they bear on the merits of some of the most influential explanations of the onset of war and the international political economy. These questions also address the extent to which international politics and international economics are related fields of inquiry, as well as the extent to which it is necessary to integrate the often-separated fields of conflict studies and international political economy.

In addition, these questions bear on a series of controversies regarding systemic approaches to the study of international relations. The analysis in this book is cast at the systemic level of analysis. One purpose of this book is to examine the general usefulness of a systemic approach to these topics, and to evaluate the competing claims of some particular systemic approaches. More specifically, one central source of disagreement among systemic theorists concerns the degree to which structural and process-level factors explain patterns of global outcomes. This issue underlies the deep and long-standing divisions among realists, liberals, and interdependence theorists. Through an analysis of the relationships among power, trade, and war, I hope to shed new light on these debates.

In this book I argue that a systemic approach to the study of international relations is extremely useful. However, I also argue that the strength and nature of the relationships among power, trade, and war often differ considerably from those which leading systemic theories predict. These differences are particularly acute in the cases of those theories that emphasize the importance of the global distribution of power. Scholars have displayed an overwhelming tendency to define the global distribution of power solely in terms of the number of poles in the system. But I maintain that polarity is a less important feature of the distribution of power than these scholars assert. I also argue that the concentration of power is a fundamentally important feature of the distribution of power, whose influence on the onset of war and patterns of international trade is often more pronounced than that of polarity.

Scholars of international relations have also displayed an overwhelming tendency to posit monotonic relationships between the distribution of power and both the onset of war and patterns of international trade. I maintain that such claims are misleading. The relationships between the concentration of power and both of these outcomes are quadratic, rather than monotonic. Thus while the distribution of power is strongly related to both war and trade, the most salient feature of this distribution and the nature of its effect on these outcomes have been mischaracterized in many leading theories of international relations. As a result, the importance of the distribution of power in studies of these topics has often been systematically underestimated.

Since the concentration of power is strongly related to the onset of war and patterns of international trade, it is important to analyze its determinants and dynamics. This topic is central to debates concerning the determinants of structural change in the international system and the extent to which neorealists have been able to explain change of this sort. While neorealists have been roundly criticized for their inability to fashion such an explanation, the simple model of structural change that I advance is consistent with many neorealist theories and helps to explain changes in the concentration of power over time.

While much of the analysis in this book centers on the effects of the distribution of power, one key argument of this study is that other systemic factors are also centrally important influences on both war and trade. Of primary importance in this regard is the impact of international trade on the onset of war and the effects of war and economic factors on patterns of international trade. Many observers conclude that trade exerts little systematic influence on war, independent of the distribution of power. Others emphasize the effects of trade on war but pay little attention to the influence of the distribution of power. Contrary to these views, I argue that both the distribution of power and international trade exert strong impacts on the outbreak of war. Moreover, because analysts of war typically ignore the effects of trade, the explanatory power of systemic analyses of war is unnecessarily and substantially reduced.

Much interest also has been expressed in the effects of war and international economic factors on patterns of international trade. Many scholars posit that war and economic factors exert few systematic effects on trade, independent of the distribution of power. Others maintain that economic factors are the primary determinants of trade and largely ignore the effects of international politics. Contrary to these views, I maintain that in addition to the distribution of power, both war and international economic factors exert strong influences on patterns of international trade. I therefore conclude that debates concerning whether political or economic factors are the central causes of war and trade are miscast. Both types of factors are important; and rather than attempting to choose between them, scholars need to devote more attention to developing theories of international relations that integrate the effects of political and economic factors.

These arguments suggest a number of broader conclusions. First, contrary to the view of purely structural theories, ignoring the effects of all process-level factors serves to degrade the explanatory power of a systemic approach to war and trade. And contrary to many critics of structural theories, the distribution of power is an important influence on war and trade. As a result, more attention needs to be devoted to integrating the effects of structural and process-level factors in studies of international relations. Second, although studies of war often give short shrift to the effects of economic variables, and studies of trade often pay little attention to the effects of global security, neither tack is adequate. Analyzing either topic in a political or an economic vacuum is counterproductive. More generally, there is a need to more fully integrate studies of international politics and international economics, and studies of war and the international political economy.

In this chapter, I elaborate on these topics. I begin by discussing systemic approaches to the study of international relations, since this type of approach forms the basis of this study. The issue of structure, which is central to most systemic theories, is then analyzed. The remainder of this chapter provides an overview of the specific issues and hypotheses that I address in this book, and the argument that I advance.

A Systemic Approach to International Relations

Since one central purpose of this book is to evaluate a variety of systemic approaches to the study of international relations, very little attention will be devoted to the "first-image" effects of attributes of individuals, such as the nature and psychology of human beings, and the perceptions of decision makers on global outcomes. In addition, this study will not address the "second-image" effects of the political and economic attributes of states on war and trade. Instead the central focus of this study is on approaches to international relations that emphasize the global context in which nation-states exist. This strategy is adopted for a number of reasons. First, as Robert Keohane argues, "systemic theory is important because we must understand the context of action before we can understand the action itself" (1986:193). Second, systemic theories are generally more parsimonious than their first-image and second-image competitors (Waltz 1979; Gilpin 1981; Keohane 1984, 1986). Given this conceptual advantage, it is important to determine whether the explanatory power of systemic theories is sufficient to warrant substantial reliance on them. Third, some analysts maintain that theories operating at other levels of analysis have, in general, fared poorly in explaining patterns of international relations. Kenneth Waltz, for example, argues that

> [i]f the organization of units affects their behavior and their interactions, then one cannot predict outcomes or understand them merely by knowing the characteristics, purposes, and interactions of the system's units. The failure of reductionist [first- and second-image] theories . . . gives us some reason to believe that a systems approach is needed. When similarity of outcomes prevails despite changes in the agents that seem to produce them, one is led to suspect that analytic approaches will fail. (1979:39)

Taken together, these factors suggest that only after a careful evaluation of the extent to which systemic theories can explain patterns of global outcomes should we reject them in favor of first-image or second-image alternatives.

While many analysts subscribe to this view, there exists considerable controversy among them regarding the extent to which systemic theories do in fact provide adequate explanations of patterns of global outcomes. One reason why these debates persist is that fully articulated systemic explanations are relatively new. As a result, "few studies examine international violence at the systemic level compared to the number of studies at the nation-state level" (Zinnes 1980: 351); and, until recently, the same was true of research on the political economy of trade. Additional research needs to be completed in order to determine whether systemic factors account for variations in international relations. The analysis of the relationships among power, trade, and war in this book will provide additional findings concerning this issue.

Structure and Process in the International System

Among scholars who agree that a systemic approach is useful, at least two sources of disagreement exist. One source of disagreement concerns the relative salience of structural and process-level factors on global outcomes. Another source of disagreement concerns the nature of structural and process-level effects on international outcomes. The analysis conducted in this book bears on both of these fundamental topics.

Systemic theorists commonly hold that "[a] system is composed of a structure and of interacting units" (Waltz 1979:79). There is also considerable agreement that the primary units in the global arena are nation-states, which can be treated as unitary, rational actors and whose interests are given by assumption. Interactions among states are considered systemic "processes." Central to many systemic theories is the argument that the structure of the system should be defined in terms of its ordering principle (anarchy or hierarchy), the functional differentiation among states (homogeneous or heterogenous), and the distribution of power among states (Waltz 1979; Gilpin 1981). Scholars who advance this argument often maintain that since the system has been characterized by anarchy, and since states have been functionally homogeneous over time, structural variations are influenced by changes in the distribution of power among the leading states in the system.

Most structural theories of international relations therefore attribute primary importance to the effects of anarchy and variations in the distribution of power on patterns of global outcomes. Most prominent among theories of this sort are neorealist explanations, although a variety of other theories are grounded on similar arguments. One central source of disagreement concerning systemic theories revolves around the extent to which the structure of the international system provides the most salient explanation for patterns of international relations.

Much of the popularity that neorealism (and other structural approaches) enjoys emanates from its elegance. Explanations of this sort suggest that we need to focus on only one variable—the distribution of power—to explain patterns of many aspects of international relations. They generally assert that the influence of systemic factors other than structure can either be endogenized, since the distribution of power explains variations in these factors, or ignored, since they are unrelated in any systematic fashion to patterns of global outcomes.

This approach, however, has come under attack from a number of sources.[1] Of central importance for the purposes of this study is the charge

[1] Many critics agree that systemic factors are central to the study of international relations, but challenge the underlying assumptions of neorealist theories. For example, Bull (1977), Ruggie (1983), and Milner (1991) argue that the system is not anarchic to the extent, and in the sense, that neorealists posit. Others maintain that states are not the only central actors in international relations (Keohane and Nye 1977), that states cannot be treated as either unitary or rational (Allison 1971), and that the interests of states are not exogenously given (Wendt 1992). Further, Ruggie (1983) argues that categorizing states as functionally homogeneous is

that systemic influences are not limited to those related to the distribution
of power. As Joseph Nye observes, "At the systemic level, in addition to the
distribution of power, states experience constraints and opportunities because of changes in levels of world economic activity, technological innovation, shifts in patterns of transnational interactions, and alterations in
international norms and institutions" (1988:250). This line of argument
challenges the assumption inherent in neorealist, and a number of other
structural, explanations that the distribution of power is the fundamental
determinant of variations in international relations. It suggests that, in
addition to (or, for some scholars, instead of) the distribution of power,
certain process-level variables—that is, variables that are systemic but not
structural—are also of considerable importance in this regard.

It is this final challenge to neorealism on which I focus in much of the
present study. The extent to which process-level variables are said to supplement or dominate the effects of structural variables differs among critics
of neorealism and other purely structural approaches. But they are all of the
opinion that the elegance of structural theories is gained at the expense of
explanatory power, and that adequate explanations of patterns of certain
aspects of international relations cannot be developed in the absence of (at
least some) reference to process-level variables.

These debates hinge largely on a series of empirical questions regarding
the respective salience of structural and process-level factors in accounting
for patterns of global outcomes. It is clear that both structural and process-
level influences could alter the calculus of the rational actors that structural
explanations view as comprising the international system. It is also clear
that process-level influences need not be epiphenomenal of the system's
structure. Indeed they may be more important determinants of international relations than the distribution of power. In the final analysis, these
are empirical issues. The deep divisions among systemic theorists concerning these issues have persisted because few empirical attempts have been
made to assess the influence of one type of systemic factor, holding constant the effect of the other.

In this study, a series of quantitative analyses are conducted that are
designed to resolve some of these issues. From this standpoint, this book's
focus on the relationships among power, trade, and war is important because many leading structural theories emphasize the importance of the
distribution of power in shaping patterns of the onset of war and aspects of
international trade. While these theories attach little importance to
process-level factors in this regard, some of their critics argue that trade
exerts a marked effect on war; and that war, as well as international eco-

---

problematic and is responsible for the inability of neorealists to explain systemic change. For
an excellent overview of these arguments, see Grieco (1988; 1990).

nomic factors, contributes to patterns of global trade. Despite the advantages of this research strategy, it is obvious that this analysis will ignore many process-level factors that might also influence war and trade. It is also obvious that debates concerning the importance of structural and process-level factors are not confined to analyses of war and trade. But war and trade are the subjects of many of the most influential systemic theories of international relations; and the process-level factors that are examined in this study are highlighted in many leading treatments of these topics. Hence, by examining the relationships among power, trade, and war, I hope to shed new light on debates concerning the emphasis that should be placed on structural and process-level factors in analyses of international relations.

In addition to disagreements over the importance of structure and process in accounting for global outcomes, systemic theorists differ in their views regarding the nature of the relationships between various systemic factors and global outcomes. Among scholars who agree that the distribution of power exerts a salient impact on international relations, fundamental debates persist regarding the manner in which the distribution of power is related to the onset of war and patterns of international trade. Similarly, among scholars who agree that process-level factors influence global outcomes, independent of the effects of the distribution of power, longstanding disagreements exist concerning, for example, the nature of the relationship between trade and the onset of war, and the nature of the influence of war and economic factors on trade.

Finally, among both adherents to, and critics of, structural approaches, there is considerable controversy regarding why changes occur in the distribution of power, and whether existing structural theories provide an adequate explanation of these changes.

The relationships among power, trade, and war bear on each of these controversies. In the face of the enormous amount of research that has been devoted to assessing the strength and nature of the relationships between systemic variables and global outcomes, it is remarkable that the debates discussed above remain unresolved. One reason why more progress has not been made on this front is that most empirical studies have not directly compared the effects of various structural and process-level factors or the explanatory power of various systemic theories. In this book, a series of empirical tests are conducted in order to assess the merits of many positions that have been expressed regarding these debates. I make no claim that the results of these tests offer the final word on these longstanding disputes: indeed no single study could hope to completely resolve them. But I believe that the results in this book shed new light on these disputes, and that this study's findings help to explain why they continue to persist.

Measuring the Distribution of Power

Central to many systemic analyses of international relations is the effect of the system's structure on patterns of global outcomes. As noted in the previous section, there is a fairly widespread consensus that the structure of the international system is defined by anarchy and the distribution of power. Since structural variations are caused by variations in the distribution of power, it is obvious that we need to be clear as to how the distribution of power should be defined and measured prior to any empirical analysis of its effects.

Any analysis of the distribution of power confronts two issues: (1) how should power be measured, and (2) which feature(s) of this distribution should be emphasized? Although the measurement of power remains the topic of considerable controversy, it has received a great deal of scholarly attention. Neorealists and a wide variety of other scholars typically rely on national capabilities to measure national power. There has been much debate concerning the merits of this approach, and the potential problems associated with using capabilities to measure power are widely documented (Lasswell and Kaplan 1950; Sprout and Sprout 1965; Frey 1971, 1986; Nagel 1975; Dahl 1976; Baldwin 1979, 1980; Keohane 1984, 1986). But despite the drawbacks of what James March (1966) refers to as a "basic-force" model, few alternatives to this approach currently exist for the study of international relations. Recognizing that capabilities are neither necessary nor sufficient for states to exercise power, this study will analyze and utilize capabilities as proxies for power. In addition to the lack of alternative indices that have been operationalized, this tack is taken because I am interested in testing structural theories on their own terms and because capabilities provide a useful first cut at measuring the power potential of states. Further, a variety of studies maintain that the widely used economic, demographic, and military capabilities that are analyzed in this study are important power resources for the purposes of waging wars and influencing trade flows.

Whereas much research has centered on the measurement of power, surprisingly little scholarly attention has been devoted to the issue of which aspect of this distribution should be emphasized in studies of international relations. In a great many studies, the global distribution of power is defined and measured in terms of polarity. It is therefore important to consider polarity in some depth.

Polarity

Most analysts of international relations characterize the distribution of power according to the number of "leading" major powers in the system.

In particular, they generally distinguish among systems characterized by a single preponderant state (hegemonic or unipolar), two dominant states (bipolar), or more than two dominant states (multipolar). Hence, scholars generally measure the structure of the system by *counting* the number of "particularly powerful" states.[2] There are, however, at least three sets of problems that this approach engenders (Mansfield 1993a).

First, this approach is subject to a variety of operational problems. One problem concerns the material bases of power: the number of poles may vary depending on which capabilities are used to measure polarity. For example, the number of poles based on military capabilities may differ from the number of poles based on economic capabilities. Another problem concerns the lack of a rigorous counting principle that can be used to distinguish polar powers from other states (Wagner 1993).[3] This not only hampers our ability to define the number of poles in any given system, it also undermines attempts to determine when changes occur in the number of poles (Knorr 1966). Many analysts seem to agree with Waltz's assertion that "[t]he question [of who is a polar power] is an empirical one, and common sense can answer it" (1979:131). But marked differences exist among scholars of international relations in their evaluations of whether various periods during the nineteenth and twentieth centuries were characterized by hegemony, bipolarity, multipolarity, or some combination of these structural conditions (Gilpin 1975, 1981, 1987; Snyder and Diesing 1977; Modelski 1978; Waltz 1979; Organski and Kugler 1980; Wallerstein 1983; Levy 1985a; Thompson 1988). This suggests that defining and measuring the number of poles in the system is not a matter of common sense, and that one reason why previous analyses have arrived at such divergent conclusions regarding the effects of the structure of the global system is that they have yet to agree on how polarity should be measured. In order to determine the extent to which this is the case, a variety of different

[2] In addition to those who measure polarity by counting poles, others define polarity in terms of coalitions of states (Singer and Small 1968; Haas 1970; Wallace 1973; Bueno de Mesquita 1975; Stoll and Champion 1985; Bueno de Mesquita and Lalman 1988). Underlying the latter definition of polarity is the view that alliances are behaviorally analogous to states. This view has come under considerable criticism, and scholars commonly distinguish between *polarization* (that is, the number and strength of alliance blocs) and *polarity* (that is, the number of preponderant states) (Nogee 1975; Jackson 1977; Rapkin and Thompson with Christopherson 1979; Waltz 1979; Wayman 1984; Hart 1985; Levy 1985a; Thompson 1988; Wayman and Morgan 1990; Wagner 1993). Since structural theories almost always define the structure of the system in terms of polarity, rather than polarization, this is the tack that is taken in this study.

[3] See Rapkin and Thompson with Christopherson (1979), Wayman (1984), and Thompson (1988) for some recent attempts to devise rigorous measures of polarity. See also Bueno de Mesquita (1975) for a measure of polarity that is based on coalitions of states, rather than the number of polar powers in the system.

classifications of polarity (that will be presented in chapter 2) are analyzed
in this study.

Second, the use of polarity is incompatible with the microeconomic
foundations of neorealism. Neorealists generally rely on analogies between
the structure of markets and industries, and that of the international system (Waltz 1979; Gilpin 1981:20–21, 85; see also Russett 1968a:131–
37).[4] They argue that, like the effects that the number and size distribution
of firms in a given industry exert on the behavior of firms in that industry,
the number of—and the distribution of capabilities among the—major
powers influence the behavior of states in the international system.

While this provides a useful framework for explaining patterns of international relations, it does not justify the use of polarity to measure the
system's structure. Neorealists often assert that polarity is the most appropriate measure of the structure of the international system because "[m]ar-
ket structure is defined by counting firms; international-political structure,
by counting states" (Waltz 1979:98–99). Market structure, however, is not
defined solely by counting firms. In addition to the number of firms in an
industry, "when . . . firms are unequally sized in a given way, the extent of
that inequality will also affect performance. . . . [Thus any measure of
market structure] should be a one-dimensional measure, incorporating the
two relevant aspects of industry structure, namely *firm numbers . . . and
size inequalities*" (Waterson 1984:166–67, emphasis added; Hannah and
Kay 1977; Scherer 1979, chap. 3; Jacquemin 1987). This suggests that,
rather than counting the number of poles in the system, a measure of the
distribution of power is needed that incorporates both the number of major
powers and the relative inequality of power among them. But the only
dimension of inequality that polarity captures is that *between* polar and
nonpolar powers; it fails to capture the inequality *among* the poles or
nonpolar major powers (Levy 1985a; Thompson 1988; Schweller 1993).

Finally, the fact that measuring the system's structure solely in terms of
the number of poles is inconsistent with measures of industry and market
structure need not pose a serious problem if the aspects of the distribution
of power that polarity captures are central to theories of international
relations and if the aspects of this distribution that it fails to capture are of
little importance. This, however, is not the case. The use of polarity requires
analysts to assume that: (1) nonpolar major powers are unimportant for
the purposes of determining the international distribution of power; and
(2) polar powers are either equally powerful or asymmetries of power
among them are of little consequence for explaining patterns of interna-

---

[4] It should be pointed out that not all analysts rely equally heavily on analogies of this sort.
For example, Gilpin qualifies the usefulness of the analogy between microeconomics and
international politics more than does Waltz.

tional outcomes (Thompson 1988:204). As the empirical results in this book demonstrate, both of these assumptions limit substantially the ability of structural theories to explain patterns of war and trade. And, as I argue in chapters 3 and 5, both of these assumptions are at odds with a variety of leading theories concerning the effects of the distribution of power on patterns of war and trade, as well as the hypotheses that I advance in this book.

This discussion is not meant to imply that polarity provides no useful information concerning the distribution of power. Nor do I argue that theories of international relations place no emphasis on this aspect of the distribution of power. It is clear that theories concerning the effects of polarity occupy a prominent position in the study of international relations—and considerable attention will therefore be devoted to analyzing the effects of polarity on patterns of war and trade.

But I do argue that this variable is fraught with both conceptual and empirical limitations, and that these limitations are especially severe when (as is often the case) scholars rely solely on the number of poles to measure the international distribution of power. A wide variety of studies posit that power inequalities among states are fundamentally important influences on international relations: polarity, as it is conventionally defined, provides an extremely crude and narrow description of global inequalities of power. I also argue that another feature of the distribution of power— concentration—provides much important information about the system's structure, and that the usefulness of concentration has not been sufficiently appreciated.

Concentration

In contrast to polarity, concentration reflects both the number of major powers and the relative inequality of power among them. In particular, I demonstrate in chapter 3 that concentration can be expressed as the coefficient of variation of the proportion of the aggregate major-power capabilities possessed by each major power divided by the square root of one less than the number of major powers. Concentration is discussed at length in chapters 3 and 5; but for present purposes, it is useful to provide a brief overview of this feature of the distribution of power, since it is central to much of the argument advanced in this study.

While polarity is a discrete variable (that is often presented as a dichotomous variable), concentration is a continuous variable that takes on values ranging from zero to one. Moreover, while polarity provides a qualitative measure of the inequality of power between all poles and the remaining states in the system, concentration captures the aggregate inequality among all the major (polar and nonpolar) powers in the system. A system in which capabilities are uniformly distributed among the major powers is clearly one that is characterized by the absence of power inequalities among these states. Under these circumstances, power is maximally dispersed and the level of concentration is minimized. A system in which capabilities are monopolized by a single state is clearly one that is characterized by the most extreme inequality of power. Under these circumstances, the level of concentration is maximized.

Although it is analytically useful to describe the characteristics of those systems in which concentration takes on its highest and lowest possible values, neither of these types of systems has existed during the period analyzed in this book. Instead the analysis in this book centers on the effects of relatively low, relatively high, and intermediate levels of concentration. A more precise and rigorous discussion of these structural conditions is presented in chapters 3 and 5; but since many of the hypotheses advanced in this book refer to relatively low, relatively high, and intermediate levels of concentration, it is important at the outset of this study to provide some illustrative historical examples of these types of systems and the differences among them.

Relatively low levels of concentration have obtained during periods in which power inequalities among the major powers have not been very pronounced. For example, the Concert of Europe era and the last quarter of the nineteenth century were periods in which the level of concentration was relatively low (Singer, Bremer, and Stuckey 1972). Referring to the former period, Gordon Craig and Alexander George point out that because decision makers at the time believed that "the eighteenth century . . . had been too loosely defined and too full of dangerous imbalances," they went to considerable effort to create a system in which capabilities were more uniformly distributed among the major powers (1983:30). Referring to the latter period, F. H. Hinsley notes that the system was characterized by "the near-equality of its component states" (1963:249).

Relatively high levels of concentration have obtained during periods in which power inequalities among the major powers have been especially pronounced. For example, concentration attained its highest level during the nineteenth and twentieth centuries in 1946. At this time, the United States was markedly stronger than the Soviet Union; and both of these states were substantially stronger than either Great Britain or France, the two remaining major powers in the system, based on the data used in this book (Singer, Bremer, and Stuckey 1972).

Finally, intermediate levels of concentration have obtained during periods characterized by moderate imbalances of power among the major powers. For example, during the period immediately after the conclusion of the Concert of Europe system, David Thomson reports that the major powers in the system remained the same as those that had forged the settlement in 1815. But "because of the economic transformations since 1815 and the events of 1848–50, the relative importance [and power] of these five powers had changed and was still changing" (1981:217). The upshot of these changes was that the relatively low levels of concentration that obtained during the Concert of Europe gave way to intermediate levels of concentration, which were marked by more pronounced inequalities of power among the leading actors.

The preceding discussion points to a number of reasons why it is important to analyze concentration in this book, rather than adopting the standard practice among scholars of international relations of defining the global distribution of power solely in terms of the number of poles in the system. First, concentration and polarity measure different features of the distribution of power, and these variables need not be strongly related (Mansfield 1993a). For example, it was noted above that the level of concentration varied considerably during the nineteenth century. But a wide variety of analysts argue that the polarity of the system did not change during this century, although they disagree over the number of poles that existed (Gilpin 1975, 1981, 1987; Snyder and Diesing 1977; Modelski 1978; Waltz 1979; Levy 1985a; Mearsheimer 1990).

Second, since concentration measures both the number of major powers and the relative inequality of power among them, it is much closer than polarity to economists' measures of market structure discussed above. In fact, it is closely related to one of the most widely used indices of this sort, the Hirschman-Herfindahl index (Ray and Singer 1973; Taagepera and Ray 1977). Not only is the use of concentration consistent with the microeconomic bases of neorealism, its use is also consistent with the specific definitions of global structure advanced by neorealists. For example, Glenn Snyder and Paul Diesing argue that "the 'structure' of an international system is defined by the *number* of major actors and the *distribution of power and potential among them*" (1977:419; emphasis in original). Similarly, Robert Gilpin defines the system's structure in terms of "[t]he number of states and the distribution of capabilities among them" (1981:88; see also Mearsheimer 1990). Whereas concentration measures both the number of major powers and the distribution of power among them, polarity, as it is usually defined, does not measure either of these structural features; it captures only the number of polar major powers, and it provides no information concerning power inequalities among all these states (Mansfield 1993a).

These are both important reasons to analyze concentration in this study. However, as I argue in chapters 3 and 5, the central reason to do so is that the aspects of the distribution of power that concentration measures—and that polarity does not measure—are emphasized in many leading theories of the onset of war, patterns of international trade, and structural change, as well as in the explanations of these outcomes that are advanced in this book. Thus, contrary to those analysts who argue that concentration is a theoretically trivial variable and that theories of international relations focus solely on the number of poles (Waltz 1979:15), I maintain that concentration is a fundamentally important aspect of the distribution of power from both a conceptual and an empirical standpoint. Further, for the purposes of explaining the onset of war, patterns of international trade, and structural change, polarity is a considerably less salient feature of the distribution of power than is commonly asserted. Because the importance of concentration has not been sufficiently appreciated among scholars of international relations, and because the overwhelming tendency among them has been to define the system's structure exclusively in terms of the number of poles, they have tended to systematically underestimate the extent to which the structure of the system explains patterns of war and trade, as well as the extent to which it is possible to explain structural change in the global system within a neorealist framework. In the following section, a series of hypotheses are advanced concerning the effects of the distribution of power on patterns of war and trade that will be tested throughout this book.

The Effects of the Distribution of Power on War and Trade

Few topics in the field of international relations have attracted more attention and have led to more disagreements than the effects of the distribution of power on patterns of global outcomes. As noted earlier, this issue underlies many contemporary discussions of the usefulness of structural theories of international relations, as well as more specific analyses of the merits of realist and neorealist approaches. This topic also bears on debates among theorists who agree that the distribution of power exerts a salient effect on international relations, but disagree over the nature of this effect. Among the most important outcomes that structural theories seek to explain are the onset of international war and aspects of international trade.

In this section, some of the most influential views concerning the nature of the relationship between the distribution of power and these outcomes are reviewed. A series of hypotheses that call into question each of these views and that form the basis of much of my analysis of the distribution of power are then advanced. Almost all the leading explanations of war and trade lead us to expect a monotonic relationship between the distribution of power and patterns of these global outcomes. But I maintain that these relationships are nonmonotonic. More specifically, I posit that an inverted U-shaped relationship exists between the concentration of capabilities and the onset of major-power war; and that a U-shaped relationship exists between the concentration of capabilities and the level of international trade.

The Distribution of Power and the Onset of War

Realists of all stripes agree that wars occur because of the anarchic character of the international system. The absence of any supranational authority in the global arena compels states to ensure their own security, and war is one (although by no means the only)[5] means of attending to this imperative. While this line of argument may help to explain why wars occur, it provides no insights into why *patterns* exist in the onset of warfare, since anarchy has been a constant feature of the international system. If, as many scholars contend, "[a] central question for a structural theory is . . . [h]ow do changes of the system affect the expected frequency of war" (Waltz 1989:44), neorealists and other structural theorists must explain how the distribution of power is related to the outbreak of war, since (in their opinion) it is the only feature of the system's structure that has changed over time.

It is on this point that theories of the distribution of power and war diverge from one another. The most marked disjunction among them concerns whether systems in which power is approximately uniformly distributed give rise to the outbreak of more or fewer wars than systems in which the distribution of power is extremely skewed.

One view concerning the relationship between the distribution of power and the onset of war holds that major-power wars are less likely to occur when power is balanced among the major powers than when it is imbalanced. For example, Arnold Wolfers maintains that "from the point of view of preserving the peace . . . it may be a valid proposition that a balance of power placing restraint on every nation is more advantageous in the long run than the hegemony even of those deemed peace-loving at a given time" (1962:120). Similarly, Inis Claude argues that

> it [is] wholly proper to evaluate the balance of power system in terms of its effectiveness in producing such management of the power situation as is necessary to prevent war. . . . The world could do much worse than manage the power relations of states so as to keep the major contestants in a position of approximate equality. There is danger when power confronts power, but there is even greater danger when power confronts weakness. (1962:55, 62)

These explanations of war generally emphasize the deterrent role played by potential blocking coalitions. They posit that systems characterized by a

---

[5] States may also form alliances, engage in military buildups, or a series of other measures short of war to ensure their security (Waltz 1979; Walt 1987).

(relatively) uniform distribution of power give rise to the onset of few wars (relative to imbalanced systems), since a variety of potential coalitions exist, each of which is able to thwart aggression on the part of any state (or small group of states) (Toynbee 1954; Gulick 1955; Herz 1959; Claude 1962; Wright 1965; Morgenthau and Thompson 1985). States have an incentive to block the aggressor(s) in order to avert the possibility that victory on its part will undermine their security. Under these circumstances, the expected costs of initiating a war are likely to exceed the expected benefits of doing so; and this is expected to enhance deterrence. Wars involving major powers, according to this variant of balance-of-power theory, are the products of power inequalities among the leading states in the system. They are one of the principal instruments that are used to "repel a bid for hegemony" and to restore a relatively uniform distribution of power among the major powers (Claude 1962:59; Toynbee 1954; Wolfers 1962; Wright 1965).[6]

A second view of the relationship between the distribution of power and war holds that wars occur most frequently when power is uniformly distributed among the major powers. Power preponderance theorists often argue that this condition tempts states to wage wars before any imbalance emerges that undermines their relative power positions. Wars involving major powers, in the opinion of power preponderance theorists, occur least frequently when this distribution is very highly skewed (Organski 1958; Modelski 1978; Organski and Kugler 1980; Gilpin 1981; Thompson 1983a, 1988; Väyrynen 1983; Kennedy 1987; Doran 1991). Under these circumstances, potential aggressors cannot hope to topple a preponderant state and the dominant state(s) has little incentive to wage war against a smaller state, since it can attain its objectives through coercion and other measures short of armed conflict. Further, wars between smaller states may begin less frequently under these conditions if the largest state pacifies smaller antagonists in order to avert the possibility that it will be dragged into the fray, thus expanding the scope of the war.

Many power preponderance theories emphasize the dynamics of power transitions as mechanisms that account for major wars (see especially Organski 1958; Organski and Kugler 1980; Gilpin 1981; Kennedy 1987). Although they offer different underlying reasons for these transitions, power preponderance theorists often suggest that both the existence of, and shifts toward, an approximately uniform distribution of power increase the likelihood of major-power war.[7]

---

[6] For excellent reviews of this literature, see Siverson and Sullivan (1983) and Levy (1985b; 1989).

[7] Some power transition theorists suggest that it is the interaction between the existence of, and shifts toward, a uniform distribution of power that gives rise to major-power wars. On this point, see Organski and Kugler (1980) and Levy (1989).

Despite the voluminous literature on balance-of-power and power preponderance theories, and the myriad tests of these competing claims, the
view is widely shared that previous studies of this topic have yielded a set of
divergent and inconclusive results (Garnham 1985; Vasquez 1987; Levy
1989). In this study, I argue that underlying the inconclusive nature of these
results have been differences regarding how both war and the distribution
of power have been and should be defined and measured, and the nature of
the relationship between the distribution of power and the onset of war.

One source of variation among previous studies of the relationship between the distribution of power and the onset of war is due to differences in
what these analyses seek to explain. Since they have relied on different data
sets of war, and since it is clear that variations in their conclusions might be
due to variations in the definition and coding of war, the effects of the
distribution of power (as well as other systemic factors) on a variety of
different data sets of war (presented in chapter 2) will be examined. Further, the effects of the distribution of power (and other systemic factors) on
various types of war will be analyzed. In particular, while systemic theories
generally seek to explain the onset of major-power wars, I argue that the
distribution of power (and other systemic factors) might also influence the
onset of all interstate wars.

In addition to analyzing various types and data sets of war, I will examine a number of different features of the distribution of power. Previous
analyses of the distribution of power and war have focused on both polarity
(Rosecrance 1963, 1966; Deutsch and Singer 1964; Waltz 1964; Modelski
1978; Organski and Kugler 1980; Gilpin 1981; Väyrynen 1983; Wayman
1984; Levy 1985a; Midlarsky 1988; Thompson 1988; Spiezo 1990; Hopf
1991) and concentration (Singer, Bremer, and Stuckey 1972; Cannizzo
1978; Bueno de Mesquita 1981a; Maoz 1982; Thompson 1983a; Wayman 1984; Stoll and Champion 1985; Bueno de Mesquita and Lalman
1988, 1992; Modelski and Thompson 1988). But very few attempts have
been made to examine simultaneously the effects of both of these features of
the distribution of power on war in a single, more inclusive analysis. The
differences that were discussed above between polarity and concentration,
as well as those among scholars regarding the number of poles which
existed during much of the nineteenth and twentieth centuries, may go a
long way toward explaining why previous studies of this topic have arrived
at such divergent conclusions. In chapters 2, 3, and 4, the extent to which
this is the case is examined.

While many systemic theorists agree that the number of poles should be
related to the onset of major-power war, the same cannot be said of concentration. As noted above, some analysts doubt that concentration is a conceptually useful variable (Duvall 1976; Waltz 1979). One of the central
arguments of this study, however, is that the importance of concentration

has not been fully appreciated in studies of international relations. In my view, concentration provides a more comprehensive measure of power inequalities among the major powers than does the number of poles; and this is important because inequalities of power among the major powers are emphasized in a wide variety of both balance-of-power and power preponderance theories, as well as in the hypothesis that I advance in the following section.

An Inverted U-Shaped Relationship Between Concentration and Major-Power War

In this book, I argue that the nature of the relationship between concentration and the onset of major-power war differs from that proposed by both balance-of-power and power preponderance explanations. On the one hand, balance-of-power theories suggest that this relationship is monotonic and direct: as the distribution of power becomes progressively imbalanced, the frequency of war is expected to increase. On the other hand, power preponderance theories imply that this relationship is monotonic and inverse: as the distribution of power becomes progressively more uniform, the frequency of war is expected to increase.

But rather than being monotonic, I hypothesize that the relationship between the concentration of capabilities and the incidence of major-power war has an inverted U-shape (like that which is shown on the right in figure 1.1): in other words, that both the highest and lowest levels of concentration give rise to the lowest incidence of major-power warfare, while intermediate levels of concentration give rise to the highest incidence of such warfare. The fact that previous studies have not examined this hypothesis suggests another reason why they have yielded such inconclu-

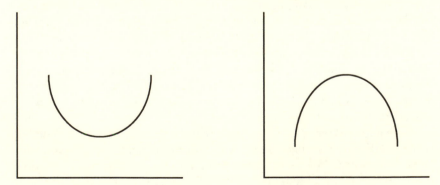

FIG. 1.1. Hypothetical U-Shaped and Inverted U-Shaped Relationships

sive and contradictory findings: these analyses have been designed primarily to test monotonic explanations of war, while the actual relationship between the distribution of power and the onset of war is nonmonotonic.

Consistent with the assumption advanced in many analyses that states can be treated as unitary, rational actors (Bueno de Mesquita 1981b; Gilpin 1981), I assume that, in deciding whether or not to initiate a war, a state compares the expected improvement in its relative position in the international system that would result from waging war with the expected costs associated with doing so. When capabilities are distributed (approximately) uniformly among the major powers, each potential aggressor (or small group of aggressors) faces the prospect of a number of potential coalitions of states forming to thwart it. This is likely to raise the expected costs of initiating a war, thus deterring states from doing so.

However, when concentration is at an intermediate level, the number of potential blocking coalitions is reduced, thereby reducing the expected costs of war. Further, under these circumstances, a large major power may determine that waging a successful military campaign against a smaller major power (or an important minor power) will be completed quickly and will improve its relative position in the international system. It is also possible that smaller states will band together and launch a war as a means to redress the disparity between them and a larger state (or group of states) if they determine that, left unchecked, their positions vis-à-vis the larger state are likely to further deteriorate.

When the system is highly concentrated, smaller states are likely to be deterred from attacking larger states because the expected costs of doing so will be substantial. Further, larger states have an incentive to manage and limit political conflicts because they can achieve their objectives through measures short of war. It is also expected that larger major powers will be deterred from attacking one another since the relative equality of capabilities among them will engender potentially high costs of initiating war.

This hypothesis will be developed in more detail in chapter 3, where the first tests of it also will be conducted. Consistent with this hypothesis, the results in chapters 3 and 4 indicate that there is considerable evidence of an inverted U-shaped relationship between the level of concentration and the incidence of major-power war.

The Distribution of Power and International Trade

Analyses of the distribution of power hold a prominent place in the study of the international political economy, as well as in the study of war. Indeed the impact of power on trade relations has long been of interest to scholars of international relations. For centuries mercantilists have stressed the fundamental importance of this relationship (Viner 1948). Further, as Albert

Hirschman notes at the outset of his seminal treatment of the effects of trade relations on power relations, "the opposite line of causation also exists and may even have had a greater historical importance: the question of how a given distribution of power influences trade relations" ([1945] 1980:13).

At the forefront of recent research in this area has been the issue of whether a single preponderant state is necessary for the coordination of the international economy. Hegemonic stability theorists argue that this is the case (Kindleberger 1973, 1981; Gilpin 1975, 1981, 1987; Krasner 1976; Lake 1988). Central to some variants of this theory is the argument that the establishment and maintenance of a liberal economic order is fraught with collective action problems. Because they view hegemonic systems as analogous to privileged groups, and because privileged groups are ones in which disproportionate amounts of collective goods will be provided (Olson 1971:49–50), these scholars maintain that hegemony is a necessary (though it need not be a sufficient) condition for a liberal economic system to obtain. Though they have not arrived at a consensus regarding either how much emphasis to place on the provision of collective goods in the international arena or why hegemons provide collective goods,[8] hegemonic stability theorists agree that the preponderant power of Great Britain and the United States, respectively, was the central cause of the relatively liberal economic systems that characterized much of the nineteenth century and the period after the conclusion of World War II.[9] They also agree that the inability of Great Britain to provide global leadership and the unwillingness of the United States to do so helped to set the stage for the Great Depression of the 1930s.

In the past decade, attacks have been leveled against hegemonic stability theory from a wide variety of quarters. Based on the logic of collective action, one central criticism is that this theory ignores the possibility that small, in addition to privileged, groups will be able to provide collective goods. As such, international economic coordination may be possible if there exist a few (approximately) equally sized states, each of which is interested in the creation and/or maintenance of a liberal economic regime (Keohane 1984; Lipson 1984; Axelrod and Keohane 1985; Oye 1985).

Other critics of this approach reject the notion that collective goods exist in the international political economy, because "goods" such as a free trade regime fail to meet the criterion of nonexcludability (Conybeare

---

[8] Kindleberger (1973; 1981), for example, implies that hegemons provide collective goods for altruistic reasons, while Gilpin (1975; 1981; 1987), Krasner (1976), and Lake (1988) argue that they do so out of self-interest.

[9] A related argument is advanced by Spiro (forthcoming), who emphasizes variations in the nature of power that a hegemon exercises as its position changes relative to the remaining states in the system.

1984; Russett 1985; Snidal 1985a). Further, some analysts argue that hegemons have an economic incentive to depart from liberal trade policies, since states with sufficient market power to influence world prices can improve their terms of trade by imposing an optimal tariff (Conybeare 1984, 1987). This suggests that the existence of a hegemon is related to whether or not the trading system is open or closed, but that, contrary to the predictions of hegemonic stability theory, this structural condition will generate closure rather than openness in trade.

One purpose of this book is to test these competing claims. To this end, the effects of hegemony on patterns of international trade are examined in chapter 5. Like the analysis of war in this study, the effects of a number of classifications of hegemony on trade will be assessed in order to determine whether the definition and measurement of hegemony influences this relationship. In addition, the effects of concentration on trade will also be analyzed. Unlike studies of war, virtually no research has been conducted on the effects of concentration in systemic studies of the international political economy (McKeown 1991). As in the case of theories of the distribution of power and war, however, theories of the international political economy that emphasize the effects of the distribution of power often highlight factors that are measured by concentration, but not by hegemony (as it is typically measured). In chapter 5, I demonstrate why this is the case. I also argue that focusing on the effects of concentration allows us to test in a preliminary fashion some of the competing claims of hegemonic stability theorists and their critics.

A U-Shaped Relationship Between Concentration and International Trade

The argument of the present study is that, just as the structural theories of war discussed above are incomplete, so too none of the positions discussed in the previous section fully captures the relationship between the distribution of power and international trade. Each of these positions posits a monotonic relationship between some feature of the distribution of power and international economic outcomes. However, I hypothesize that the relationship between the concentration of capabilities and the level of international trade is U-shaped (like that which is shown on the left in figure 1.1): in other words, that both the highest and lowest levels of concentration give rise to the highest levels of global trade, while intermediate levels of concentration give rise to the lowest levels of such trade.

Underlying this hypothesis is the assumption that the capabilities that are used to measure concentration can be viewed as rough proxies for a state's market power. John Conybeare (1984; 1987) argues that when market power is dispersed (and hence concentration is at a low level) tariff levels will be relatively low, since no state has sufficient influence over its terms of trade to gain economically from the imposition of an optimal tariff. To the extent that tariff and trade levels are inversely related, high levels of trade are expected to obtain under these conditions. As the level of concentration increases, so too does the disparity among major powers in the system. Large states are more likely to be able to use optimal protection to their advantage. All other things being equal, this should depress the level of international commerce.

However, beyond some level of concentration at which the level of global trade is minimized, I hypothesize that increases in concentration will tend to produce higher levels of commerce. Joanne Gowa (1989a; 1989b) suggests that a rational, nonmyopic state with substantial market power may forgo the use of an optimal tariff in order to maintain its monopoly power in the international economy, as well as for political reasons. To the extent that this is the case, the level of global protectionism may be lowest (and hence the level of trade may be greatest) both when concentration is lowest *and* highest. And the level of global commerce may be minimized when concentration lies somewhere between its highest and lowest levels.

Here, as in my analysis of war, my analysis of the effects of the distribution of power will center on both polarity and concentration. While the former has been the subject of much interest, the latter has received almost no attention in studies of the international political economy. As noted above, this is unfortunate because the use of concentration is consistent with the general framework of existing structural theories, and the aspects of the distribution of power that it measures (and that polarity does not measure) are emphasized in many leading explanations of trade, as well as the hypothesis that I advance. Moreover, I maintain that, like structural theories of war, the underlying relationship between the distribution of power and trade is misspecified by a wide variety of leading explanations of the international political economy. These factors, in turn, go a long way toward accounting for the inconclusive and contradictory conclusions arrived at by many previous studies of the effects of the distribution of power on patterns of global commerce.

This hypothesis is further developed in chapter 5, where the first tests of it are conducted. Consistent with this hypothesis, the results in chapter 5 indicate that there is substantial evidence of a U-shaped relationship between the level of concentration and the level of international trade.

PROCESS-LEVEL EFFECTS ON WAR AND TRADE

As noted at the outset of this chapter, one purpose of this book is to examine the relative importance of structural and process-level factors on the onset of war and international trade flows. Inherent in structural theories is the view that: (1) process-level variables have no strong and system-atic effects on patterns of international relations; and (2) whatever system-atic effects process-level factors do have on patterns of global outcomes are due to the influence of the structure of the system on both the process-level variables and the particular outcome in question. Thus while they do not dismiss entirely the importance of process-level factors, neorealists and others do regard them as considerably less important influences on pat-terns of war and trade than the distribution of power.

In the final analysis, the relative importance of structural and process-level variables is an empirical question, but this question has not been addressed fully to date. Features of the international system other than the distribution of power obviously *could* constrain, or pose opportunities for, states that help to explain patterns of the outbreak of war or patterns of trade. It is clear that assessing these claims entails an analysis of the effects of process-level factors, holding constant the effects of structural influ-ences. One purpose of this book is to conduct a series of analyses bearing on this issue.

International Trade and War

For the purposes of explaining patterns of warfare, the process-level vari-ables that I examine are (primarily) features of the international economy. Among these international economic factors are Kondratieff cycles, short-term fluctuations in the business cycle, and aspects of international trade. Primary attention, however, is focused on the effects of trade.

While the effects of trade on war bear on a series of contemporary theoretical debates, interest in this topic is far from new. As Gilpin points out,

> Thucydides' *History* can be read as an examination of the impact of a pro-found commercial revolution on a relatively static international political sys-tem. The expansion of trade, the monetization of traditional agrarian econ-omies, and the rise of new commercial powers (especially Athens and Corinth), as he tells us, transformed fifth-century Greek international politics and laid the basis for the great war that eviscerated Greek civilization. (1986:308; 1989)

More recently, the strength and nature of the effects of trade on war has been a persistent source of disagreement among liberals, (neo)mercantil-ists, interdependence theorists, (neo)realists, and others.

Many scholars seem to doubt that any systematic association exists between trade and war (Kahler 1979–80; Wilkinson 1980; Buzan 1984; Gaddis 1986; Gilpin 1987; Mearsheimer 1990; Jervis 1991–92). This position is characteristic of, but by no means limited to, neorealists. The events that preceded World Wars I and II are often presented as evidence to support this argument: trade was expanding among future antagonists until the first shots were fired in 1914; and trade was depressed among future antagonists prior to the onset of World War II. It may be, however, that commerce is related in a systematic manner to some larger sample of wars, but that one of these events is anomolous. Commercial liberals and interdependence theorists suggest that World War I was the anomaly. They maintain that, in general, an inverse relationship exists between the density of commercial flows and the onset of war (Keynes [1935] 1964; Mitrany 1975; Keohane and Nye 1977, 1987; Rosecrance 1986; Nye 1988; Mueller 1989). Mercantilists and neomercantilists, on the other hand, imply that the conditions surrounding World War II were exceptional. They suggest that, on average, a direct relationship exists between the level of trade and the outbreak of war (Viner 1948; Waltz 1970).

Although the relationship between trade and war has been emphasized in numerous theoretical studies, very little empirical research has been conducted on this topic; and none of this research has been cast at the systemic level of analysis. Indeed scholars often lament the fact that "[t]here has been no convincing test of . . . hypotheses regarding [trade and] the causes of war" (Levy 1989:261). In chapters 2 and 4, the first statistical tests of these hypotheses concerning the effects of trade on war at the level of the international system will be conducted. These results will inform two related issues in the field of international relations. First, by examining the effects of a number of aspects of global trade on a variety of different types of wars, this study will provide some initial findings concerning the strength and nature of the relationship between commerce and war. This issue is clearly central to the study of war. It is also fundamental to the study of the international political economy since, as Gilpin argues, the effect of economic relations on political conflict is one topic "that pervade[s] the historic controversies in the field of international political economy" (1987:12).

Second, in addition to evaluating the effects of commerce on war, the influences on war of both trade and the distribution of power will be compared. This analysis will therefore provide some preliminary evidence bearing on the relative importance of structural and process-level impacts on the onset of war. These results will also inform debates concerning the relationships between international political and economic factors. Comparisons of these types of variables seldom have been pursued in previous studies of war. But they are important because these comparisons may help to resolve some of the most persistent and significant disagreements among scholars of international relations.

The argument of this study is that certain aspects of trade exert an important influence on patterns of war. More specifically, I maintain that the level of international trade is inversely related to the probability of the onset of a wide variety of types of wars, and that this probably reflects the fact that the expected costs of war are greater when trade levels are higher, since the possibility that political conflict will stem the flow of commerce increases the trade-related opportunity costs of war. Moreover, the effects of trade on war complement the effects of the distribution of power. Both aspects of the international system serve to influence the cost-benefit calculus of policymakers regarding decisions to engage in warfare. But contrary to the claims of many realists, the effects of trade on war are not epiphenomenal of the distribution of power; and contrary to the assertions of many liberals, high levels of trade do not serve as a more salient deterrent than do certain configurations of the distribution of power. The results in chapter 4 bear out these arguments; and they indicate that, as Robert Keohane and Joseph Nye (1977; 1987) suggest, both the distribution of power and international trade help to shape patterns of international war.

The International Economy, War, and Trade

Like theories of war, structural theories of the international political economy have downplayed process-level influences on trade. However, a variety of studies (that are discussed below) have concluded that process-level variables are of considerable importance in this regard. In chapter 5, the effects on global commerce of two types of process-level variables are considered: global income and war.

A number of scholars—including some hegemonic stability theorists—have noted that "[t]he theory of hegemonic stability (at least in its cruder forms) . . . has underemphasized the importance of [among other things] . . . the market itself in determining outcomes" (Gilpin 1987:91; Krasner 1976; Cowhey and Long 1983; Gowa 1984; Stein 1984; Gallarotti 1985; Cassing, McKeown, and Ochs 1986; Strange 1987; McKeown 1991). This tendency poses few problems for hegemonic stability theory if the distribution of power helps to account for both the economic determinants of trade as well as trade itself. But if economic factors exert an exogenous impact on trade and this impact is substantial relative to that of the distribution of power, many variants of this influential theory would be called into question.

Although these issues have not been addressed adequately to date, they are central to the study of international relations. The study of the international political economy has enjoyed much popularity, in part, because it is widely believed that political factors influence economic outcomes. At the systemic level, the distribution of power is often held to be the most salient political influence on commerce. But in order to establish that political effects should be considered in studies of the international economy, it is necessary to evaluate the importance of these factors, *relative to economic influences* (Conybeare 1983; Pollins 1989a, 1989b; McKeown 1991; Gowa and Mansfield 1993). Of course, it is often difficult to disentangle the influence of economic and political variables, since there is likely to be considerable overlap among them. Nonetheless, if the impact of factors, such as global income, that economists have relied on to explain patterns of trade flows prove to be far more salient than political effects in this regard, one case for emphasizing the relationship between economics and security, and studying the international political economy, would be weakened. On the other hand, if the distribution of power is also important in this respect, the case for highlighting the impact of political (and security-related) factors on trade would be strengthened.

However, it is obvious that the systemic effects of politics on economic outcomes need not be limited to the distribution of power. Both economists and political scientists have suggested that war has a substantial impact on the volume of trade (Kindleberger 1966; Leamer and Stern 1970; Krasner 1976; Stein 1984; Strange 1988). This study will therefore examine whether, in addition to the distribution of power and economic variables, war influences global commerce; and if so, whether the magnitude of its effect depends on the type of war that is analyzed.

In sum, the analysis of trade in this book will provide evidence bearing on a number of fundamental topics in international relations. First, some of the first statistical tests of (at least some variants of) hegemonic stability theory, as well as a number of prominent critiques of this theory, will be conducted. Second, and related to the first point, the effects of structural and process-level variables on international economic outcomes will be estimated and compared. Finally, some insights into the relative importance of systemic economic and political influences on trade relations, and hence the relationship between economics and security, will be provided.

In this study, I argue that, as in the case of war, certain process-level factors exert substantial effects on the level of international trade. During major-power wars, states have an incentive to limit commerce. Under these circumstances, the belligerents are better served by producing goods to aid the war effort rather than for foreign trade. They may also forgo importing goods that are not vital to the war effort. And states (including those that are not directly involved in the conflict) may view war as a possible threat to the integrity of goods that are being transported.

In addition to war, the business cycle is also expected to influence the level of trade. Consistent with the results of a wide variety of studies, I conclude that global income is directly related to the level of international trade. This is to be expected, since (among other things) lower levels of global income depress the demand for imports and the supply of exports. As in the case of war, however, I do not argue that these factors are more important determinants of trade than the distribution of power. Rather, as the results in chapter 5 indicate, these process-level effects complement the effects of aspects of the distribution of power.

EXPLAINING STRUCTURAL CHANGE

Neorealist theories have been challenged on the grounds that the distribution of power does not satisfactorily explain patterns of international outcomes and that process-level variables are more important than is granted by these explanations. Much of this study is devoted to examining the strength of these criticisms. In addition, I will also address another prominent criticism of neorealist theories: the charge that they have failed to provide an adequate explanation of structural change (Ruggie 1983; Keohane 1986; Keohane and Nye 1987).

This is clearly an important issue. If the distribution of power helps to explain patterns of warfare and trade (and/or other outcomes), it is useful to examine both the determinants of the structure of the system and why the distribution of power has changed over time. A number of studies have analyzed these issues (Organski 1958; Russett 1968b; Wallerstein 1974; Organski and Kugler 1980; Gilpin 1981; Kennedy 1987; Thompson and Rasler 1988; Doran 1991). However, these topics have not received as much attention as they warrant.

Many explanations of structural change center on the rise and decline of hegemonic states. While this is obviously one important dimension of structural change, a different tack is taken in this study. As I argue throughout this book, it is useful to examine a variety of features of the distribution of power in studies of international relations. Focusing only on the existence or absence of one (or even a few) preponderant state(s) leads analysts to ignore the concentration of capabilities (among other dimensions of the system's structure), which is closely related to patterns of warfare and trade. It is therefore useful to examine changes in the distribution of power among a larger sample of states than has been the topic of previous studies.

Neorealists argue that variations in the structure of the international system are due to changes in the distribution of capabilities. They also suggest that changes in the distribution of capabilities are likely to be guided by strategic interdependence among the leading states in the system (Waltz 1979; Gilpin 1981:87; Walt 1987). The anarchic nature of the international system compels states to attend to the power of others, because it is possible for states to resort to force in order to further their interests and because the likelihood that states will do so depends, in part, on the distribution of capabilities. As a result, each leading state has an incentive to increase its capabilities at a rate that is roughly proportionate to that of its competitors in order to forestall the erosion of its power vis-à-vis these states.

Many neorealists caution, however, that this dynamic may fail to describe patterns of the growth of capabilities during periods surrounding major-power wars. Indeed one of the most common explanations of structural change is that shocks to the system brought on by the conclusion of these wars produce fundamental alterations in the distribution of power (Modelski 1978; Waltz 1979; Gilpin 1981; Levy 1985b; Thompson and Rasler 1988). But there is no consensus regarding exactly which wars have led to changes of this sort; and few empirical analyses of this important issue have been conducted.[10]

A Model of Structural Change

The analysis of the dynamics of the system's structure that is conducted in chapter 6 builds on a body of microeconomic research designed to explain changes in industry structure. As noted above, analogies between the structure of markets and industries and that of the international system form the basis of many neorealist explanations. Analyses of industry structure often focus on concentration, and a variety of studies conclude that changes in market structure can be modeled as a stochastic process. In particular, considerable use has been made of Gibrat's law, which holds that, during a given interval, firms in a given industry grow at a rate that is independent of their sizes at the outset of the interval.

The usefulness of this model for explaining structural change in the global system is not only due to the similarities between the structures of industries and the international system that neorealists emphasize or to the similarities between measures of industrial concentration and global concentration that were noted above. As I argue in chapter 6, most important for the purposes of this study is the fact that this model is consistent with a variety of neorealist explanations, which suggest that, aside from periods surrounding systemic wars, Gibrat's law may characterize structural change in the international system (Waltz 1979; Gilpin 1981).

Further, a number of empirical studies have found that Gibrat's law might prove useful in modeling changes in the distribution of capabilities (Russett 1968b; Midlarsky 1988). But despite calls for further research on this topic (Zinnes 1976; Hart 1985), few analyses of this sort have been conducted. In chapter 6, the issue of whether Gibrat's law can be used to model structural change in the international system is therefore analyzed. The results indicate that the explanatory power of Gibrat's law depends

---

[10] One exception is Thompson and Rasler (1988). For a discussion of many leading arguments concerning the effects of war on structural change, see Levy (1985b).

upon which states and capabilities are examined. The rates of change for demographic, economic, and military capabilities among the largest twelve (or fifteen) states in the system are in accord with Gibrat's law. Further, when the growth of capabilities of major powers and nonmajor powers are examined separately, there continues to be substantial evidence that the growth in economic capabilities conforms to this model. However, the growth of military and demographic capabilities among major powers often departs from this model. The periods in which the growth of military capabilities departs from Gibrat's law tend to be clustered around the occurrence of systemic wars, which is consistent with a variety of neorealist explanations of international relations.

THE ARGUMENT IN BRIEF

In this book, I argue that structural theories correctly identify the distribution of power as an important determinant of patterns of war and trade. Contrary to some critiques of neorealism, I also maintain that it is possible to explain structural change within a neorealist framework. However, neorealist explanations are hampered by their failure to appreciate the importance of process-level factors. Both structural and process-level factors help to explain patterns of war and trade during the nineteenth and twentieth centuries. Relying exclusively on either a structural or a process-level approach degrades the explanatory power of systemic models of international relations.

My empirical findings bear out this position. For example, both the distribution of power and the level of international trade exert substantial influences on the incidence of war. Moreover, there is considerable evidence of an inverse relationship between commerce and conflict. In addition, the distribution of power, war, and global income each affect the level of international trade. Hence, while they provide the bedrock for an understanding of war and trade, structural approaches are by themselves insufficient to fully explain these outcomes.

Further, I argue that those explanations that posit a monotonic relationship between (1) the distribution of power and war and (2) the distribution of power and trade misconstrue the nature of these relationships. The concentration of capabilities exerts a nonmonotonic influence on both of these outcomes. More specifically, there is considerable evidence of an inverted U-shaped relationship between concentration and the incidence of major-power war, and of a U-shaped relationship between the distribution of power and the level of international trade. These findings are at odds with most standard views of the effects of the distribution of power; and they help to explain why partial support continues to be found for many of the competing theories outlined above. These findings also suggest that,

because previous systemic studies have examined only whether these relationships are monotonic, they have systematically underestimated the influence of the distribution of power on these outcomes.

Another reason why debates persist in this area is that scholars often
define the distribution of power in an overly restrictive manner. A wide
variety of studies assume that polarity is the defining feature of the distribution of power, and that theories of international relations should center
solely on this variable. In this study, I argue that this view is inconsistent
with both the theoretical literature and the empirical record. Many leading
theories of international relations emphasize the importance of aspects of
the distribution of power that are measured best by concentration. It is
therefore not surprising that, in many cases, concentration is related more
strongly than polarity to patterns of war and trade. Because many analysts
have focused solely on the effects of polarity in analyses of these topics, as
well as for the reason given in the previous paragraph, it is not surprising
that many previous analyses have concluded that the distribution of power
has little effect on patterns of war and trade.

At a more general level, I argue that studies of war and studies of the
international political economy have become increasingly distanced from
one another, to the detriment of each. One consequence of this separation
is that scholars seldom emphasize potential economic influences on war,
such as trade. Similarly, analysts often fail to consider the impact of war on
commerce. But these research strategies serve to mask the common ground
held by scholars of war and scholars of the international political economy.
Central to an understanding of the international political economy is the
relationship between economics and security in the global arena. Fundamental to the study of war is an understanding of the causes and effects of
political conflict. There are serious problems engendered by analyzing
issues related to security and conflict in an economic vacuum, and by
examining the international political economy in a political vacuum.
While this may strike some readers as self-evident, research in international relations all too often displays these tendencies. As a result, scholars
often fail to appreciate the extent to which economic phenomena both
influence and are influenced by political conflict.

Moreover, these effects are often mutually reinforcing. Both the distribution of power and international trade influence the incidence of war by
influencing the expected costs and benefits of initiating war. Wars begin
most frequently when both the distribution of power and the level of
international trade produce conditions that decrease the expected costs of
waging war relative to the expected benefits. Hence, rather than being
competing explanations of international relations, neorealism and liberalism are compatible approaches, both of which offer important insights into
patterns of international relations.

Organization of the Book

This book is organized as follows. Chapters 2, 3, and 4 examine the systemic conditions under which wars begin. Chapter 2 analyzes the distribution of wars over time and the extent to which various data sets of war differ. In it, preliminary tests of hypotheses concerning the effects on the outbreak of various types of war of the distribution of power and the international economy are conducted. Chapter 3 focuses on the relationship between the distribution of power and the incidence of war. The effects on the frequency of war of both polarity and concentration are analyzed and compared. In addition, tests are conducted to determine whether a nonmonotonic relationship exists between concentration and the onset of war; and whether the effects of structural variables differ among major-power wars, all interstate wars, and interstate wars that do not involve a major power. Chapter 4 addresses the relationship between international trade and war. Further, the effects of the business cycle and interstate militarized disputes on the frequency of war are also examined.

Chapter 5 examines the determinants of the level of international trade. A test of hegemonic stability theory is conducted, and the relationship between concentration and trade is analyzed. Further, the effects of certain economic variables, as well as war, on the level of global commerce are considered. Chapter 6 analyzes the determinants of concentration and sketches a model of the change in capabilities over time. Chapter 7 summarizes the findings of this book. Further, the utility of systemic approaches to international relations is addressed, and the importance of integrating more fully the study of war and the study of the international political economy is emphasized.

Chapter 2

THE DISTRIBUTION OF WARS OVER TIME:
A BASIC EMPIRICAL ANALYSIS

As INDICATED in chapter 1, one purpose of this book is to determine the effects of power and trade on war. In this chapter, some preliminary empirical results are presented that bear on these relationships and that will guide the analyses in chapters 3 and 4. In particular, the effects of polarity, aspects of the international trading system, and economic cycles on the onset of war will be examined.

Prior to any empirical analysis of the systemic conditions that give rise to wars, it is important to be clear as to what is meant by war and to describe the various types of wars that will be considered in this book. As the analysis in this chapter makes apparent, there is much disagreement concerning how war should be defined and operationalized, and differences between various data sets of war often produce divergences in the effects of polarity, commerce, and the business cycle on the onset of war. In addition, this chapter addresses whether the effects of these systemic factors vary depending on whether all wars or major-power wars are considered. Since many previous empirical studies have utilized only a single type, and data set, of war, it is important to determine whether differences among the dependent variables in these studies account for the differences in their conclusions that were described in chapter 1.

DISTINGUISHING AMONG ALL WARS, ALL INTERSTATE WARS, AND MAJOR-POWER WARS

Fundamental to the study of war is the issue of whether different *types* of war have different causes. Many scholars argue that major-power wars begin for different reasons than other types of wars. Other analysts maintain that wars between nation-states are the products of different factors than wars involving nonstate actors. Systemic theories of war have sought primarily to explain patterns of the onset of major-power wars. One purpose of this book is to evaluate these explanations. However, I am also interested in applying systemic explanations to a wider range of wars than has been typical of previous studies. Hence, in addition to wars involving major powers, the issue of whether power and trade (as well as other systemic variables) provide insights into the conditions under which all wars and all interstate wars begin is also examined. I am unaware of any previous attempt to examine statistically the effects of systemic factors on such a wide variety of wars.

At the outset, it is also important to recognize that the causes of some types of war are not analyzed separately in this book. In particular, no separate analysis is conducted of the determinants of the incidence of hegemonic wars—that is, wars between a hegemon and a rising challenger (Organski 1958; Modelski 1978; Organski and Kugler 1980; Gilpin 1981; Kennedy 1987)—or wars between major powers, although the effects of the latter wars on patterns of international commerce (in chapter 5) and of the distribution of power (in chapter 6) are considered. This research strategy is adopted because hegemonic wars and wars between major powers have generally occurred too infrequently during the period covered in this study to permit reliable tests (of the sort conducted in this book) of the conditions that give rise to their onset. However, it is important to note that hegemonic wars and wars between major powers are included in each of the data sets that are used in the following analyses. Thus while they are not treated separately, these wars will be examined in conjunction with other types of wars in this (and the following two) chapter(s).

Since systemic explanations are typically applied solely to major-power wars, and since one purpose of this study is to determine whether systemic factors are related to all interstate wars, as well as wars involving major powers, it is useful to consider briefly some of the possible connections between systemic aspects of power and trade and the onset of wars that do not involve major powers. A number of scholars suggest that the international distribution of power might be related to the outbreak of minor-power wars. Hans Morgenthau, for example, asserts that "[t]he more intimately a local balance of power system is connected with the dominant [global] one, the less opportunity it has to operate autonomously and the more it tends to become merely a localized manifestation of the dominant balance of power" (Morgenthau and Thompson 1985:219). If this is the case, the structural conditions that shape patterns of major-power wars may also encourage the outbreak of minor-power wars. Kenneth Waltz also implies that structural variables may influence patterns of warfare among smaller states. He notes that the management of international affairs is easier in bipolar than multipolar systems, since management of the global system is a collective good and collective action problems are more easily overcome as the number of polar powers declines. Further,

[t]he size of the two great powers gives them some capacity for control and at the same time insulates them to a considerable extent from the effects of other states' behavior. The inequality of nations produces a condition of equilibrium at low levels of interdependence. In the absence of authoritative regula-

tion, loose coupling and a certain amount of control exercised by large states help to promote *peace* and stability. (1979:209; emphasis added)

To the extent that management involves (among other things) "promoting peace" among smaller, as well as larger, states, Waltz implies that wars among minor powers may be less likely to begin in bipolar than in multipolar systems.

Aside from the distribution of power, process-level factors also may be related to the frequency of minor-power wars. In particular, systemic influences derived from the global economy are likely to influence both major powers and smaller states. Smaller states are, in general, more heavily dependent on international commerce than their major-power counterparts. By virtue of their small size, domestic demand in such states is less than what is required to support some indigenous industries. This tends to result in a dependence on export markets. Further, because their domestic economies are not highly diversified, smaller states also depend on imports more heavily than major powers. Fluctuations in trade might therefore be expected to exert a marked influence on minor-power wars. The same may also be true of the influence of the global business cycle, since it also would be expected to impact heavily the economies of smaller states in the international arena.

Another reason why systemic factors might be related to the incidence of minor-power wars is related to the "stability-instability paradox" (Snyder 1965; Jervis 1984:29–34, 1989:19–22). The thrust of this paradox is that when deterrence is strongest among the major powers (and hence the incidence of war among the major powers is likely to be lowest), "this very stability allows either side to use limited violence because the other's threat to respond by all-out retaliation cannot be very credible" (Jervis 1984:31). While this argument has arisen primarily in discussions of the effects of nuclear weapons on international relations, a similar dynamic may apply to conventional situations as well. If it does, this would suggest that periods in which few (many) major-power wars begin would experience the outbreak of many (few) minor-power wars. For example, this hypothesis is consistent with Inis Claude's observation that "the classic era of the balance of power system in Europe was marked by many minor wars and occasional major conflicts" (1962:71).

Further, the possibility that systemic factors influence the incidence of minor-power wars should be considered because "[t]he extent to which [structure and] changes in structure influence behavior *throughout the world system* is still very much an important and ongoing theoretical and empirical question" (Thompson 1983a:160; emphasis added). It is on this question that much of the present study will focus.

DEFINING AND CODING WAR

Even among scholars who are interested in explaining the onset of the same type of war, there is considerable variation regarding how war is defined and the data sets that are generated based on these definitions. In this book, I will address the extent to which empirical results concerning the determinants of war differ, depending on both the type, and data set, of war that is analyzed. However, it is useful to begin by describing the definitions and data that will be used for this purpose.

In this chapter, five different definitions of war, and nine data sets that have been derived from these definitions, are used. In particular, the well-known data sets compiled by Lewis Richardson (1960a), Quincy Wright (1965), J. David Singer and Melvin Small (1972), Bruce Bueno de Mesquita (1981b), Melvin Small and J. David Singer (1982), and Jack Levy (1983) are analyzed.

Wright's list is intended to include all hostilities involving members of the "family" of nations,

> whether international, civil, colonial, or imperial, which were recognized as states of war in the legal sense or which involved over 50,000 troops. Some other incidents are included in which hostilities of considerable but lesser magnitude, not recognized at the time as legal states of war, led to important legal results such as the creation or extinction of states, territorial transfers, or changes of government. (1965:636)

Wright's data are plotted in figure 2.3 (the entire compilation of wars) and figure 2.4 (interstate wars only) in the appendix at the end of this chapter.

Richardson's list "is classified . . . in seven broad classes by the number killed" (1960a:3).

> The war dead were taken to include all those, on both sides, whether armed personnel or civilians, who were killed fighting, or drowned by enemy action, or who died from wounds or from poisonous gas, or from starvation in a siege, or from other malicious acts of their enemies. Moreover, deaths from disease or exposure of armed personnel during a campaign were included. (Richardson 1944:247)

He is not concerned with whether the deadly quarrels "occurred in Europe, America, Asia, or Africa, whether between recognized states, between revolutionary groups within a state, between primitive tribes, or between governments and rebels, insurgents, or colonials" (1960a:vii). Richardson's data are shown in figure 2.5 in the appendix.

Small and Singer list all wars that were identified between 1816 and 1980 by Wright, Richardson, and diplomatic and military historians; they then screen out "those quarrels which failed of inclusion because of: (a) the inadequate political status of the participants; or (b) their failure to meet a minimum threshold of battle-connected casualties of troops in combat" (1982:38). They also include civil wars between 1816 and 1980 in their data set. Civil wars are defined by "(a) military action internal to the metropole, (b) the active participation of the national government, and (c) effective resistance by both sides" (1982:210). International civil wars are also recognized by Small and Singer if a second state commits one thousand troops to the combat zone or, in the event that the deployed force is smaller than this figure or the number is not known, at least one hundred deaths are sustained (1982:218–19). Small and Singer's data are plotted in figure 2.6 (the entire data set) and figure 2.7 (interstate wars only) of the appendix. Singer and Small (1972) have also compiled a list of major-power wars, which will be analyzed below. These data are shown in figure 2.8 of the appendix.

Bueno de Mesquita began by utilizing Singer and Small's data. He mentions that "using the coding rules of Singer and Small and extending their [1972] data through 1974 gives me 79 interstate war initiations, for which I have sufficient data to test my theory on all but 3" (1981b:101). He does not include civil wars in his compilation. Of particular importance for present purposes is the fact that he lists wars in terms of dyadic relationships between individual antagonists. Figures 2.9 and 2.10 of the appendix show his data—the latter after adjustments are made that are described below.

Levy defines a war as "a substantial armed conflict between the organized military forces of independent military units" (1983:51). He argues that because Great Powers occupy a unique position in the international system, have been involved "in a disproportionately high percentage of history's wars," and "many theories of international politics are essentially theories of Great Power behavior," wars involving these states deserve special attention (3). For these reasons, Levy excludes hostilities that do not involve a Great Power, civil wars, and "imperial or colonial wars, unless they expand through the intervention of another state" (51). Because his data pertain solely to Great Powers, they will be utilized in this chapter only when the results based on all wars are compared with those restricted to major powers. Figure 2.11 of the appendix shows Levy's data involving major powers.

As noted above, one purpose of this book is to determine whether systemic factors influence the onset of all wars and all interstate wars, as well as wars involving major powers. To this end, we begin by examining the former two types of wars. But prior to analyzing the effects of power and trade (and the business cycle) on wars of this sort, it is useful to determine whether differences exist among data sets of these wars, and, if so, how pronounced are these differences. This is an important issue because if the data sets of a given type of war are sufficiently similar, it may be possible to choose one of them for the purposes of testing whether systemic factors help to explain the onset of all wars and all interstate wars; otherwise, it will be necessary to compare empirical results of this sort across a variety of data sets.

A Statistical Comparison of the Data Sets for All Wars and All Interstate Wars

Because of the differences in the definitions of war in the compilations described above, some variation would be expected among these data sets. Thus it is not surprising that differences exist in the summary statistics (presented in table 2.1) among these seven data sets of all wars and all interstate wars. For example, as shown in table 2.1, the mean number of wars breaking out annually tends to be higher based on Small and Singer's data and lower based on Wright's (interstate war) data than is the case when the other compilations are analyzed. Similarly, the standard deviation of the number of wars beginning per year varies substantially from data set to data set.

However, as noted above, the *extent* of this variation is a matter of considerable significance. These findings indicate that this variation is quite pronounced. Indeed *there is a relatively low correlation between the number of wars begun in any particular year according to one data set and the number of wars begun in the same year in another compilation.* Specifically, as shown in table 2.2, the average value of the coefficient of determination (r^2) is only about 0.22. Moreover, the correlation remains low when Wright's and Small and Singer's data are adjusted to include only interstate wars.[1]

Three factors seem to account for most of the differences that are observed between these compilations. First, as mentioned earlier, there is considerable debate about what constitutes a war. Various definitions of war would be expected to produce different results. For example, Richardson cautions, "[l]et no one suppose that the present list ought to agree with Wright's. Their principles are different; because his [Wright's] rule for selecting incidents does not mention the number of deaths, and may involve the importance of legal results" (1960a:30). Similarly, the decision to include hostilities involving nonstate actors has a marked impact on the

---

[1] For the purposes of making these adjustments, extrasystemic and civil wars were excluded from Small and Singer's data; only their list of interstate wars was employed. Further, civil and imperial wars were deleted from Wright's compilation; only the wars he classified as defensive and balance-of-power conflicts are utilized in the subsequent analysis. Richardson's data were not broken down because it was difficult to determine which "deadly quarrels" were (and were not) between nation-states.

TABLE 2.1
Summary Statistics and Results of Tests of Poisson Distribution, Linear Trend, and Effects of Kondratieff Cycles

	Richardson	Wright[a]		Bueno de Mesquita		Small and Singer	
		All Wars	Interstate Wars	Unadjusted	Adjusted	All Wars	Interstate Wars
Mean number of wars beginning per year	.81	.60	.34	.48	.35	1.35	.41
Standard deviation of wars beginning per year	.93	.81	.60	1.03	.64	1.29	.64
Number of years	130	462	462	159	159	165	165
Time period	1820–1949	1480–1941	1480–1941	1816–1974	1816–1974	1816–1980	1816–1980
Poisson distribution: Chi-square statistic	—[b]	2.40	0.79	9.93	.19	1.31	.02
Linear regression of annual number of wars begun on time:							

Regression coefficient	−0.00032	0.00057	0.00008	0.0023	0.0017	0.0057	0.00227
t-statistic	−0.15	2.03	0.38	1.31	1.55	2.72	2.19
r^2 (adjusted for degrees of freedom)	−.008	.007	−.002	.005	.009	.038	.023
Durbin-Watson statistic	2.11	1.99	2.06	2.06	2.07	2.09	1.90
Mean number of wars beginning per year:							
Kondratieff upward phase	.81	.62	.32	.70	.47	1.63	.50
Kondratieff downward phase	.81	.62	.37	.28	.24	1.07	.30

[a] Wright lists the Napoleonic Wars, World War I, and World War II as single wars and also breaks them down into a series of smaller wars. In the present analysis, these conflicts are each considered as a single war.

[b] No Chi-square statistic is provided by Richardson (1944:248); however, he notes that his data are in "agreement with the Poisson law" and he asserts that "there is considerable resemblance between the historical facts and the Poisson law" (1960a:128). In order to observe the rule that the expected frequency be no less than 5, the Chi-square statistic for Bueno de Mesquita and Bueno de Mesquita (adjusted), respectively, was computed by categorizing the number of wars breaking out in a particular year as 0, 1, and 2 or more. The Chi-square statistic for Wright is from Richardson (1944:243). To observe the same rule, the number of wars beginning per year is classified as 0, 1, 2, and 3 or more. Small and Singer's Chi-square statistic is from Houweling and Kune (1984:56); the wars per year were classified as 0, 1, 2, 3, and 4 or more.

TABLE 2.2
Coefficient of Determination Between the Number of Wars Beginning in a Particular Year
in One Data Set and the Number Beginning in the Same Year in Another Data Set,
1820–1941[a]

Data Set	Small and Singer (Interstate Wars)	Richardson	Wright[b] (All Wars)	Wright[b] (Interstate Wars)	Bueno de Mesquita (Unadjusted)	Bueno de Mesquita (Adjusted)
Small and Singer (all wars)	.38	.07	.20	.12	.15	.31
Small and Singer (interstate wars)	—	.02	.13	.28	.40	.79
Richardson	—	—	.05	.04	.00	.02
Wright[b] (all wars)	—	—	—	.42	.11	.12
Wright[b] (interstate wars)	—	—	—	—	.14	.29
Bueno de Mesquita	—	—	—	—	—	.54

[a] All coefficients of determination are adjusted for degrees of freedom. The time frame employed in this analysis is from 1820 to 1941, since it is the only period common to all seven data sets. Richardson's data include only wars of magnitude ranging from $7 \pm \frac{1}{2}$ to $4 \pm \frac{1}{2}$ because, as Richardson notes, his data for lesser magnitudes are quite vague, sketchy, and incomplete (1960a:73).

[b] See table 2.1, note a.

compilations. Table 2.2 indicates that data sets that include such wars agree little with those lists that are restricted to international wars. More is at work, however: substantial divergencies exist even among data sets that follow similar rules for inclusion regarding nonstate actors.

Second, the level at which war is analyzed explains some of the difference among data sets. This apparently accounts for much of the variation between Bueno de Mesquita's compilation and the other lists. Bueno de Mesquita is interested in modeling the calculus that decision makers employ when evaluating whether or not to go to war; thus he focuses on dyadic relations between states. For example, he identifies eight separate dyads in 1866 involving Germany and a series of states, rather than classifying the incident as the Seven Weeks' War or the Austro-Prussian War, as other scholars have.

Third, there are differences in the dating of wars. Wright and Small and Singer, for example, date the onset of the Russian Revolution in 1917, while Levy places its origin in 1918. Richardson breaks the Russian Revolution into two deadly quarrels, one beginning in 1917, the other beginning in 1918.[2] Such discrepancies seem minor, but they help to reduce the correlation between the data sets.

Given the relatively low correlation between these data sets, analysts should be hesitant to use them interchangeably. This is not to imply that any of these data sets is "wrong" or misleading. Each is useful contingent on the objectives of the particular analysis.[3] But analysts should be aware that results may vary depending on which list is employed. Throughout this study, tests of the systemic influences on war will therefore be conducted using a variety of these compilations. It is also useful to adopt this approach because, in previous research on war, "[r]arely [have] two studies' dependent variables been sufficiently similar to permit a direct comparison of results" (Bueno de Mesquita 1985:132; Krasner 1985). This approach will permit us to determine the extent to which hypotheses derived from leading theories produce similar results when both different types of wars and different data sets of the same type of war are analyzed.

CONTAGION EFFECTS AMONG ALL WARS AND ALL INTERSTATE WARS

Since there is relatively little agreement among Richardson's, Wright's, Small and Singer's, and Bueno de Mesquita's data, it is important to determine what are the substantive implications of the low correlation among

[2] Bueno de Mesquita's dating of the Russian Revolution is not considered because he does not include civil wars in his data. Small and Singer, on the other hand, list this conflict twice, once as an extrasystemic war and once as a civil war (1982:311, 321).

[3] Singer and Small (1972:78–128) provide an analysis of the agreement between Richardson's, Wright's, and their own data for all wars. However, they are concerned with different measures of agreement than the one used in this study. They compute the "commonality in percentage terms by . . . divid[ing] the number of wars which [a pair of data sets] included by the number which *either* of them included, for the period covered by both studies" (1972:78; emphasis in original). Their results indicate only moderate agreement between the lists, and the "commonality declines even further [when they] compute . . . the number of wars found in *every* one of the . . . lists . . . and divide by the total found in *any* one of them" during the time period when the studies overlap (1972:79; emphasis in original).

However, when Singer and Small analyze "for each pair of studies, what percentage of the first's wars are also in the second's list, and what percentage of the second's wars are found in the first's list . . . the discrepancies are not so great as they first appeared" (1972:79). Although Singer and Small find evidence of some commonality among the compilations that they compare, table 2.2 indicates that there is little correlation between the data sets used in these compilations. One very basic issue of this sort is whether the distribution of war's onset differs across these data sets. To this end, two issues are examined: (1) whether the data fit the Poisson distribution; and (2) whether any linear trend exists in the data.

These topics also bear on long-standing debates concerning "war contagion." Much interest has been expressed in whether or not the onset of war in one period increases or decreases the likelihood that war will begin in a subsequent time period (Richardson 1960a; Starr and Most 1976; Davis, Duncan, and Siverson 1978; Siverson and King 1979; Most and Starr 1980; Levy 1983, chap. 7; Most, Starr, and Siverson 1989). As Levy notes, "This question has attracted considerable attention in the literature on international conflict" (1983:150). But few analyses have examined this issue at the level of this international system;[4] and systemic studies rarely have considered whether war contagion characterizes the onset of all wars and all interstate wars.[5] For present purposes, it is important to answer this question because the existence of contagion effects would have implications for the subsequent statistical analyses in this study.

If the data do not fit the Poisson distribution or if the residuals from the trend over time in the onset of war are correlated with one another, the null hypothesis that no contagion exists in the onset of war might be rejected (Levy 1983, chap. 7). (However, it is also clear that departures from the Poisson distribution need not be caused by contagion effects among wars.) In the following two sections, these hypotheses are tested.

How Robust Is the Poisson Distribution?

If wars occur at random, one would expect the number of wars beginning each year to conform to the Poisson distribution.[6] That is, if the probability

---

this study. Even though a considerable percentage of wars may be common to a pair of data sets, the noncommon outbreak of wars in a particular year seems to reduce the correlation significantly. Thus the present analysis is a useful supplement to Singer and Small's seminal work on this topic.

[4] One exception is Levy (1983, chap. 7).

[5] It should be noted that some systemic studies of war diffusion have analyzed all interstate wars, as well as major-power wars (for example, Siverson and Starr 1990). However, while this topic is related to war contagion, analyses of diffusion generally focus on the expansion of ongoing conflict, whereas analyses of contagion generally center on whether the onset of war in one period influences the probability of war in a subsequent period.

[6] The Poisson distribution occurs under the following circumstances: (1) the probability that an event (in this case, a war) occurs in a short period of time that is proportional to the length of the period; (2) the probability that more than one event occurs in any very short period of time is zero; (3) the events are independent of one another; (4) the probability that an event occurs in a short period of time does not depend on when the period begins. Regardless of whether these assumptions hold, the Poisson distribution may be a good approximation to the distribution of wars. If that is true, it is important to know since this has

equals $\lambda\Delta$ that a war begins in a short period of time of Δ years, the probability that x wars begin in a year equals $[(\lambda\Delta)^x e^{-\lambda\Delta}]/x!$. In view of the relatively low correlation among the data sets found earlier, it is interesting to note that the Poisson distribution provides a good approximation to the data, regardless of whether Wright's, Richardson's, or Small and Singer's compilations are used (Richardson 1944, 1960a; Moyal 1949:447; Wright 1965; Singer and Small 1972; Houweling and Kune 1984). Thus the fit of the Poisson distribution to these data is remarkably robust.[7] Table 2.1 shows the results of the Chi-square goodness-of-fit tests for each of these studies.

To determine if Bueno de Mesquita's data also conform to the Poisson distribution, a Chi-square test was carried out. Table 2.1 indicates that his data do not fit the Poisson distribution at all well. Apparently, this is because he frames the outbreak of hostilities in terms of dyadic conflicts (which is more appropriate for his purposes), and does not employ the more conventional definition in which all combatants are viewed as engaging in a single war. When his data are adjusted to aggregate wars (from dyads) in cases in which at least two of the other three data sets agreed that this could be done, the adjusted data (plotted in figure 2.10 in the appendix) fit the Poisson distribution remarkably well.[8]

---

implications for war contagion hypotheses and for purposes of prediction. (For an example of the usefulness of the Poisson distribution for major-power wars, see figures 2.1 and 2.2.)

[7] A Poisson process is not necessarily at work just because the data fit the Poisson distribution. A tight fit does not necessarily imply randomness. For example, Houweling and Kune (1984) find that Small and Singer's data do not follow a Poisson process although they are closely approximated by a Poisson distribution. Interestingly, they are not able to reject the hypothesis that a Poisson process is at work when they analyze Small and Singer's "international wars, excluding civil wars" (1984:60). See Houweling and Kune (1984) for a more complete discussion of this issue.

[8] The following adjustments were made: (1) The three dyads in 1827 involving Great Britain, France, and Russia versus Turkey were aggregated into the Battle of Navarino Bay. (2) The eight dyads that Bueno de Mesquita identifies in 1866 between Germany and eight states are aggregated into either the Seven Weeks' War or the Austro-Prussian War. (3) In both 1906 and 1907, Bueno de Mesquita lists two dyads that Wright aggregates into the Central American War; Small and Singer list one war between the combatants each year. The latter position is adopted as a compromise among Bueno de Mesquita, Wright, and Small and Singer. (4) The two dyads that appear in 1913 between Yugoslavia and Bulgaria, and Greece and Bulgaria, were aggregated into the Second Balkan War to conform with the other scholars. (5) The five dyads in 1948 were aggregated into one war in Palestine to conform with both Richardson and Small and Singer. (6) The two dyads in 1965 between North Vietnam and both South Vietnam and the United States were aggregated into one war, consistent with Small and Singer (the only other study including wars as recent as this one). (7) The three dyads in 1967 between Israel and Egypt, Syria, and Jordan, respectively, were aggregated into the Six-Day War. (8) The two dyads in 1973 between Israel and both Egypt and Syria were aggregated into the Yom Kippur War. Adjustments (7) and (8) are also in accord with Small and Singer's compilation.

Because students of international politics have traditionally focused their attention on relations between nation-states, it is important to consider this class of wars separately. When Small and Singer's and Wright's compilations are restricted to international wars, the Poisson distribution again approximates the data extremely well (see table 2.1). Hence, the fit to the data appears to be quite robust.

TREND AND AUTOCORRELATION

In addition to testing whether the Poisson distribution provides a good fit, many major studies attempt to determine whether there is a trend in the data. Richardson (1960a:141), for example, concludes that no trend exists, and Small and Singer note the "absence of any clear trend," (1982: 132) although they do find a slight upward drift in the data.[9] To see whether this is true regardless of which data set is used, the least-squares regression of the annual number of wars begun in a particular year on the year itself was calculated.[10]

The results (shown in table 2.1) indicate that, except for Richardson's list, there does seem to be an upward drift in all cases. However, it is statistically significant only for Wright's and Small and Singer's data.[11] Further, the coefficient of determination (r^2) for each set is quite small, indicating that these trends explain very little of the variation in the outbreak of warfare.[12] It is also interesting to note that Wright's and Small and Singer's data produce upward trends when only international wars are analyzed, and that r^2 remains small. As Small and Singer note, this upward

---

[9] In earlier research, Small and Singer argue that not only is there "no long range secular trend" in the data as a whole, but that there is also no clear trend in the separate compilations of international wars, military confrontations, and civil wars, respectively (Small and Singer 1979:73).

[10] It should be noted that ordinary least-squares regression is a somewhat rudimentary technique for analyzing trends in data. It is frequently used for this purpose, however, and is the natural starting point in a comparative study of this sort. See, for example, Richardson (1960a), Small and Singer (1982), and Levy (1983).

[11] The use of tests of statistical significance is appropriate when a researcher is analyzing a sample and wants to generalize from the sample to the population. Such tests are inappropriate when the population is being studied. The data sets that are being used in this analysis can be thought of as the population of all wars during the time frames that each compilation covers. However, these data can also be considered a sample of the hypothetical population of all wars over all times. Tests of significance are often used in this book, but depending upon the assumptions that are made about the data, these tests may or may not be meaningful.

[12] The regression coefficients are quite small for each data set. However, it is possible that over the course of hundreds of years, the average number of wars could go up by a significant amount. Consequently, the percentage change was calculated between the predicted number of wars at the beginning of the time period and that at the end. The change exceeded 20 percent only in the case of Wright's data for all wars.

drift may be due to nothing more than an increase in the number of states in the international system over time. They find that, when their subset of data on international wars is normalized to account for the number of nations in the international system, a "discernible downward trend" exists (1979:64).[13] But the results in the following chapter indicate that there is an upward trend in the incidence of all interstate wars over time even after controlling for the number of states in the system.

Investigators such as H. Houweling and J. Kune (1984) and J. Moyal (1949) have found that there is autocorrelation in the distribution of wars over time. For example, Moyal concludes that there is "some small positive correlation for intervals greater than one year, though only the values for 5 and 15 years are distinctly significant" (1949:447). To determine whether the residuals from the regressions in this section are serially correlated, the Durbin-Watson statistic for each compilation was calculated[14] (shown in table 2.1). In each case, there exists no evidence of serial correlation of this sort.[15] In this regard, the results are quite robust.

In sum, the results of this, and the previous, section suggest that contagion effects do not exist in the onset of all wars and all interstate wars. In almost every case, the Poisson distribution provides a good fit to the data; and there is no evidence of autocorrelation.

THE EFFECTS OF POLARITY ON ALL WARS AND ALL INTERSTATE WARS

Having described and compared some of the data that will be used throughout this study, we should turn to a preliminary examination of whether systemic aspects of power and trade influence the onset of all wars and all interstate wars. In the opening section of this chapter, some possible connections between the distribution of power and wars of this sort were

[13] It is important to note that the decision to normalize or not to normalize these compilations "rests on an implied null model: that system size, population growth, or number of possible pairs, etc., should have *no effect* on the incidence of violence and conflict" (Small and Singer 1979:72; emphasis in original). This issue will be dealt with at greater length in chapters 3 and 4.

[14] If the value of a time series at time t is correlated with its value k periods before, the time series exhibits serial correlation (also known as autocorrelation). The assumption in classical linear regression is that there will be no serial correlation of the residuals. For present purposes, it is useful to determine whether the residuals are serially correlated because, if they are, this might help us predict and understand the incidence of war.

[15] This is true if we use the standard table of the Durbin-Watson statistic and let $n = 100$. Alternatively, the von Neumann ratio can be used, which is $n/(n - 1)$ multiplied by the Durbin-Watson statistic. Since for large n it may be taken as approximately normally distributed (its mean being $2n/(n - 1)$ and its variance being $[4n^2(n - 2)]/[(n + 1)(n - 1)^3])$, this statistic can be used to test for serial correlation of the residuals. In no case is the result statistically significant. For a more detailed explanation of this method, see Johnston (1972:250–51).

presented. In this section, some preliminary empirical tests of this relationship are conducted. As noted in chapter 1, this book focuses on two features of the system's structure—polarity and concentration. Initially, the
effects of polarity on the onset of war are analyzed. In the following chapter, this analysis is supplemented by comparing the influence on war of
both polarity and concentration.

There is a widespread belief among scholars of international relations
that polarity is the most salient feature of the global distribution of power.
As pointed out earlier, however, there is little consensus regarding the type
of polarity that characterized many periods covered in this study. As a
result of these disagreements, a variety of different classifications of polarity are considered in this study. Waltz (1979), Glenn Snyder and Paul
Diesing (1977), and Levy (1985a), for example, argue that the system was
never characterized by unipolarity during the period after the conclusion of
the Napoleonic Wars; instead the relevant distinction in this respect is
between periods of multipolarity and bipolarity. They maintain that the
system was multipolar until the conclusion of World War II, and bipolar
thereafter. On the other hand, a variety of scholars suggest that the system
has been characterized by a single preponderant power during portions of
the nineteenth and twentieth centuries, and that the most important structural distinction is between hegemonic periods and periods that lacked a
hegemon. However, these scholars are divided on which periods were
hegemonic and which were not. As a result, the effects of hegemony will be
examined and compared, using Robert Gilpin's (1975; 1981; 1987),
George Modelski's (1978), and Immanuel Wallerstein's (1983) classifications. As noted above, Levy (1985a) argues that no hegemon existed after
the conclusion of the Napoleonic Wars; however, he also maintains that
periods of hegemony existed prior to the nineteenth century. His classifications of hegemony will be examined in the analysis of major-power wars,
below.[16]

[16] Gilpin's periods of hegemony are: 1815–1914 (Great Britain) and 1945–1980 (United
States). He does not specify exactly when or whether U.S. hegemony has ended; however, he
asserts that "by the 1980s, American hegemonic leadership . . . had greatly eroded"
(1987:345). For this reason, and because no data set extends beyond that year, 1980 is used as
the final year of American hegemony.
    Modelski (1978; 1981) points out that he is interested in periods of "world leadership"
rather than of hegemony. In such eras, power is less highly concentrated than during periods
of hegemony. Modelski's periods are: 1494–1580 (Portugal); 1609–1688 (United Provinces
of the Netherlands); 1713–1802 (Great Britain); 1815–1937 (Great Britain); and 1945–
1980 (United States). The beginning of each cycle is given by the year Modelski provides for
the "legitimizing settlement." When more than one year is provided, the most recent is
employed. The end of each cycle is marked by "landmarks of descent." For each cycle, the
final year of the most recent landmark is utilized (Modelski 1978:225). The war data em-

It was also pointed out in chapter 1 that power preponderance and balance-of-power theories are two leading views regarding the relationship between the distribution of power and the onset of war. Power preponderance theorists suggest that periods of hegemony are associated with fewer wars than periods in which no hegemon exists, since they argue that "an inequality of power is likely to prevent war"; this hypothesis is contrary to those variants of balance-of-power theory that argue that a relatively equal distribution of power makes war relatively unlikely (Siverson and Sullivan 1983:474). More will be said about these explanations of war in chapter 3, but for present purposes it is important to note that scholars who advance the argument that a preponderance of power deters war differ over the type(s) of war that this perspective explains.

Some focus on the (dyadic) distribution of power between the two most powerful states in the global system and the incidence of war between these states (Organski 1958; Organski and Kugler 1980; Gilpin 1981; Kennedy 1987). Others have extended this dyadic theory of war to the international system in general and posit that "when global capabilities are highly concentrated, the . . . prevalence of global warfare is lower than when global capabilities are more widely dispersed" (Thompson 1983b:344, 1983a; Modelski 1978; Doran and Parsons 1980; Väyrynen 1983).[17] Because I do not seek to explain separately the incidence of hegemonic wars, the primary focus of this study is on the latter variant of power preponderance theory.

Initially, the effects of hegemony on the onset of all wars and all interstate wars are examined. Table 2.3 shows that the mean number of wars begun per year tends to be higher during hegemonic periods than during non-hegemonic periods. For Gilpin's classifications, this holds true in six out of seven data sets; for Wallerstein's, in five out of seven cases; and for Modelski's, in four out of seven cases.[18] Thus this evidence does not seem to

---

ployed do not extend beyond 1980; moreover, no landmarks of descent are provided for the United States. Hence, 1980 is used as the final year of American leadership.

Wallerstein's periods are: 1625–1672 (United Provinces of the Netherlands); 1815–1873 (Great Britain); and 1945–1967 (United States). Any data prior to 1600 were excluded for Wallerstein's periods because this is when he dates the start of the modern world-system and it would be inappropriate to compare wars in different systems. Levy (1985b) also designates three periods of hegemony: 1556–1588, 1659–1713, and 1797–1815. However, because Wright's data set is the only one that includes wars that begin prior to 1815, Levy's eras of hegemony are not analyzed in this section (although they are considered in the analysis of wars involving major powers, below).

[17] This hypothesis is also suggested by Wagner (1986), Niou, Ordeshook, and Rose (1989), and Niou and Ordeshook (1990).

[18] If, in fact, a preponderance of power increases the probability of war, this could explain why the results based on Modelski's classifications are weaker than those based on the others.

TABLE 2.3

Mean Number of Wars Beginning per Year During Periods of Hegemony and Nonhegemony, and During Periods of Bipolarity and Multipolarity

	Richardson	Wright		Bueno de Mesquita		Small and Singer	
		All Wars	Interstate Wars	Unadjusted	Adjusted	All Wars	Interstate Wars
Bipolar	—[a]	—[a]	—[a]	.76	.48	2.03	.51
Multipolar	—[a]	—[a]	—[a]	.42	.32	1.17	.38
Gilpin's classification							
Hegemony	.81	.89	.43	.51	.36	1.44	.40
Nonhegemony	.80	.52	.31	.33	.33	.97	.43
Modelski's classification							
Leadership	.82	.65	.36	.47	.34	1.37	.39
Nonleadership	.57	.38	.23	.57	.57	.86	.71
Wallerstein's classification							
Hegemony	.75	.85	.38	.57	.37	1.42	.35
Nonhegemony	.86	.53	.31	.38	.33	1.29	.46

[a] Too few observations exist for bipolar periods to permit reasonably reliable calculations of this sort.

bear out the power preponderance hypothesis; instead it generally seems to support the balance-of-power hypothesis. The preliminary nature of this analysis is obvious, however.

Because these theories seek to explain only international hostilities, wars involving nonstate actors should be excluded from this analysis. Using Wright's list of international wars only, the results are consistent with the earlier analysis: periods of hegemony produce a higher incidence of warfare. Using Small and Singer's data on international wars, however, precisely the opposite is the case. (See table 2.3.) Thus here is still another case where the results differ, depending on whose data sets are used.[19]

This analysis of hegemony seems to lend credence to balance-of-power theory, though the evidence is mixed. But, as noted earlier, other scholars argue that rather than distinguishing between periods of hegemony and nonhegemony, the relevant distinction is between bipolar and multipolar periods. These analysts often disagree, however, over whether bipolar systems are more or less war-prone than their multipolar counterparts.

As a preliminary analysis of this issue, the mean number of wars beginning per year was compared for each structural configuration. This test can only be conducted using Singer and Small's and Bueno de Mesquita's data, because Wright's and Richardson's data sets contain few (if any) observations after 1945. The results, shown in table 2.3, indicate that wars tend to begin more frequently during bipolar than multipolar periods: the mean number of wars is higher during bipolar periods for both all wars and all interstate wars.

Like the earlier analysis of the relationship between hegemony and war, the tentative nature of these findings is apparent. However, while the strength of these relationships often varies, the analyses in the following two chapters yield additional evidence that all interstate wars tend to begin most frequently during periods of hegemony and bipolarity. As a result, these tests offer a useful first cut at the systemic effects of power on wars of this sort.

HEGEMONIC TRANSITIONS AND THE ONSET OF ALL WARS AND ALL INTERSTATE WARS

Besides analyzing static features of polarity, it is also important to determine whether dynamic aspects of this dimension of the system's structure are associated with the onset of war. As noted in chapter 1, many power

---

Modelski is referring to leadership, not hegemony. Leadership is clearly a weaker form of power disparity than hegemony. Thus the relationship might be expected to be weaker when his classifications are used than when the others are used.

[19] Various datings of hegemony also elicit different results. When Modelski's periods are examined and only international wars are employed, the lack of leadership seems to be

preponderance theories emphasize dynamic aspects of the distribution of power. They argue that it is not only the existence or absence of a hegemonic power that renders major-power war more or less likely, but also that transition periods—when either hegemony breaks down (and a balance ensues) or a hegemon emerges—encourage the outbreak of wars. And some balance-of-power theorists also highlight dynamic features of the distribution of power in their explanations of war. Wars are often said to be the products of inequalities among the leading states in the system.

Hence, it is important to know whether warfare clusters around transitions from nonhegemony to hegemony and from hegemony to nonhegemony. This might indicate that the breakdown of the existing system, rather than the mere presence or absence of a hegemon, helps to explain the onset of warfare. To find out, the mean number of wars during each quarter of periods of hegemony and nonhegemony was compared. Table 2.4 shows that only in the cases of Bueno de Mesquita's and Small and Singer's (interstate war) data does the last quarter of periods of nonhegemony tend to have a higher incidence of war than other quarters. In few cases does the first quarter of a period of hegemony have a higher incidence of war than the other three quarters. Thus there seems to be limited evidence of such clustering.

It has also been hypothesized that the breakdown of hegemony is associated with a high incidence of warfare. If Wallerstein's classifications are used, the incidence of war is higher in the last quarter of hegemonic periods than in the other quarters of such periods (or of nonhegemonic periods). The evidence is much weaker when it is based on Gilpin's or Modelski's classifications. These results provide additional, although tentative, support for the balance-of-power hypothesis; it is important, however, to recognize their roughness.

The Effects of International Trade on All Wars and All Interstate Wars

In addition to the effects of power on war, the influence of trade on war is central to this study. In this section, one aspect of this relationship is considered in a preliminary manner. For present purposes, my focus is on whether an open international trading system results in a diminished incidence of war. As pointed out in chapter 1, this position would seem to be consistent with the view of commercial liberals and others who "believe that the mutual benefits of trade and the expanding web of interdependence among national economies tend to foster cooperative relations," but

---

associated with a relatively high incidence of war; Gilpin's and Wallerstein's periods produce very different results.

inconsistent with the view of mercantilists and others who argue that openness and greater interdependence is "a cause of conflict and insecurity" (Gilpin 1987:56, 57).

To test this hypothesis, Stephen Krasner's (1976) classifications of periods of openness and closure during the nineteenth and twentieth centuries were used.[20] As shown in table 2.5, the mean number of wars per year has tended to be greater during periods of openness than during periods of closure. This observation seems to support the position that "trade is not a guarantor of peace" (Gilpin 1987:58).

Again, it is important to analyze international wars separately because many theories of trade and war do not purport to explain civil or extrasystemic wars. When Small and Singer's data on international wars are examined, the mean number of wars during periods of closure exceeds the mean during periods of openness. But for Wright's data and each of Bueno de Mesquita's compilations, interstate wars begin more frequently during periods of openness. Here is another case in which different data sets yield different results.

It is also important to determine whether the transitions between periods of openness and closure produce substantial changes in the frequency of warfare. Because many structural explanations suggest that trade relations may be symptomatic of political relations between states, there is reason to believe that this is the case. In order to test the hypothesis that transition periods are ones in which the incidence of war is higher than other phases, each of Krasner's periods of openness and closure was divided into quarters, and the mean number of wars per year in each quarter was computed. For all seven data sets, the incidence of war tends to be higher during the last half of openness than during the first half. (See table 2.6.) This is consistent with the notion that the breakdown of economic relations is reflected in the breakdown of political relations between nations. In five of seven cases, however, the final quarter of periods of closure also appears to produce an increase in hostilities, which may suggest that transition periods are the ones that are most likely to witness the outbreak of war.

Like the earlier analysis in this chapter of the effects of the distribution of power on war, the roughness of this analysis is obvious. Since a variety of other factors are not held constant in these exploratory tests, the results in this section can be regarded only as suggestive and tentative. But these

---

[20] By increasingly "open" trading systems, Krasner is referring to those in which "tariffs are falling, trade proportions are rising, and regional trading patterns are becoming less extreme" (1976:324). The time periods that he utilizes and the commensurate degrees of openness and closure are: 1820–1879—openness; 1879–1900—closure; 1900–1913—openness; 1918–1939—closure; and 1945–1970—openness.

TABLE 2.4

Mean Number of Wars Beginning per Year During Each Quarter of Periods of Hegemony and Nonhegemony

Classification	Hegemony (Quarter of Period)[a]				Nonhegemony (Quarter of Period)[a]			
	First	Second	Third	Fourth	First	Second	Third	Fourth
Gilpin:								
Richardson	.90	.68	.72	1.04	1.43	.57	.75	.50
Wright (all wars)	1.04	1.00	.80	.72	.64	.60	.48	.44
Wright (interstate wars)	.44	.44	.40	.44	.43	.31	.30	.25
Bueno de Mesquita	.21	.56	.48	.52	.29	0	.38	.63
Bueno de Mesquita (adjusted)	.13	.56	.20	.40	.29	0	.38	.63
Small and Singer (all wars)	.79	1.64	1.04	1.40	1.00	.86	1.13	.88
Small and Singer (interstate wars)	.08	.60	.28	.48	.43	0	.50	.75
Modelski:[b]								
Richardson	.80	.74	.87	.94	—	—	—	—
Wright (all wars)	.59	.72	.63	.67	.35	.44	.59	.31
Wright (interstate wars)	.34	.37	.38	.35	.18	.33	.29	.19

Bueno de Mesquita[b]	.17	.77	.23	.45	—	—	—	—
Bueno de Mesquita (adjusted)[b]	.10	.55	.19	.39	—	—	—	—
Small and Singer (all wars)[b]	.76	1.61	1.10	1.23	—	—	—	—
Small and Singer (interstate wars)[b]	.07	.58	.32	.45	—	—	—	—
Wallerstein:								
Richardson	.71	.80	.60	.87	.65	.94	1.17	.67
Wright (all wars)	.54	1.04	.74	1.07	.64	.47	.52	.48
Wright (interstate wars)	.31	.30	.41	.52	.34	.36	.27	.29
Bueno de Mesquita	.56	.05	.43	1.24	.12	.39	.44	.44
Bueno de Mesquita (adjusted)	.22	.05	.43	.76	.12	.28	.39	.44
Small and Singer (all wars)	1.22	1.00	1.48	1.95	.88	1.28	1.33	.94
Small and Singer (interstate wars)	.17	.05	.43	.71	.24	.39	.44	.56

[a] When the number of years in a period of hegemony or nonhegemony equals $4m + 1$, where m is an integer, the last $(m + 1)$ years are regarded as the last quarter of the period. When the number equals $4m + 2$, the last $(m + 1)$ years are regarded as the last quarter, and the previous $(m + 1)$ years are regarded as the third quarter. When the number equals $4m + 3$, the second, third, and last quarters contain $(m + 1)$ years. The initial year for the analysis of each classification was 1495 for Gilpin, 1494 for Modelski, and 1600 for Wallerstein.

[b] Too few observations exist for nonhegemonic periods to permit reasonably reliable calculations of this sort.

Table 2.5
Mean Number of Wars Beginning During Periods of
Openness and Closure, Seven Data Sets[a]

Data Set	Openness	Closure
Richardson	.81	.89
Wright (all wars)	.93	.73
Wright (interstate wars)	.42	.41
Bueno de Mesquita	.58	.30
Bueno de Mesquita (adjusted)	.39	.30
Small and Singer	1.45	1.14
Small and Singer (interstate wars)	.40	.43

[a] Krasner (1976) includes 1879 and 1900 in periods of both openness and closure. For this reason, these two years were each employed in the analysis of both types of periods.

Table 2.6
Mean Number of Wars Beginning per Year During Each Quarter of Periods
of Openness and Closure

Data Set	Closure (Quarter of Period)[a]				Openness (Quarter of Period)[a]			
	First	Second	Third	Fourth	First	Second	Third	Fourth
Richardson	1.30	.40	1.00	.83	.61	.83	.74	1.11
Wright (all wars)	1.20	.20	.33	1.17	1.00	.83	1.00	.89
Wright (interstate wars)	.50	.20	.33	.58	.39	.44	.42	.42
Bueno de Mesquita	.20	.10	.17	.67	.46	.29	.69	.85
Bueno de Mesquita (adjusted)	.20	.10	.17	.67	.21	.29	.62	.42
Small and Singer (all wars)	1.00	.90	1.08	1.50	1.29	1.25	1.73	1.50
Small and Singer (interstate wars)	.40	.20	.33	.75	.21	.29	.58	.50
Singer and Small	0	.10	.17	.58	.17	.25	.31	.19
Levy	.10	.10	.08	.42	.17	.25	.23	.19

[a] See table 2.4, note a.

results are useful because they indicate that aspects of trade may influence the outbreak of all wars and all interstate wars. This issue will therefore be examined further in chapter 4.

THE EFFECTS OF KONDRATIEFF CYCLES ON ALL WARS AND ALL INTERSTATE WARS

In this book, my analysis of process-level effects on war centers on trade. But it is clear that other factors of this sort could contribute to the onset of war. One leading candidate is the global business cycle.

In recent years, there has been a renewed interest in whether the occurrence of hostilities is correlated with so-called Kondratieff cycles of approximately fifty to sixty years in length.[21] Nikolai Kondratieff asserts that "it is during the period of the rise of long waves . . . that, as a rule, the most disastrous and extensive wars and revolutions occur" ([1926] 1979:536). He speculates that the explanation for this finding may be that "wars originate in the acceleration of the pace and the increased tension of economic life, in the heightened economic struggle for markets and raw materials, and . . . social shocks happen most easily under the pressure of new economic forces" (539). Although many scholars are not convinced that such cycles exist, others postulate that economic upswings provide the wealth to finance wars, technological advances that enhance war-fighting capacities, and increases in international tensions that can boil over into conflict.[22]

A number of studies have investigated whether there is a difference in the incidence of the outbreak of war between the upswings and the downswings of the Kondratieff cycle. Joshua Goldstein utilized Levy's data on Great Power wars for this purpose and concludes that a "roughly equal number of wars took place on downswings as on upswings" (1985:424). In other words, with respect to these economic cycles, wars involving major powers seem to occur at random. Raimo Väyrynen (1983) argues, however, that major wars are more likely to begin in the upswing stages. William Thompson and L. Gary Zuk (1982) corroborate these results, finding that 80 percent of the wars beginning between 1816 and 1914 occurred during upswings.

[21] Kondratieff identifies a series of cycles in the international economy. Specifically, he argues that long waves existed in the wholesale price level, interest rates, wages, turnover in foreign trade, and the production and consumption of certain raw materials. Other researchers have found evidence of long cycles in investment, innovation, and profit levels. See Goldstein (1985; 1988) and Thompson (1988, chap. 8) for discussions of this literature.

[22] Conversely, it has been suggested that war gives rise to upswings in the economy. For example, Thompson and Zuk (1982) argue that major wars may be responsible for reinforcing upswings in price series, but that the conclusion of such hostilities usually signals a price downswing.

To see whether the average number of wars begun per year differed between the upward and downward phases of the cycles, the mean number of wars begun per year for each phase was calculated (using Goldstein's 1985, 1988 dating of the phases). When all wars are considered, the mean number of wars during the upward phase equals or exceeds that of the downward phase, regardless of which data set is used. (See table 2.1.) The differences in the mean number of wars between upswings and downswings are statistically significant only in the cases of Bueno de Mesquita (both adjusted and unadjusted) and Small and Singer. Nonetheless, the results suggest that the outbreak of wars may be correlated with long-term movements in the global economy, a topic that will be considered at greater length in chapter 4.

While Kondratieff expressed interest in the relationship between long waves of economic activity and both international wars and revolutions, it is useful to analyze the former types of conflict separately for a better illustration of the role that such cycles play in the global arena. When the lists of Small and Singer and Wright are adjusted to include only wars between states, the results are not quite so robust. Whereas Small and Singer's data still produce a higher mean number of wars in the upward phases of the Kondratieff cycles, the opposite is true for Wright's adjusted compilation (see table 2.1). This illustrates the fact that researchers should be careful when choosing a data set because the outcomes may vary considerably.[23]

Since Kondratieff suggests that the rise in upswings in these cycles may be most strongly associated with the onset of war, it would also be useful to examine whether differences exist in the frequency of war among various phases of upswings and downswings. To this end, the upswings and downswings of the Kondratieff cycle were divided into quarters, and the mean number of wars beginning per quarter was calculated. The results, shown in table 2.7, indicate that, for all wars, there is weak evidence that transition periods between the final quarter of downswings and the initial quarter of upswings lead to an increase in the mean number of wars breaking out per year. But there is no evidence that wars occur more frequently during various quarters of either type of phase of these cycles. The results for interstate wars are somewhat different: the mean number of wars tends to decline during transitions from upswings to downswings (in three out of four cases); and the incidence of war also tends to be lower during the first half than the last half of both types of periods.

[23] The causal connections between economic fluctuations and warfare (in both directions) remain ambiguous. Although these findings are interesting and potentially useful theoretically, one must be careful to distinguish between causality and correlation.

TABLE 2.7

Mean Number of Wars Beginning per Year During Each Quarter of Upswings and Downswings in the Kondratieff Cycle

Data Set	Upswing (Quarter of Period)[a]				Downswing (Quarter of Period)[a]			
	First	Second	Third	Fourth	First	Second	Third	Fourth
Richardson	.84	.67	.83	.92	1.08	1.00	.65	.62
Wright (all wars)	.69	.44	.71	.62	.62	.59	.63	.63
Wright (interstate wars)	.31	.27	.38	.32	.40	.29	.34	.43
Bueno de Mesquita	.37	.53	.68	1.21	.17	.33	.23	.36
Bueno de Mesquita (adjusted)	.37	.32	.58	.63	.17	.24	.18	.36
Small and Singer (all wars)	1.53	1.53	1.89	1.58	.89	.19	1.14	1.04
Small and Singer (interstate wars)	.47	.37	.63	.53	.28	.24	.27	.39
Singer and Small	.21	.26	.32	.32	0	.14	.14	.26
Levy	.23	.17	.29	.28	.28	.22	.20	.31

[a] See table 2.1, note a. See also table 2.4, note a.

THE EFFECTS OF POWER, TRADE, AND THE BUSINESS CYCLE ON MAJOR-POWER WARS

As noted in the first section of this chapter, one purpose of this book is to determine whether systemic variables influence the onset of all wars and all interstate wars, as well as major-power wars. The results in this chapter indicate that certain systemic factors may be of considerable use in explaining the onset of all wars and all interstate wars. But it was also pointed out above that, for many purposes, primary attention should be focused on hostilities involving major powers.[24]

For 1495 to 1975, Levy (1983) provides data for wars involving major powers; for 1816 to 1980, Singer and Small (1972) and Small and Singer

[24] These data sets include wars that involve one, as well as more than one, major power. As pointed out above, wars between major powers are not examined separately. For an analysis of the following hypotheses when the data are restricted to wars between major powers, see Mansfield (1988).

(1982) provide data for wars involving major powers.[25] Singer and Small (1972:70) and Small and Singer (1982:45) categorize Austria-Hungary (1816–1918), Prussia/Germany (1816–1870; 1871–1918; 1925–1945), Russia/the Soviet Union (1816–1917; 1922–1980), France (1816–1940; 1945–1980), Great Britain (1816–1980), Italy (1860–1943), Japan (1895–1945), China (1949–1980), and the United States (1898–1980) as major powers. Levy (1983:24–43) identifies France (1495–1975), England/Great Britain (1495–1975), the Hapsburg Dynasty/Austria/ Austria-Hungary (1495–1519; 1519–1556; 1556–1918), Spain (1495– 1519; 1556–1808), the Ottoman Empire (1495–1699), the Netherlands (1609–1713), Sweden (1617–1721), Russia/the Soviet Union (1721– 1975), Prussia/Germany/West Germany (1740–1975), Italy (1861– 1943), the United States (1898–1975), Japan (1905–1945), and China (1949–1975) as Great Powers. These classifications will be used for various purposes throughout this book. For present purposes, these data are used to determine whether the results obtained in previous sections remain robust if we narrow our focus to wars with at least one major-power participant.

In many respects, the results for major-power wars (shown in tables 2.6, 2.7, 2.8, and 2.9) differ little from those for all wars and all interstate wars. For wars with major-power participants, as for these other types of war, the Poisson distribution provides a remarkably good fit. (See figures 2.1 and 2.2.)[26] When the number of wars per year is regressed on time, the value of r^2 is very low, and there is no evidence of autocorrelation of the residuals. Hence, there is no evidence of contagion among the onset of major-power wars, a result that is consistent with Levy's findings (1983, chap. 7).

There is also a tendency for the mean number of major-power wars per year to be higher during periods of increased openness than during periods of closure, although the evidence is quite weak. Some of the reasons why the relationship between openness and closure and the onset of major-

[25] Singer and Small (1972:70) provide an initial compilation of thirty major-power wars. Using their coding scheme, this list was updated using the data they provide in *Resort to Arms*, thereby adding three other wars to their original data: the Vietnam War (1965), the Russo-Afghan War (1979), and the Sino-Vietnamese War (1979). In addition, Navarino Bay (1827) was no longer considered a war in their updated study (1982). It should be noted that further analysis has led to minor differences between some of the results reported in Mansfield (1988) and those in the present study for Singer and Small's data.

[26] The incidence of wars involving major powers for Singer and Small's list was too small to conduct a Chi-square test for goodness-of-fit: if the expected number in each class does not exceed five, no degrees of freedom exist. These conclusions, then, are based on the comparison of histograms in figures 2.1 and 2.2 showing the theoretical and observed frequency distributions. For Levy's data involving major powers, a Chi-square test was conducted ($\chi^2 =$ 1.69, .10 $< p <$ .20). Clearly, the null hypothesis that the data conform to the Poisson distribution cannot be rejected. On this point, see also Levy (1983, chap. 7).

TABLE 2.8
Linear Trend and Effects of Kondratieff Cycles, Openness, Hegemony, and
Polarity on the Number of Major-Power Wars Beginning per Year

	Singer and Small	Levy
Linear regression of annual number of wars begun on time:		
Regression coefficient	0.00037	−0.00049
t-statistic	0.45	−2.88
r^2 (adjusted for degrees of freedom)	−.005	.015
Durbin-Watson statistic	1.98	2.22
Mean number of wars beginning per year:		
Kondratieff upward phase	.26	.24
Kondratieff downward phase	.12	.25
Openness	.230	.21
Closure	.227	.18
Gilpin's classifications:		
Hegemony	.20	.18
Nonhegemony	.26	.27
Modelski's classifications:		
Leadership	.20	.25
Nonleadership	.57	.21
Wallerstein's classifications:		
Hegemony	.23	.28
Nonhegemony	.19	.18
Levy's classifications:		
Hegemony	—[a]	.26
Nonhegemony	—[a]	.24
Bipolarity	.20	.17
Multipolarity	.22	.25

[a] No mean number of wars can be computed for Singer and Small's data using Levy's periods because Levy's final period of unipolarity ends in 1815 and Singer and Small's data begin in 1816.

power wars is so weak will be addressed in chapter 4. Further, table 2.6 shows that the incidence of major-power war tends to be higher in the last half of periods of openness than in the first half of such periods, but that this difference is not very pronounced; and that the final quarter of closure again witnesses much more war than earlier quarters of closure. As was the case for all wars, table 2.9 indicates that the evidence that the incidence of major-power war is higher in the last quarter of hegemonic periods than in

TABLE 2.9

Mean Number of Major-Power Wars Beginning per Year During Each Quarter
of Periods of Hegemony and Nonhegemony

Classifications	Hegemony (Quarter of Period)[a]				Nonhegemony (Quarter of Period)[a]			
	First	Second	Third	Fourth	First	Second	Third	Fourth
Gilpin:								
Singer and Small	.09	.38	.15	.18	0	0	.38	.63
Levy	.16	.32	.16	.12	.37	.28	.23	.22
Modelski:								
Singer and Small[b]	.07	.39	.10	.16	—	—	—	—
Levy	.27	.28	.26	.23	.24	.44	.11	.06
Wallerstein:								
Singer and Small	.11	.05	.33	.43	.10	.10	.10	.45
Levy	.23	.12	.39	.36	.16	.15	.18	.26
Levy:								
Singer and Small[c]	—	—	—	—	—	—	—	—
Levy	.32	.30	.19	.25	.25	.32	.20	.36

[a] See table 2.4, note a. The initial year used for the analysis of Levy's classification was 1495.
[b] See table 2.4, note b.
[c] See table 2.8, note a.

other quarters is much stronger when Wallerstein's classifications are used than when the other classifications are employed.

In four noteworthy respects, however, the results do change. First, although there has been a mild upward trend in the total number of wars per year, the trend in wars involving major powers depends on the data set that is analyzed. For Singer and Small's data, there is a weak upward trend; for Levy's data, there has been a downward trend in the number of major-power wars per year.[27] Second, although for all wars and all interstate wars the mean number of hostilities per year during the upward phase of the Kondratieff cycle generally has been higher than during the downward phase, the mean number of wars per year involving major powers does not seem to have varied appreciably between these phases.[28] (See table 2.8.)

Third, although the presence of a hegemon seems to have been associ-

[27] Levy (1983:112–49) also finds a downward trend in the onset of wars involving major powers.
[28] Goldstein (1985) makes the same observation, based on Levy's data. However, Singer and Small's data support the thesis that more wars tend to begin in upswings than in downswings of the Kondratieff cycle. (See table 2.8.) This issue will be addressed further in chapter 4.

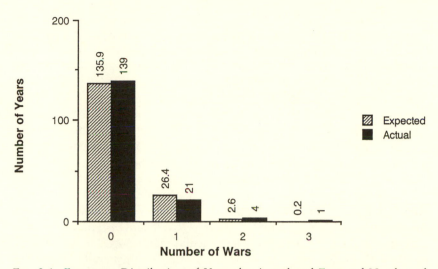

FIG. 2.1. Frequency Distribution of Years, by Actual and Expected Number of Singer and Small's Wars Involving Major Powers, Based on the Poisson Distribution

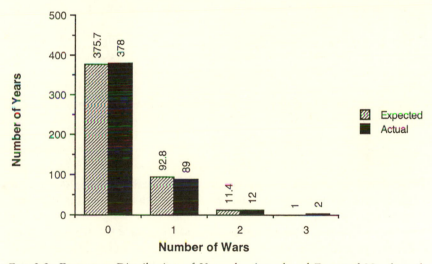

FIG. 2.2. Frequency Distribution of Years, by Actual and Expected Number of Levy's Wars Involving Major Powers, Based on the Poisson Distribution

ated with a higher incidence of all wars than the absence of such a power, the results are more ambiguous for wars involving major powers. When the four classifications (including Levy's [1985a]) are compared across the two data sets, no clear relationship seems to exist between hegemony and wars of this sort.[29] Further, table 2.9 indicates little clear evidence of clustering around changes from hegemony to nonhegemony and vice versa. However, there are some notable differences between Singer and Small's and Levy's data in this respect. In the former case, the last quarter of nonhegemony is related to the highest mean number of wars: this is consistent with the power transition hypothesis. In the latter case, there is no evidence of clustering. (It should be noted that these differences, as well as those in the trends in the number of wars beginning over time, between Singer and Small's and Levy's data are probably due at least as much to variations in the time period that these data sets cover as to differences in the events that are coded as wars and the dating of particular major-power wars.) In sum, although the data for all wars and all interstate wars generally seem to be consistent with balance-of-power theory, the data for wars involving major powers do not support strongly either power preponderance or balance-of-power explanations. In the following chapter, some reasons why this might be the case will be considered.

Finally, whereas the mean number of all wars beginning per year tended to be greater in bipolar periods, table 2.8 shows that the mean number of major-power wars beginning per year is greater during multipolar periods. These results are consistent with the predictions of Waltz (1964) and others who argue that bipolar systems should witness fewer major-power wars than multipolar systems.

CONCLUSIONS

In this chapter, I examined in a preliminary fashion the effects of power and trade on the outbreak of all wars, all interstate wars, and major-power wars. These findings have a number of implications for the analyses that will be conducted in the following chapters. First, there was no evidence of contagion regarding the onset of war. As a result, contagion effects will not be considered in the subsequent models of war. Second, there is often relatively little agreement among the various data sets of all wars and all interstate wars. The subsequent analyses of war will therefore continue to compare empirical results across a variety of data sets.

Third, evidence derived from this chapter suggests that systemic vari-

---

[29] There do seem to be important differences across classifications of hegemony and nonhegemony. Gilpin's classifications consistently elicit a higher mean number during periods of nonhegemony, whereas Wallerstein's and Levy's classifications provide consistent results that point in the opposite direction.

ables influence the incidence of all wars and all interstate wars, as well as those involving major powers. In particular, all wars and all interstate wars seem to begin most frequently during periods of hegemony, bipolarity, openness, and upswings in the Kondratieff cycle, respectively. These are important findings since, as noted above, empirical analyses have rarely addressed all wars and all interstate wars in systemic studies. However, it is clear that further analysis is needed before we can be confident that power, trade, and economic cycles influence minor-power wars, and if so, the nature of these relationships. Such analysis will be conducted in the following two chapters.

Fourth, these results indicate that certain systemic factors impact the onset of major-power wars. For example, wars involving major powers tend to begin more frequently during periods of openness and multipolarity than during periods of closure and bipolarity. But in many cases, systemic variables seem to have surprisingly little effect on the outbreak of major-power wars, given that systemic explanations are generally designed to explain major-power behavior. For example, hegemony and the international trading system appear to be very weakly related to the onset of wars involving major powers. These relationships will be examined further, and a number of explanations for the weakness of these findings will be presented, in chapters 3 and 4.

The results of this chapter offer a useful start to this study's analysis of the systemic determinants of war. However, as stressed throughout this chapter, these findings are only a beginning. It is necessary to isolate the effects of various systemic influences on war, holding constant other systemic factors that might be important in this regard. And as I argued in chapter 1, it is useful to compare the impact of various aspects of power and trade on war. It is to these tasks that I turn in the following two chapters.

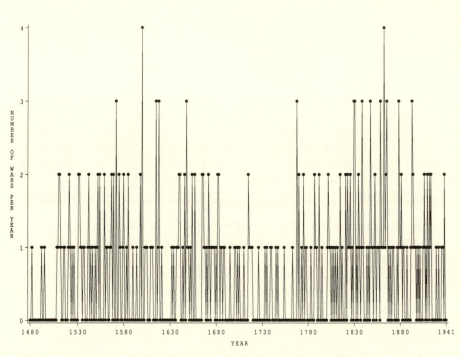

FIG. 2.3. Number of Wars Beginning Each Year, Based on Wright's Data, from 1480 to 1941

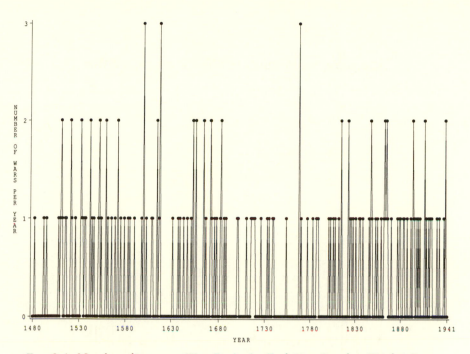

FIG. 2.4. Number of Interstate Wars Beginning Each Year, Based on Wright's Data, from 1480 to 1941

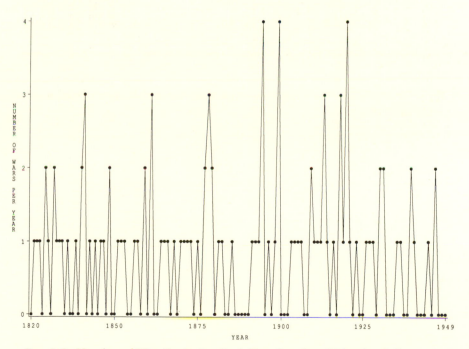

FIG. 2.5. Number of Wars Beginning Each Year, Based on Richardson's Data, from 1820 to 1949

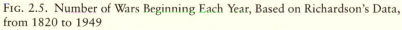

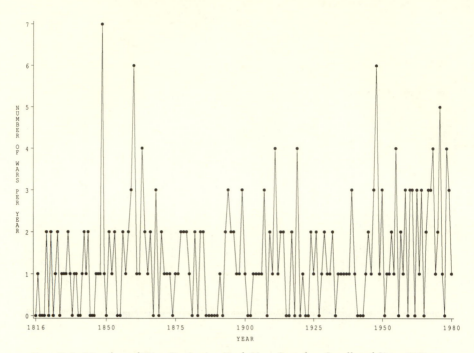

FIG. 2.6. Number of Wars Beginning Each Year, Based on Small and Singer's Data, from 1816 to 1980

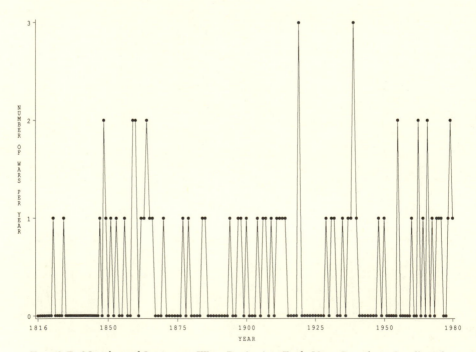

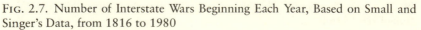

FIG. 2.7. Number of Interstate Wars Beginning Each Year, Based on Small and Singer's Data, from 1816 to 1980

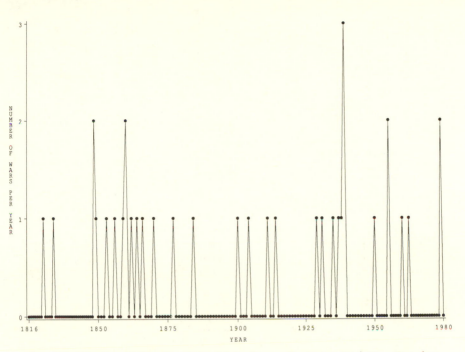

FIG. 2.8. Number of Wars Involving Major Powers Beginning Each Year, Based on Singer and Small's Data, from 1816 to 1980

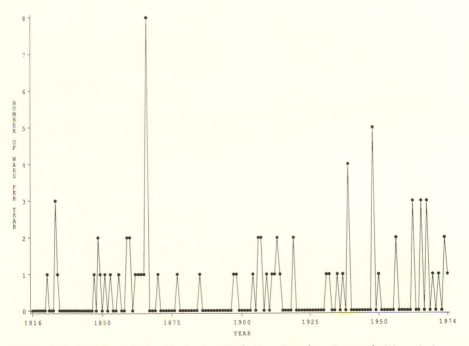

FIG. 2.9. Number of Wars Beginning Each Year, Based on Bueno de Mesquita's Data, from 1816 to 1974

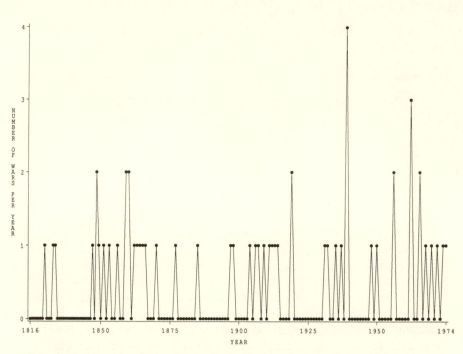

FIG. 2.10. Number of Wars Beginning Each Year, Based on Bueno de Mesquita's (Adjusted) Data, from 1816 to 1974

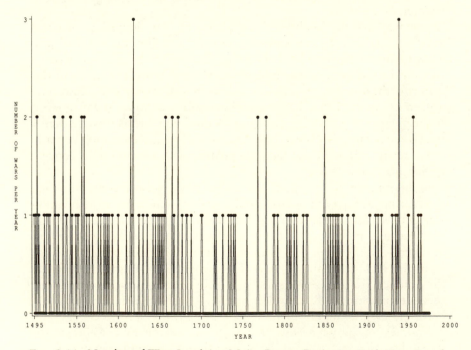

FIG. 2.11. Number of Wars Involving Major Powers Beginning Each Year, Based on Levy's Data, from 1495 to 1975

Chapter 3

THE DISTRIBUTION OF POWER
AND THE ONSET OF WAR

FEW TOPICS in international relations have generated as much interest, and as little agreement, as the relationship between the distribution of power and the onset of war. A wide variety of realist and other theories place primary emphasis on the distribution of power in their explanations of war. The *strength* of this relationship clearly bears heavily on the merits of these theories, and the *nature* of this relationship is clearly central to many debates among scholars of war. The previous chapter presented some preliminary findings regarding these topics. But it was also pointed out that additional tests of the effects of the distribution of power on the onset of war needed to be conducted in order to more fully address the strength and nature of this relationship. The purpose of this chapter is to further examine this relationship, and to extend in a number of ways the analysis in chapter 2.

One way that this analysis is extended is by considering the effects of both polarity and the concentration of capabilities on the onset of war. Since many previous studies concerning the impact of the system's structure on the outbreak of war have centered on polarity, the effects of this feature of the distribution of power were examined in chapter 2. However, I argued in chapter 1 that defining the distribution of power solely in terms of the number of poles courts a variety of important problems, and that at least some of these problems could be avoided by supplementing the traditional realist and neorealist focus on polarity with a focus on the concentration of capabilities.

In this chapter, I argue that, in addition to the general conceptual reasons for analyzing both polarity and concentration, tests of the relationship between the distribution of power and war should include concentration because many leading theories of war—and the hypothesis that I advance—highlight the effects of the number of major powers and the inequalities of power among them. It is demonstrated in this chapter that the number of major powers and the inequalities of capabilities among them determine the level of concentration. Counting the number of poles, however, provides no information concerning either of these factors.

Another way in which this analysis is extended is by considering the possibility that the nature of the relationship between the distribution of power and the onset of war may not accord with predictions based on either balance-of-power or power preponderance theories. I argued in chapter 1 that, rather than the monotonic relationship that both sets of theories lead us to expect, there is reason to believe that an inverted U-shaped relationship exists between the concentration of capabilities and the onset of major-power war. In this chapter, this hypothesis is further developed, and the first tests of it are conducted.

THE CONCENTRATION OF CAPABILITIES

In chapter 2 the analysis of the distribution of power centered on polarity. This approach was entirely appropriate since many analysts consider the number of poles to be the most important dimension of the global distribution of power. But as I argued in chapter 1, relying solely on polarity to measure the distribution of power entails a number of limitations. Most important is the failure of this variable to measure the number of major powers and the inequalities of power among these states. As a result, scholars who rely exclusively on polarity to measure the distribution of power must assume that: (1) either the poles in any given system are structurally equivalent or inequalities of power among the poles are of little consequence for the purposes of explaining patterns of global outcomes; and (2) those major powers that are not poles exert no influence on the distribution of power, and hence on patterns of global outcomes (Mansfield 1993a).

I argue that these assumptions pose both conceptual and empirical problems for analyses of the distribution of power and war (and for analyses of the international political economy, as discussed in chapter 5). Rather than assuming that the number of major powers and the level of inequality among them are unimportant, it is useful to directly examine their effects on the incidence of war. One well-known index (Ray and Singer 1973) that directly measures these aspects of the distribution of power, and that will be used extensively throughout the remainder of this book, is *concentration*, which is defined as follows:

$$
(3.1) \qquad CON_t = \sqrt{\frac{\sum\limits_{i=1}^{N_t} (S_{it})^2 - 1/N_t}{1 - 1/N_t}} \, ,
$$

where S_{it} is the proportion of the aggregate capabilities possessed by the major powers that major-power i controls in year t, and N_t is the number of major powers in the system in year t. CON_t is thus a continuous index that takes on values ranging from zero to one and measures the aggregate inequality of capabilities among all the major powers in the system. It is clear that when each major power possesses the identical proportion of the aggregate capabilities controlled by the major powers, CON equals zero; when one major power monopolizes the aggregate capabilities possessed by the major powers, CON equals one; and when neither of these conditions obtain, $0 < CON < 1$ (where more [less] skewed distributions of capabilities produce higher [lower] levels of CON).

At the outset, it is important to make clear that concentration and polarity, as it is conventionally defined, measure different features of the distribution of power. To briefly illustrate some of these differences, consider a hegemonic (or unipolar) system—that is, a system characterized by a "large" relative disparity between the *two* most powerful states (and, by extension, between the largest state and every other state) in the international system. Assume also that in addition to the hegemon four nonpolar major powers exist, so that the system is comprised of five (polar and nonpolar) major powers.

The level of concentration will decrease if, holding the number of major powers (and the capabilities of all but the two largest major powers) constant, the proportion of the aggregate major-power capabilities that the hegemon controls declines and the proportion controlled by the strongest nonpolar major power increases (since this will reduce the value of the sum of the squared proportions of the capabilities possessed by the major powers, and hence the numerator in equation 3.1). In the event that this change in the distribution of capabilities between these two states is large enough to generate a rough balance between them, a bipolar system would emerge. In this sense, concentration is related to polarity. But the level of concentration will also decrease if: (1) holding the number of major powers constant, a "small" major power's capabilities increase relative to the other major powers in the system (since this will also decrease the sum of the squared proportions of the capabilities possessed by the major powers, and hence the value of the numerator in equation 3.1), even though no change occurs in the distribution of capabilities between the two largest states; or (2) holding constant the proportion of the aggregate major-power capabilities possessed by each major power, the number of major powers in the system increases. In neither of these cases would a change in the level of concentration be related to a change in the number of poles.

To further illustrate the differences between concentration and polarity, consider table 3.1. In it, rough estimates of the share of the aggregate major-power capabilities that is possessed by each major power and the corresponding level of concentration are presented for each of four years. These shares were computed based on the equally weighted average of economic, military, and demographic capabilities described below, using the Correlates of War Project's "National Material Capabilities Data"

TABLE 3.1
Shares of Major-Power Capabilities and Levels of Concentration
in 1840, 1855, 1920, and 1955[a]

	Major Power					
	A	B	C	D	E	CON
1840	.320	.240	.240	.130	.070	.222
1855	.340	.270	.220	.120	.050	.259
1920	.450	.230	.150	.090	.080	.326
1955	.390	.290	.190	.080	.050	.319

[a] These shares of major-power capabilities and levels of concentration are rough approximations that are computed based on the Correlates of War Project's "National Material Capabilities Data" (1991).

(1991). (Note that the major powers are not identified by name because their identities differ across some of these years.) Since each system is comprised of five major powers, variations among these systems concerning the level of concentration are due solely to differences in the shares of the aggregate major-power capabilities that each state controls and hence to differences in the relative inequality of capabilities among the major powers.

The entries in table 3.1 indicate that as power inequalities become increasingly pronounced (particularly among the three largest major powers), the level of concentration rises accordingly. Table 3.1 also illustrates quite starkly some differences between concentration and polarity. Many scholars who emphasize the distinction between bipolarity and multipolarity consider the systems in 1840, 1855, and 1920 to be structurally equivalent, since, as noted in chapter 2, they classify each of these years as multipolar. A wide variety of other analysts who highlight the distinction between hegemony and nonhegemony consider the systems in 1840, 1855, and 1955 to be structurally equivalent, since, as noted in chapter 2, they classify each of these years as hegemonic. Yet it is clear that the level of concentration varies markedly among these multipolar and hegemonic systems. The level is relatively low in 1840, it is relatively high in 1920 and 1955, and it is at an intermediate level in 1855. Moreover, the level of concentration in 1920, which is considered multipolar and nonhegemonic, respectively, exceeds that in 1955, which is considered bipolar and nonhegemonic, respectively.[1]

These examples indicate some of the differences between polarity and

[1] See Mansfield (1992a; 1993a) and Wayman and Morgan (1990) for further discussions of the differences between concentration and polarity.

concentration. However, the fact that they measure different features of the distribution of power provides little inherent justification for analyzing both of them in structural analyses of war. Studies of concentration have been criticized on the grounds that the aspects of the distribution of power that it measures are not emphasized in leading theories of international relations, and that concentration therefore has little theoretical content. In the following section, I argue that this view is mistaken.

SOME CONCEPTUAL FOUNDATIONS OF CONCENTRATION

It was noted in chapter 1 that analyzing concentration in structural studies of international relations is appropriate because it is consistent with both the microeconomic bases of neorealist theories and the ways in which these explanations often define the system's structure. These issues are addressed below. But the central reason for analyzing concentration in this study is that the effects of the number of major powers and the distribution of capabilities among them, which determine the level of concentration, are highlighted in many balance-of-power and power preponderance theories of war—as well as in the hypothesis that I advance below. Since one purpose of this book is to test these explanations, an emphasis on concentration is clearly warranted.

As pointed out in chapters 1 and 2, both power preponderance theorists and those balance-of-power theorists who seek to explain the onset of war often focus on the effects of inequalities of power among the leading states in the system. The differences between these groups of theories stem primarily from disagreements concerning whether inequalities of power enhance or undermine deterrence.

For many balance-of-power theorists, a uniform distribution of power among the major powers deters war involving these states because potential aggressors are likely to be dissuaded from war if a state or coalition of states exists that could defeat them. As Quincy Wright argues, "The balance of power is a system designed to maintain a continuous conviction in every state that if it attempted aggression it would encounter an invincible combination of the others" (1965:254; see also Toynbee 1954; Gulick 1955; Herz 1959; Claude 1962; Wolfers 1962; Morgenthau and Thompson 1985). According to these explanations, the more uniform the distribution of power among the leading states, the greater the number of potential blocking coalitions that exist. And the more potential blocking coalitions that exist, the greater the expected costs of initiating war relative to the expected benefits of doing so, all other things being equal. As the distribution of power becomes increasingly skewed, fewer blocking coalitions exist, thus tempting aggression on the part of stronger states.

For power preponderance theorists, a highly skewed distribution of power deters the onset of certain types of war. Aggression against preponderant states is likely to be fruitless, and preponderant states can achieve political goals vis-à-vis smaller states through means other than war. When inequalities of power are less pronounced, states are likely to engage in wars for (among other reasons) the purposes of bolstering their positions in the system.

It is clear that the distribution of power among all the major powers is central to both of these explanations of major-power war. A wide variety of studies suggest that the distribution of power among the major powers is an important influence on the coalitions among them that are likely to form (Russett 1968c; Zinnes 1970; Gilpin 1981:88; Wagner 1986; Niou, Ordeshook, and Rose 1989; Niou and Ordeshook 1990). This issue is fundamental to many balance-of-power theories. Further, a variety of studies conclude that, consistent with predictions based on power preponderance explanations, "near-preponderant" systems (that is, systems in which a single state controls precisely half of the relevant power capabilities) are unlikely to experience the onset of certain types of major-power wars (Wagner 1986; Niou, Ordeshook, and Rose 1989; Niou and Ordeshook 1990). Concentration provides a summary measure of the number of major powers and the distribution of capabilities among them, which are emphasized by many balance-of-power and power preponderance theories. It was pointed out in chapter 1 that polarity provides little information concerning either of these factors: the only dimension of inequality that it measures is that between polar and nonpolar states; polarity does not measure power inequalities among (between) poles and/or nonpolar major powers. Since one purpose of this study is to test certain balance-of-power and power preponderance theories, a focus on concentration is necessary.

Aside from the fact that these explanations focus on the effects of factors that are measured well by concentration, there are a number of more general reasons to examine concentration in a study of this sort. For example, as indicated in chapter 1, a wide variety of scholars define the system's structure in terms of the number of major powers and the distribution of power among them (Russett 1968a:131–37; Snyder and Diesing 1977:419; Gilpin 1981:88; Mearsheimer 1990). These factors are measured by concentration, but not by the number of poles.

In addition, it was also indicated in chapter 1 that neorealist theories of international relations are often based on analogies between the structure of industries and markets and the structure of the global system. Measuring the distribution of power solely in terms of the number of poles is inconsistent with the manner in which industry structure is typically measured. Economists generally posit that both the number of firms in an industry and the size inequality among them influence industry outcomes.

Concentration is closely related to the most widely used measure of this sort, the Hirschman-Herfindahl index; in fact, it "is a perfectly predictable function of [the Hirschman-Herfindahl index], as long as we know the value of N" (Ray and Singer 1973:430).[2] Hence, the conceptual bases for the use of concentration inhere in both the factors emphasized by the explanations of war that are tested in this book and the analytic foundations of many structural approaches to the study of international relations.

Previous Empirical Studies of Concentration and War

As noted in chapter 1, many tests of balance-of-power and power preponderance theories have centered on the effects of polarity. But a number of other major studies have tested these theories by focusing on the relationship between concentration and features of major-power war. Their conclusions have differed substantially.

[2] For the original derivation of the Hirschman-Herfindahl index (HH), see Hirschman (1945 [1980]:xviii–xx, 87–88, 157–62). This index is defined as follows:

$$(a) \qquad HH_t = \sum_{i=1}^{N_t} (S_{it})^2.$$

Hence,

$$(b) \qquad CON_t = \sqrt{\frac{HH_t - 1/N_t}{1 - 1/N_t}}.$$

It is clear that the primary difference between HH and CON is that the latter is somewhat less sensitive than HH to the size of N. More specifically, the upper bound of both indices is one, but the lower bound of CON is zero, while the lower bound of HH is $1/N$ (Ray and Singer 1973; Taagepera and Ray 1977).

This is not to suggest that the Hirschman-Herfindahl index is the sole measure of its kind. However, a number of well-known alternative measures (Theil 1967; Hannah and Kay 1977) are closely related to the Hirschman-Herfindahl index, and, hence, to Ray and Singer's index of concentration (Taagepera and Ray 1977).

Nor is this to suggest that Ray and Singer's index is the only measure of global structure that is consistent with existing measures of industry and market structure. For example, Wayman's (1984) index of polarity is quite similar to N-firm ratios of industry structure, which measure the aggregate market share possessed by a given number (N) of firms in an industry. Wayman defines a bipolar system as one in which the two largest major powers control over half of the aggregate major-power capabilities, and a multipolar system as one in which the two largest major powers control less than half of these capabilities. The effects of this index of polarity on major-power war are considered briefly (see footnote 18, below). But it is important to note that this index departs from most neorealist definitions of polarity, since Wayman's "two-state" ratio measures the proportion of the aggregate major-power capabilities controlled by the largest two states, rather than counting the number of poles. As

The initial empirical study of this sort was conducted by J. David Singer, Stuart Bremer, and John Stuckey (1972), who examined the extent to which the magnitude of wars involving major powers (operationalized as the number of nation-months of war involving at least one major power that are underway in a given period) was explained by the concentration of capabilities, the change in concentration, and the amount of movement in capabilities among the major powers. (These variables, which were measured at five-year intervals from 1820 to 1960, are defined and discussed further below.) On the whole, their results supported the power preponderance hypothesis, though the "goodness of fit was not very impressive" (1972:46). When the data were split into the nineteenth and twentieth centuries, the results were much stronger. The balance-of-power hypothesis was supported during the nineteenth century, whereas the power preponderance hypothesis was supported during the twentieth century.[3]

In 1981 Bruce Bueno de Mesquita (1981a) extended Singer, Bremer, and Stuckey's study. However, a number of important alterations were made in both the independent and dependent variables. First, Bueno de Mesquita incorporated "[a]ssumptions [about decision makers] related to variable attitudes toward risk-taking [in order] to build a simulation of decision-making under the constraint of expected utility maximization" (1981a: 541). To this end, concentration was calculated in a somewhat different fashion than in Singer, Bremer, and Stuckey's study.[4] Second, his model included variables to indicate whether the distribution of power among alliances affects the likelihood of war. Third, rather than explaining the magnitude of war, he utilized a binary dependent variable, the value of which depended on whether or not any wars began in a given period of time. Contrary to Singer, Bremer, and Stuckey's findings, Bueno de Mesquita concluded that *"no particular distribution of power has exclusive claim as a predictor of peace or war in theory or in the historical record of the period 1816–1965"* (1981a:541; emphasis in original).

The controversy in this area continued in 1983, with a study by William Thompson (1983a). Like Bueno de Mesquita, Thompson altered both the independent and dependent variables used in Singer, Bremer, and Stuckey's analysis. The most notable difference between his study and the preceding analyses was his use of naval expenditures and capital ships to measure capabilities, and his use of a somewhat different major-power subsystem.[5]

---

a result, analyses of polarity based on these ratios may differ considerably from those based on counting poles (Mansfield 1993a).

[3] See also Cannizzo (1978) who arrives at a similar conclusion based on analysis of both the aggregate magnitude of major-power war and the magnitude of war for individual major powers. However, she finds some variation concerning the effects of concentration on the magnitude of war for individual major powers, particularly during the nineteenth century.

[4] See Bueno de Mesquita (1981a:556–59).

[5] Thompson argues that, based on the "sea power criteria," Austria-Hungary, Prussia, Italy, and China should not be included as major powers, that the United States and Japan

He also restricted his study to bivariate analyses of the relationship between concentration and "the nation-months of global power participation" (1983a:150) for both wars involving and between major powers. Unlike Bueno de Mesquita, he found evidence of a strong relationship between concentration and war. Thompson concluded that "the magnitude of war underway does tend to increase as systemic capability concentration declines. It also does not seem to make much empirical difference how one slices the 1816–1964 time frame" (1983a:153).[6]

More recently, Bruce Bueno de Mesquita and David Lalman (1988) analyzed the relationship between concentration and the onset of European wars involving and between major powers. They relied on the same capabilities used by Singer, Bremer, and Stuckey to measure concentration, but since their interest was in European wars, concentration (and the other independent variables in their model) was calculated among the *European* major powers.[7] Besides concentration, they analyzed the effects of polarity, the "tightness" of polarity, and the interaction effects among these variables on the onset of war. As in the case of Bueno de Mesquita (1981a), they treated the onset of war as a binary variable and concluded that "[t]hese structural dimensions . . . show no sign of significantly altering the likelihood of international war" (1988:13). In their latest study, Bueno de Mesquita and Lalman (1992) also analyzed whether the concentration of capabilities among European powers influences the onset of all dyadic disputes and wars among European states during the nineteenth and twentieth centuries. They found that the likelihood of war depended far more heavily on the expected utility of war and aspects of the dyadic distribution of power than on concentration.[8]

THE RELATIONSHIP BETWEEN CONCENTRATION AND WAR

Both balance-of-power theory and power preponderance theory posit that the relationship between the distribution of power and the onset of major-power war is monotonic, although they disagree over whether the relationship should be direct or inverse. By virtue of their interest in testing these explanations, the studies summarized above (as well as other analyses) restricted their analyses to testing whether a monotonic relationship exists

should be "introduced [as major powers] at earlier points in time," and that "France and Britain [sh]ould be dropped from the list [of major powers] after 1945" (1983a:147).

[6] This finding is in accord with Boswell and Sweat's (1991) results concerning the relationship between concentration and the intensity of major-power wars.

[7] In addition to the European major powers, "the United States is included as a European major power after 1939, when it chose to play an active diplomatic, strategic, and military role in European affairs" (Bueno de Mesquita and Lalman 1988:9).

[8] Among other analyses of the effects of concentration on war are Maoz (1982), Wayman (1984), Stoll and Champion (1985), Modelski and Thompson (1988), Midlarsky (1988), and Boswell and Sweat (1991).

between concentration and war. However, as I argued in chapter 1, it is important to recognize that this relationship may have an inverted U-shape.

A number of previous studies have pointed out that a curvilinear relationship may exist between features of the distribution of power and the onset of war, but none of them has focused on the effects of concentration. Some scholars have suggested that the relationship between the *dyadic* distribution of power and the onset of war is curvilinear (Herz 1959; Claude 1962; Most and Starr 1987, 1989; Midlarsky 1988; Wolfson, Puri, and Martelli 1992). Others have noted that, at the systemic level, it is not theoretically clear why the relationship between the distribution of power and the onset of war should be monotonic (Thompson 1983a:150; Modelski and Thompson 1987; Levy 1989:232–33); and a number of studies have examined whether the relationship between *polarity* and the onset of war is nonmonotonic (Rosecrance 1966; Wallace 1973; Garnham 1985; Levy 1985a).[9] Yet no tests of whether a nonmonotonic relationship exists between concentration and the outbreak of war have been conducted to date. Since the factors that are measured by concentration are central to many leading explanations of war, this is an important gap in the literature. But prior to testing this hypothesis, it is important to discuss why such a relationship might be expected.

An Inverted U-Shaped Relationship Between Concentration and Major-Power War

It was noted in chapter 1 that if an inverted U-shaped relationship exists between the concentration of capabilities and the onset of major-power war, both the highest and lowest levels of concentration are associated with the lowest incidence of warfare while intermediate levels of concentration are associated with the highest incidence of warfare. Like most systemic studies, it is assumed in the following analysis that states are rational

[9] These studies suggest that a curvilinear relationship may exist between polarity and war. Specifically, Rosecrance argues that "tight bipolar" and "loose multipolar" systems are the most likely to witness the onset of war. Garnham maintains that "[t]here is a curvilinear relationship between the number of poles in the interstate system and the probability of major power war. The likelihood of war is lowest for a tripolar system, higher for a bipolar system, highest in a system with five poles, and less likely in larger systems" (1985:20). In contrast to this argument, Levy (1985a) finds that the frequency of warfare is highest when the system is bipolar, lowest when the system is multipolar, and at an intermediate level when the system is unipolar.

This hypothesis is not examined in the present study because few analysts who define polarity in terms of the number of poles in the system argue that more than two types of systems (either hegemonic and nonhegemonic or bipolar and multipolar) existed during the nineteenth and twentieth centuries. (See Thompson 1988 for an exception.)

actors: each state makes decisions concerning whether or not to initiate a war based on a comparison of the expected improvement in its relative position in the international system that would result from waging war with the expected costs associated with doing so.

Systems characterized by a (relatively) uniform distribution of capabilities—and therefore low levels of concentration—are expected to experience the onset of few wars (relative to imbalanced systems), since this condition gives rise to a variety of potential coalitions, each of which is able to thwart any aggressor(s). States have an incentive to block the aggressor in order to avert the possibility that victory on its part will undermine their respective positions vis-à-vis the initiator. And this has the effect of increasing the expected costs of initiating a war relative to the expected benefits, and hence deterring states that are considering doing so.

Of course, these expected benefits and costs may not be so easy to evaluate. The expected costs of initiating a war depend on, among other things, the likelihood that a blocking coalition will actually form. Kenneth Waltz argues that this likelihood will be influenced by "the size of the group and the inequalities within it, as well as on the character of its members" (1979:165). As a result, collective action problems may lead states to "buck-pass" and fail to block an aggressor if many states of equal size are required to do so.[10] Further, the expected benefits and costs that a potential aggressor faces depends on its expectation of winning the war, the costs of war, and the consequences of defeat.[11] If it determines that war can be waged successfully, or if it calculates that defeat will be cheap and inconsequential, a state may choose to initiate hostilities.

But in a system characterized by a relatively uniform distribution of capabilities, only a small number of states are likely to be needed in order to block an initiator (or group of initiators). Since, as Mancur Olson points out, "sufficiently small groups can provide themselves with some amount of a collective good through the voluntary and rational action of one or more of their members" (1971:32–33), there is likely to be a high probability that some type of blocking coalition will form. Further, the potential targets of aggression are likely to be highly dependent on one another in matters of security, and to share a strategic interest in defending one another, since if the defeat of one (or more) of them enhances the power of an aggressor, the security of the remaining states will be jeopardized. This mitigates the possibility that potential allies will abandon one another in the face of a hostile power when capabilities are (approximately) uniformly distributed.[12] In addition, if capabilities are (approximately) uniformly

---

[10] See also Posen (1984) and Christensen and Snyder (1990) on this issue.

[11] I am grateful to Robert Jervis for bringing these points to my attention.

[12] On this point, see Snyder (1984).

distributed among the major powers, a war undertaken by a major power against a very weak state is unlikely to bolster substantially its international position. As a result, the expected benefits of such actions are likely to be small, and to be outweighed by the expected costs of doing so.

On the other hand, when concentration is at an intermediate level, the moderate imbalances that obtain among the major powers are expected to tempt them to aggression since, as John Mearsheimer argues, "when power is unbalanced, the strong become hard to deter" (1990:15). Further, under these conditions, fewer potential blocking coalitions exist, which (all other things being equal) weakens deterrence by reducing the expected costs of war. And as the distribution of capabilities becomes increasingly skewed, a large major power may determine that war against a smaller major power or an important minor power is worth undertaking if victory will improve its position relative to the other large major powers and is likely to be completed quickly (before any of the few potential blocking coalitions that do exist are able to form and assist the smaller state). Further, the threat posed by a large major power may lead weaker states to band together and launch a preventive war against it, since, if this major power is left unchecked, the disparity between it and smaller states might further widen. Under these circumstances, smaller states have reason to conclude that the expected costs of waging war are likely to be outweighed by the consequences of inaction.

Indeed a number of studies suggest that the imbalances fostered by intermediate levels of concentration contribute to the onset of war. John Herz, for example, argues that war is most likely to begin when there exists a "slight imbalance" among the major powers (1959:154; see also Claude 1962). Further, Mearsheimer argues that wars prior to 1945 were the product of both "multipolarity and *the imbalances of power that often occurred among the major states in that multipolar system*" (1990:11, emphasis added; see also Wolfers 1962).

When concentration is at a high level, deterrence is expected to be enhanced. A system of this sort is likely to be characterized by the preponderance of one or two states, and even "[b]alance of power theorists concede that a given state is more likely to be deterred by a preponderance of power" (Levy 1989:232; Blainey 1973). In a highly concentrated system characterized by one preponderant state and a host of weaker states, each of the smaller states is expected to be deterred from attacking the preponderant state, and the dominant state is likely to try to manage and limit conflict, rather than participate in (or encourage) it, because it can achieve its own objectives through coercion, intimidation, and other measures short of war. In a highly concentrated system characterized by two preponderant powers and a series of smaller states, we would expect: (1) smaller states to be deterred from attacking the dominant states because the expected costs of doing so are likely to be prohibitive; (2) the dominant states to be deterred from attacking one another since the disparity of capabilities between them is relatively small and thus the potential costs of war are again quite high (Waltz 1979; Mearsheimer 1990); (3) relatively few wars involving smaller major powers since the dominant states have an incentive to manage conflicts among the smaller states (Waltz 1979); and (4) the dominant states to refrain from attacking smaller states since the defeat of the latter states can do little to improve the position of one superpower vis-à-vis the other.

THE STATISTICAL MODEL

The previous section indicated why an inverted U-shaped relationship might exist between concentration and the onset of major-power war. In this section, the statistical model that will be used to test this hypothesis is described. At the outset, it should be pointed out that this analysis focuses on the relationship between the distribution of power and the onset of war during the period after the conclusion of the Napoleonic Wars. This time period is chosen because it has been the focus of most previous empirical studies of this topic, and because data limitations preclude the examination of earlier eras.

Like Singer, Bremer, and Stuckey's and Bueno de Mesquita's studies described above, the present analysis centers on the effects of concentration, the change in concentration, and the movement in capabilities among the major powers on warfare.[13] The present analysis will also compare the effects of aspects of both polarity and concentration on war because it is important to determine whether these structural variables exert different influences on war, and whether the impact of polarity on war varies from that in chapter 2 when other features of the distribution of power are held constant. However, unlike Singer, Bremer, and Stuckey's and Thompson's studies, this analysis will center on the *onset* of war. After all, if one is interested in the causes of war, the magnitude of war does not seem to be the most appropriate dependent variable (Duvall 1976; Siverson and Sullivan 1983; Most and Starr 1989). And unlike Bueno de Mesquita's and Bueno de Mesquita and Lalman's studies, the *frequency of war's onset* (and, in particular, the mean number of wars that began in a given period of time) will be analyzed because it is important to understand whether the system's structure can explain variations in how many wars began, as well as whether or not any war began.

---

[13] Thompson's analysis was restricted to bivariate tests of the relationship between concentration and war.

With these considerations in mind, the statistical model is as follows:

$$(3.2) \quad War_t = A + B_1 Hegemony_t + B_2 Polarity_t + B_3 CON_t$$
$$+ B_4 delta\ CON_t + B_5 MOVE_t + B_6 CON_t^2 + B_7 Year_t + e_t.$$

The dependent variable (War_t) and the independent variables ($Hegemony_t$, $Polarity_t$, CON_t, $delta\ CON_t$, $MOVE_t$, CON_t^2, and $Year_t$) are defined and discussed below. The parameters are A, B_1, B_2, B_3, B_4, B_5, B_6, and B_7; e_t is a random error term.

The dependent variable, War_t, is the mean number (that is, the frequency) of wars per five-year period (beginning in 1825), where t is the first year of the period.[14] As in chapter 2, the effects of the distribution of power on a number of different types of wars are examined. Since most structural explanations focus on major-power behavior, the following analysis continues to center on the impact of the distribution of power on major-power wars. And because the results in chapter 2 indicated that certain differences exist between Singer and Small's and Levy's data, the results continue to be compared across both compilations.

As in chapter 2, the relationship between the distribution of power and all interstate wars is also examined. Since there is little reason to expect the structure of the system to impact the incidence of extrasystemic, civil, and colonial wars, only those data sets that focus solely on interstate wars are considered. Further, Wright's interstate war data are not considered in this chapter, because his compilation does not include wars beginning after 1941 and there is no variation in *Polarity* until 1946. The results in the previous chapter suggested that the effects of the distribution of power on all interstate wars may depend on which compilation of war is used. Hence, results based on Bueno de Mesquita's, Bueno de Mesquita's (adjusted), and Small and Singer's (interstate war) data continue to be generated and compared.

The independent variables are defined as follows:

Hegemony is a dummy variable that takes on a value of one if a hegemon exists in year t, and zero if year t is classified as nonhegemonic. Because the results in chapter 2 indicated that different classifications of hegemony may be related to war in different ways, both Gilpin's and Wallerstein's data on hegemony are examined. (Levy's and Modelski's classifications are not

---

[14] For example, if CON is measured in 1900, the dependent variable is the mean number of wars from 1900 to 1904. It should be noted that the correlation between CON and the number of wars beginning in the first year of each period (year t) is quite low and hence we need not worry that a simultaneous relationship exists between concentration and war.

Five-year periods are used in all cases except the following: 1910–1912, 1913–1919, 1935–1937, 1938–1945, and 1946–1949. These exceptions were made to replicate Singer, Bremer, and Stuckey's analysis. They did not use five-year periods in these cases to avoid measuring the independent variables during World Wars I and II.

analyzed because the former does not define any period from 1825 to 1964 as hegemonic and the latter defines very few years during this era as non-hegemonic.)

Polarity is a dummy variable that takes on a value of one if the system is multipolar in year *t*, and zero if the system is bipolar in year *t*. As in chapter 2, Snyder and Diesing's (1977), Waltz's (1979), and Levy's (1985a) classifications of polarity are analyzed: the system is considered multipolar until 1945, and bipolar thereafter.

Year is the value of year in year *t*. This variable is included because, in a number of cases, there was evidence of a secular trend in the onset of major-power wars and all interstate wars in chapter 2. Further, it is important to ensure that any observed relationship between the distribution of power and war is not due to a secular trend in both variables.

Except for the quadratic term, the remaining independent variables are the same as those used by Singer, Bremer, and Stuckey: (1) *CON;* (2) *delta CON;* and (3) *MOVE*. Prior to describing these variables, it should be pointed out that two sets of estimates of *CON, delta CON,* and *MOVE* are analyzed in this and the following chapters. The first set is taken directly from Singer, Bremer, and Stuckey's study; the second set is derived from more recent data on national capabilities compiled by the Correlates of War Project. (When the more recent data are used, the analysis in this and the following chapter is extended to 1974, and the analysis in chapter 5 is extended to 1975.)[15] All the following analyses in this book are conducted using both sets of estimates; and it is important to note that the results of these analyses are generally quite robust with respect to which set of estimates is used. There is therefore little need to report findings based on both sets of estimates, except in those specific cases in which the results differ substantially. Since a wide variety of previous studies have relied on Singer, Bremer, and Stuckey's estimates of *CON, delta CON,* and *MOVE,* and to enhance the comparability of the present study's findings with those of previous studies, the results in the remainder of this study are based on Singer, Bremer, and Stuckey's estimates, unless otherwise noted.

CON is the index developed by Ray and Singer (1973), which is described above (see equation 3.1). Consistent with Singer, Bremer, and Stuckey, as well as a wide variety of other studies, the proportion of the aggregate capabilities possessed by the major powers that each major power controls in year *t* (S_{it}) is based on an equally weighted average of national population, urban population in cities with more than 20,000

---

[15] The newer data were taken from the Correlates of War Project's "National Material Capabilities Data" (1991). While these data extend until 1990, estimates of concentration based on these data were only derived for the period from 1820 to 1970 because many of the data on war and trade used in this study do not extend beyond 1975.

residents, energy consumption (from 1885 on), iron/steel production,[16] military personnel, and military expenditures among the major powers in the international system. Further, in keeping with many previous studies, including Singer, Bremer, and Stuckey's, the number of major powers in the system in year t (N_t) is based on the compilation of major powers by Singer and Small (1972) and Small and Singer (1982) that was described in chapter 2.

Delta CON and MOVE measure dynamic features of concentration. The change in concentration is measured as follows:

$$(3.3) \qquad delta\ CON_t = \frac{CON_t - CON_{(t-5)}}{t - (t - 5)}$$

where CON_t is the level of concentration at the beginning of each five-year period (year t) and $CON_{(t-5)}$ is the level of concentration at the beginning of the previous period (year $t - 5$).

MOVE "reflects the number of percentage shares which have been exchanged between and among the major powers during each period" (Singer, Bremer, and Stuckey 1972:27). MOVE is measured as follows:

$$(3.4) \qquad MOVE_t = \frac{\sum_{i=1}^{N_t} \left| S_{it} - S_{i(t-5)} \right|}{2(1 - S_{mt})}$$

where m is the major power that possesses the smallest proportion of capabilities.

Since both *delta* CON and MOVE are used extensively in this study, it is useful to elaborate on the aspects of the distribution of power that they measure. On the one hand, *delta* CON measures the average annual change in concentration during each five-year period. On the other hand, MOVE measures changes in the proportion that each major power controls of the capabilities possessed by all major powers. To illustrate the difference between these features of the distribution of power, consider a system comprised of three major powers, A, B, and C. Assume that in year $t - 5$ the distribution of the proportion of major-power capabilities among these states is as follows: A = .50; B = .25; C = .25. Assume that in year t this distribution becomes: A = .25; B = .50; C = .25. CON is clearly the same (about .251) in years $t - 5$ and t; as a result, *delta* CON equals zero. However, because the proportion of capabilities possessed by A and B has changed, MOVE is not equal to zero; in fact, MOVE = .333. Since shifts in

---

[16] Iron is used until 1895; thereafter, steel is used.

capabilities among major powers may generate (im)balances among them, and because (im)balances have been linked to the onset of war by a variety of the explanations discussed above, it is important to consider the effects of *MOVE*, as well as *delta CON*, in any study of this sort.

Estimates of the Parameters for Major-Power Wars

It was noted earlier that one purpose of this book is to examine the structural conditions that give rise to major-power wars. To help shed new light on this topic, ordinary least squares (OLS) was used to estimate the values of A, B_1, B_2, B_3, B_4, B_5, B_6, and B_7 for Singer and Small's and Levy's data on wars involving major powers. These results (in table 3.2) indicate that the aspects of the distribution of power included in equation 3.2 and time explain only a modest percentage (about 10 to 15 percent) of the variation in major-power wars. They also indicate that there is no evidence of a secular trend in the incidence of wars involving major powers.[17] However, the relationship between *certain* features of the distribution of power and the frequency of major-power war is quite strong.

As I hypothesized, *an inverted U-shaped relationship exists between the concentration of capabilities and the frequency of wars involving major powers*. The regression coefficient of CON is positive and statistically significant, and the regression coefficient of CON^2 is negative and statistically significant in all four cases. Further, dynamic features of concentration also are associated with the frequency of war. The regression coefficients of both *delta CON* and *MOVE* are positive (although they are statistically significant only when Levy's data are used), which suggests that increases in concentration and greater movement have been catalysts to major-power wars.

Singer, Bremer, and Stuckey argue that, if the results are consistent with power preponderance theory, it should be the case that: (1) a negative correlation exists between CON and war; (2) a negative correlation exists between *delta CON* and war; and (3) a positive correlation exists between MOVE and war. If, on the other hand, the results are consistent with balance-of-power theory, the respective regression coefficients should point in the opposite directions. Their findings provide weak support for the power preponderance hypothesis. The results in table 3.2 do not lend

[17] It should be noted that when the more recent data on national capabilities described above were used to estimate concentration during the period from 1820 to 1974, there were two cases in which *Year* was both positive and statistically significant (at the .10 level). It should also be noted that one reason why there was evidence of a statistically significant downward trend over time in Levy's data in chapter 2, but not in the present analysis, is that Levy's entire data set was analyzed in chapter 2. The present analysis is concerned only with wars involving major powers that began during the nineteenth and twentieth centuries.

TABLE 3.2

Regression of the Mean Number of Wars Involving Major Powers per Year
for Each Five-Year Period (1825–1964) on *Hegemony, Polarity,* CON,
delta CON, MOVE, CON², and *Year,* Two Data Sets[a]

	Classifications of Hegemony			
	Gilpin		Wallerstein	
	Levy	Singer and Small	Levy	Singer and Small
Intercept	−6.17	−10.19	−6.48	−11.14*
	(−1.23)	(−1.70)	(−1.21)	(−1.75)
Hegemony	0.15	0.24	0.15	0.27
	(0.71)	(0.97)	(0.71)	(1.06)
Polarity	0.06	0.37	0.05	0.39
	(0.18)	(0.99)	(0.16)	(1.06)
CON	27.83***	31.23***	19.45**	16.93*
	(2.99)	(2.80)	(1.89)	(1.38)
delta CON	11.98**	7.00	11.92**	6.82
	(2.13)	(1.04)	(2.11)	(1.02)
MOVE	19.53*	18.82	12.02	6.09
	(2.04)	(1.64)	(1.27)	(0.54)
CON²	−51.76***	−54.62***	−38.44**	−31.83*
	(−3.12)	(−2.83)	(−2.12)	(−1.47)
Year	0.001	0.003	0.002	0.005
	(0.65)	(1.21)	(0.72)	(1.28)
$\bar{R}^2$ [b]	.16	.09	.16	.09

[a] The *t*-statistic of each regression coefficient is reported in parentheses below the coefficient.

[b] All values of R^2 are adjusted for degrees of freedom.

* Significant at the .10 level. One-tailed tests are conducted for the regression coefficients of CON and CON² because their signs are specified by the model. Two-tailed tests are conducted for all other regression coefficients.

** Significant at the .05 level. See note *.

*** Significant at the .01 level. See note *.

any clear support to either power preponderance or balance-of-power
theories. In no case does the set of regression coefficients point in the
direction predicted by either theory. Instead there is strong evidence of an
inverted U-shaped relationship between concentration and the frequency
of wars involving major powers.

This may help to explain why the results in table 3.2 show that *neither
Hegemony nor Polarity is associated with the incidence of major-power*

wars.[18] These findings are consistent with the results in chapter 2, and (in conjunction with the findings concerning the relationship between concentration and wars involving major powers) support the argument that, by themselves, neither power preponderance nor balance-of-power theory explains fully the onset of major-power war.[19]

If there is an inverted U-shaped relationship between the concentration of capabilities and the incidence of wars involving major powers, it follows that there is a level of concentration that maximizes the frequency of war. Taking the first derivative of the regression equation with respect to *CON* and setting it equal to zero will provide the level of concentration that maximizes the incidence of major-power war (so long as the second derivative is negative). This value will identify the periods that historically have experienced the highest frequency of major-power wars. In the following section, the issue of why wars began particularly often during these eras is considered. For Singer and Small's compilation, a concentration level of about .275 is associated with the maximum frequency of the onset of war; for Levy's compilation, a concentration level of about .260 is associated with the maximum frequency of war. In interpreting these results, it is important to bear in mind that the level of concentration has varied from .202 to .417. Obviously, the regression equations in table 3.2 should not be extrapolated beyond this range.

The period from 1845 to 1869 contains the years that most closely resemble the level of concentration at which the incidence of war is maximized, according to the regression equation. Taken together, it is clear that this period (during which the Austro-Sardinian War, the first Schleswig-Holstein War, the Roman Republic War, the Crimean War, the Anglo-Persian War, the War of Italian Unification, the Franco-Mexican War, the

[18] It is important to note that these results are very insensitive to how the number of poles is measured. For example, in addition to the classifications of polarity and hegemony that have been used throughout this study, Wayman's (1984; see also Wayman and Morgan 1990) classifications of polarity were also analyzed. Based on Wayman's data (see footnote 2, above), two analyses were conducted. First, *Polarity* was defined as the proportion of the major-power capabilities possessed by the largest two major powers. Second, *Polarity* was defined as a dummy variable that equaled one if the two largest states possessed more than half of the aggregate major-power capabilities, and zero otherwise. In both cases, the results were virtually identical to those in table 3.2.

[19] When this analysis is based on the newer data on national capabilities described above and extended to 1974 (rather than using Singer, Bremer, and Stuckey's data), and when Wallerstein's classifications of hegemony are used, the regression coefficient of *Hegemony* is positive and statistically significant in both cases, and the regression coefficient of *Polarity* is positive and statistically significant in one instance. However, it is important to point out that results in the following chapter, based on a more complete model which includes international trade as well as the variables in equation 3.2, indicate that there is no evidence that either *Hegemony* or *Polarity* is related to the frequency of major-power wars, regardless of which estimates of concentration or classifications of hegemony are used (see table 4.1).

second Schleswig-Holstein War, the Austro-Prussian War, and [for Singer and Small] the Italo-Roman and Italo-Sicilian wars began) was the most war-prone since the conclusion of the Napoleonic Wars. On the other hand, periods of lowest (1825–1844 and 1870–1919) and highest (1920–1924 and 1946–1964) levels of concentration witnessed the onset of very few wars involving major powers.

WHY DO INTERMEDIATE LEVELS OF CONCENTRATION CONTRIBUTE TO THE ONSET OF MAJOR-POWER WARS?

The findings in the previous section indicated that an inverted U-shaped relationship exists between concentration and the incidence of wars involving major powers, and that the third quarter of the nineteenth century is the period (during the nineteenth and twentieth centuries) that most closely approximates the level of concentration that has maximized the frequency of this type of war. At this point, it is useful to examine whether the structural consequences of intermediate levels of concentration described above help to explain why major-power wars began especially often during the era from 1845 to 1869.

A number of studies have concluded that, during this period, power became more asymmetrically distributed among the major powers than in any era since the conclusion of the Napoleonic Wars (Hinsley 1963:238–71; Thomson 1981:217–19). One consequence of this intermediate level of concentration among the major powers was that moderate inequalities of power obtained among many of these states (as well as between major powers and smaller states). These imbalances of power had two implications that are especially relevant for present purposes.

First, certain stronger states seemed to believe that wars could be waged successfully and at relatively low cost against certain weaker, but important, states. Moreover, stronger states often appeared to believe that if they did not press their advantage quickly, the opportunity to do so would soon be foreclosed, since smaller states were likely to become stronger in the near future. In addition, there were, according to some observers, also cases in which weaker states launched preventive wars against stronger foes, fearing that the power imbalance among them was likely to worsen if no action was taken. Arnold Wolfers, for example, maintains that throughout this period, "Again and again, a country believing it had attained a position of superiority struck out against its rivals, or another country fearing an increasingly adverse balance initiated war before the balance had tilted too far against it" (1962:122). And Alfred Vagts argues that, during this era, "When, in the cycle of competition, [certain] elements made one Power or group of Powers superior to the expected opponents, who might themselves become superior at a later date, the temptation to plead for or to undertake . . . war remained great" (1956:283). Second, and related to the first consequence of intermediate levels of concentration, these imbalances reduced the number of potential coalitions that could thwart aggression on the parts of the largest states in the system. This had the effect of undermining deterrence during the era from 1845 to 1869.

A number of cases suggest that the factors described above help to explain why wars involving major powers began relatively frequently during this period. The circumstances surrounding the outbreak of the Crimean War provide one especially useful illustration of the salience of these factors. On the eve of this war, it was widely recognized that Russia was in a position to wage war successfully against Turkey, and that doing so would improve substantially its international position. As the Duke of Argyll, a British cabinet member at the time, stated:

> There was in the mind of all of us one unspoken but indelible opinion—that the absorption by Russia of Turkey in Europe, and the seating of the Russian Emperor on the throne of Constantinople, would give to Russia an overbearing weight in Europe, dangerous to all the other Powers and to the liberties of the world. . . . Men do not discuss opinions which are considered axiomatic. But it [this potential increase in Russian power] underlay every motive to action and every thought of policy. Moreover, the absorption of Turkey by Russia was not regarded by us at this time as so difficult as to be at all necessarily a very remote contingency. (quoted in Rich 1985:40)

However, it was not just the favorable distribution of power that led Russia to wage war against Turkey; it was also the belief that no coalition would form that could thwart Russian ambitions. In his analysis of the Crimean War, A. J. P. Taylor attaches much weight to this cause of war.

> On 2 June the British fleet was ordered to Besika bay, outside the Dardanelles. It was joined by the French fleet a few days later; the Anglo-French alliance thus came into being literally by a side wind. This development was unwanted to the tsar, rather than alarming. He had often faced Anglo-French opposition at Constantinople; and he felt secure of the Holy Alliance. He said to the French ambassador: "*The four of you could dictate to me; but that will never happen. I can count on Vienna and Berlin.*" (1971:54; emphasis added; see also Hinsley 1963:213–37)

This suggests that Russia initiated war against Turkey because it was confident that the constellation of states that would be necessary to hamper its effort would not form. Paul Schroeder echoes this view: "It was the Tsar's own foolish pride that led him into trouble, but Russia's conservative diplomats helped by failing to warn him sufficiently about the likely attitude of the European powers. They even shared his basic illusions[, one of which was] *that an anti-Russian coalition was impossible*" (1977:42, emphasis added; 1986:10).

In addition to the Crimean War, there is evidence that the structural factors that intermediate levels of concentration give rise to also help to explain a number of other wars involving major powers that began during the third quarter of the nineteenth century. For example, these factors appear to have played a role in the timing of Prussia's war against Austria in 1866. Vagts argues that

> [d]uring the negotiations with Austria early in 1866, when the outlook for peace seemed to improve under the influence of the pacific Prussian King, Bismarck, although obedient, remonstrated with the monarch that if the endeavor to maintain peace "should be successful now, the danger of war would threaten us later, perhaps in months, under more unfavorable circumstances." For Austria would in the meantime try to get on better terms with France and Italy. (1956:284)

This suggests that Bismarck was anxious to wage war with Austria while the distribution of power was tilted in Prussia's favor and before any potential blocking coalition could come to the assistance of Austria. Similarly, prior to Prussia's war with France, one fear of Moltke, the Prussian Chief of Staff, was that the favorable imbalance of power be acted upon before the Franco-Austrian alliance that was being negotiated could serve as a blocking coalition.

> Accordingly, his war plans of 1869 envisaged such a constellation. "If Austria arms," he told Schweinitz, now ambassador to Vienna, "we really ought to declare war against France at once so that we shall have settled with her before Austria is ready for war, which will take her three months. For this would be a sure sign that there is an agreement with Napoleon and that the latter intends to attack, something for which he by himself is not strong enough." (Vagts 1956:286)

This brief discussion suggests that intermediate levels of concentration encourage the outbreak of wars involving major powers because of the moderate imbalances that inhere during periods of this sort and the few potential blocking coalitions that might form to deter potential aggressors. Moreover, during the middle of the nineteenth century, many small states were viewed as being attractive targets by their stronger adversaries. While these conditions certainly did not *cause* the numerous wars involving major powers that began during this period, they seem to have created a *context* in which wars of this sort were more likely to begin.

ESTIMATES OF THE PARAMETERS FOR ALL INTERSTATE WARS

I argued in chapter 2 that systemic variables might be related to the frequency of all interstate wars, as well as of major-power wars. The results in the previous chapter suggested that aspects of polarity were associated with the frequency of all interstate wars. In this section, the relationship between polarity and the frequency of wars of this sort is examined further. In addition, the importance of concentration in this regard is evaluated. Ordinary least-squares estimates of the parameters in equation 3.2 (shown in table 3.3) demonstrate that certain features of the distribution of power are related to the incidence of all interstate wars. But like the findings in chapter 2, these effects are not identical to those for wars involving major powers.

First, whereas it has little influence on major-power wars, *Hegemony seems to have a strong and quantitatively large effect on the incidence of all interstate wars*, according to the results in table 3.3. The regression coefficient of *Hegemony* is positive in all six cases and statistically significant in five instances, which (as in chapter 2) indicates that all interstate wars have begun more frequently during hegemonic periods than during periods in which no hegemon existed. Moreover, the quantitative effect of *Hegemony* on the incidence of interstate war is considerable. For both Gilpin's and Wallerstein's classifications, the mean number of all interstate wars beginning per year is, on average, about .80 greater during periods of hegemony than nonhegemony. Indeed this is quite substantial, since the mean number of wars of this sort beginning per year rarely exceeded 1.0 during the nineteenth and twentieth centuries.

The effect of Polarity *on war, however, seems to depend on whose data are analyzed.* The regression coefficient of *Polarity* is positive in each case and, like *Hegemony,* it is usually quite large. This suggests that wars occur more frequently during periods of multipolarity than during periods of bipolarity, a finding that is at odds with the results in chapter 2. But unlike *Hegemony,* the regression coefficient of *Polarity* is statistically significant only when Small and Singer's compilation is analyzed; it is not statistically significant when either of Bueno de Mesquita's data sets are examined. Thus, as in the previous chapter, the effects of polarity on the outbreak of all interstate wars often depend on whose compilation is used.

Moreover, the effects of *Hegemony* and *Polarity* on the incidence of all interstate wars are weaker when concentration is estimated based on the more recent data on national capabilities described above, rather than on Singer, Bremer, and Stuckey's data (in table 3.3). The regression coefficients of *Hegemony* and *Polarity* continue to be positive when the newer estimates of concentration are used, but there is no instance in which they are statistically significant and these regression coefficients are considera-

TABLE 3.3

Regression of the Mean Number of Interstate Wars per Year for Each Five-Year Period (1825–1964) on *Hegemony, Polarity, CON, delta CON, MOVE, CON²,* and *Year,* Three Data Sets[a]

| | Gilpin's Classifications of Hegemony | | | Wallerstein's Classifications of Hegemony | | |
| | Small and Singer | Bueno de Mesquita | | Small and Singer | Bueno de Mesquita | |
		(Unadjusted)	(Adjusted)		(Unadjusted)	(Adjusted)
Intercept	−22.07*** (−2.98)	−18.79 (−1.49)	−19.47** (−2.73)	−19.47** (−2.31)	−24.15* (−1.85)	−20.34** (−2.65)
Hegemony	0.74** (2.44)	1.08* (2.08)	0.64** (2.20)	0.57 (1.70)	1.26** (2.44)	0.64** (2.11)
Polarity	1.10** (2.36)	1.14 (1.43)	0.67 (1.50)	0.84* (1.72)	1.28 (1.69)	0.62 (1.40)
CON	35.44** (2.57)	32.77 (1.40)	43.47*** (3.28)	−0.83 (−0.05)	−33.54 (−1.34)	7.32 (0.50)

	(1)	(2)	(3)	(4)	(5)	(6)
delta CON	8.59	8.50	16.10*	9.01	7.49	15.91*
	(1.03)	(0.60)	(2.01)	(1.01)	(0.55)	(1.97)
MOVE	20.49	43.21*	24.57*	-12.79	-15.64	-7.92
	(1.44)	(1.79)	(1.80)	(-0.86)	(-0.68)	(-0.58)
CON²	-59.66**	-51.74	-76.40***	-2.50	54.09	-18.97
	(-2.50)	(-1.27)	(-3.33)	(-0.09)	(1.22)	(-0.73)
Year	0.008***	0.006	0.007**	0.010**	0.015*	0.010**
	(2.82)	(1.28)	(2.35)	(2.15)	(2.01)	(2.36)
$\bar{R}^2$ [b]	.14	-.02	.18	.03	.05	.17

[a]See table 3.2, note a.
[b]See table 3.2, note b.
* Significant at the .10 level. Two-tailed tests are conducted for all regression coefficients.
** Significant at the .05 level. See note *.
*** Significant at the .01 level. See note *.

bly smaller than those in table 3.3. This suggests that the relationship between aspects of polarity and the incidence of all interstate wars depends on the data used to measure national capabilities (and concentration), as well as on the data on war that are analyzed.

Differences in the effects of structural variables are not due solely to variations in data on war and national capabilities: they are also due to differences in how hegemony is defined, measured, and operationalized. While the effects of *Hegemony* and *Polarity* on war do not depend on whether Gilpin's or Wallerstein's classifications of hegemony are analyzed, the relationship between concentration and war depends markedly on which of these classifications is utilized. In particular, features of concentration are largely unrelated to the frequency of war when Wallerstein's data are used, but they are often strongly related to war when Gilpin's data are analyzed. On the one hand, the results (in table 3.3) show that, *for Gilpin's data, the relationship between concentration and all interstate wars is much the same as that for major-power wars*. Although the strength of the relationship differs somewhat across the three data sets, there is considerable evidence of an inverted U-shaped relationship between concentration and war; and both *delta CON* and *MOVE* are directly related to the incidence of war. On the other hand, *when Wallerstein's data are utilized, features of concentration seem to have little impact on the frequency of all interstate wars*.[20]

In addition, there is strong evidence of an upward trend over time in the incidence of all interstate wars. As pointed out in chapter 2, a number of studies have speculated that this trend may reflect increases in the number of states over time (Small and Singer 1982). However, this does not appear to be the case. To test this hypothesis, the average number of states in the system during each five-year period, according to Small and Singer (1982:118–22), was included in equation 3.2. There is no evidence that this variable has a statistically significant or quantitatively large impact on the incidence of all interstate (or major-power) wars, regardless of whose data set or classifications of hegemony are analyzed. There is also no evidence that either the size or statistical significance of the regression coefficients of the remaining variables in equation 3.2 changes appreciably when the number of states in the system is introduced into this model of war.

It should also be noted that, as in the case of major-power wars, this model explains little of the variation in interstate wars. This is what many

[20] Whereas the findings in table 3.3 indicate that the existence and strength of an inverted U-shaped relationship between concentration and the incidence of all interstate wars depend on whose classifications of hegemony are used, results based on the newer estimates of concentration described above indicate that there is substantial evidence of this type of relationship regardless of whether Gilpin's or Wallerstein's classifications are analyzed.

structural theories lead us to believe should occur, since these explanations are designed primarily to explain the onset of major-power wars. However, the relationships between features of the distribution of power and the incidence of interstate wars are often much stronger than many structural theories imply.

ESTIMATES OF THE PARAMETERS FOR INTERSTATE WARS THAT DO NOT INVOLVE MAJOR POWERS

Thus far, the analyses of all interstate wars in this (and the previous) chapter have been conducted by treating as similar each war between nation-states. Major-power wars and interstate wars that do not involve a major power therefore have been aggregated. Since the distribution of power may have different effects on major-power wars than on those interstate wars that do not involve a major power, it is useful to examine separately non-major-power interstate wars. Thus, in this section, the parameters in equation 3.2 are estimated for Small and Singer's, Bueno de Mesquita's, and Bueno de Mesquita's (adjusted) data after excluding major-power wars from these compilations.

The results indicate that the disturbances are characterized by a first-order autoregressive process (AR[1]). As a result, OLS will produce inefficient estimates of the parameters in equation 3.2 and biased estimates of the error variance. However, it is widely recognized that, under these circumstances, generalized least-squares (GLS) estimates will be both unbiased and efficient (Hibbs 1974; Hanushek and Jackson 1977, chap. 6; Harvey 1981, chap. 6; Kmenta 1986). GLS estimates of equation 3.2 are therefore presented in table 3.4.[21]

These findings indicate that like all interstate wars, *non-major-power wars begin more frequently during periods of hegemony than during non-hegemonic periods*: the regression coefficient of *Hegemony* is positive and statistically significant in all six cases, and the size of these regression coefficients continues to be relatively large. Further, there is evidence that *multipolar periods experience a higher frequency of wars that do not involve major powers than bipolar periods*, particularly when Wallerstein's classifications of hegemony are analyzed. The regression coefficient of

[21] To test whether the residuals are first-order autoregressive, Durbin-Watson statistics were computed. The results of these tests were inconclusive. However, Rao and Griliches (1969) conclude that for small samples, when $|\hat{\rho}|$ (the absolute value of the estimate of the first-order correlation among the residuals) is greater than, or equal to, .30, better estimates than those derived using OLS can be obtained by using methods that correct for autocorrelation (see also Maddala 1988:199). Since $|\hat{\rho}| > .30$ in each case in table 3.4, the first-order autocorrelation was dealt with by using GLS. For descriptions of this procedure, see Hibbs (1974), Gallant and Goebel (1976), Hanushek and Jackson (1977, chap. 6), Harvey (1981, chap. 6), and Kmenta (1986).

TABLE 3.4

Regression of the Mean Number of Non-Major-Power Interstate Wars per Year for Each Five-Year Period (1825–1964) on Hegemony, Polarity, CON, delta CON, MOVE, CON^2, and Year, Three Data Sets[a]

	Gilpin's Classifications of Hegemony			Wallerstein's Classifications of Hegemony		
	Small and Singer	Bueno de Mesquita		Small and Singer	Bueno de Mesquita	
		(Unadjusted)	(Adjusted)		(Unadjusted)	(Adjusted)
Intercept	−12.03***	−8.23	−11.84***	−12.02***	−14.15**	−14.38***
	(−3.55)	(−1.41)	(−3.39)	(−2.92)	(−2.71)	(−4.34)
Hegemony	0.51***	0.54**	0.42***	0.48**	0.79***	0.51***
	(3.58)	(2.21)	(2.86)	(2.78)	(3.57)	(3.67)
Polarity	0.77***	0.39	0.38	0.68***	0.65**	0.46**
	(3.61)	(1.07)	(1.71)	(2.89)	(2.18)	(2.42)
CON	5.12	−9.67	10.67	−25.23***	−52.20***	−19.03**
	(0.76)	(−0.84)	(1.56)	(−2.88)	(−4.60)	(−2.66)

delta CON	1.95	2.01	3.97	2.23	1.44	4.20
	(0.42)	(0.27)	(0.88)	(0.44)	(0.21)	(1.00)
MOVE	3.61	8.14	−0.22	−25.44***	−30.90***	−28.11***
	(0.50)	(0.67)	(−0.03)	(−3.36)	(−3.20)	(−4.60)
CON²	−6.14	20.40	−17.26	42.52**	89.59***	30.91**
	(−0.52)	(1.02)	(−1.44)	(2.76)	(4.49)	(2.46)
Year	0.005***	0.005*	0.005***	0.008***	0.011***	0.009***
	(4.12)	(2.02)	(3.81)	(3.36)	(3.64)	(4.65)
$\bar{R}^2$ [b]	.49	.46	.40	.39	.62	.54

[a] All regression coefficients are generalized least-squares estimates. The t-statistic of each coefficient is reported in parentheses below the coefficient.
[b] See table 3.2, note b.
* Significant at the .10 level. See table 3.3, note *.
** Significant at the .05 level. See table 3.3, note *.
*** Significant at the .01 level. See table 3.3, note *.

Polarity is positive in all six cases, and it is statistically significant in four instances. Moreover, whether the system is bipolar or multipolar seems to exert a substantial quantitative effect on the mean number of non-major-power wars beginning per year. Based on the results derived using Wallerstein's classifications, multipolar systems, on average, give rise to the onset of about .60 more wars of this sort per year than do bipolar systems, which is substantial. There is also evidence of an upward trend over time in the incidence of non-major-power interstate wars. It should also be noted that, as in the case of all interstate wars, there is no evidence that the number of states in the system accounts for this trend, or that including this variable in the model influences substantially the effects on war of the other variables in equation 3.2.

While the effects of *Hegemony, Polarity,* and *Year* on the incidence of interstate wars are much the same, regardless of whether or not major-power wars are included in data sets of this sort, the influence of concentration on non-major-power interstate wars is markedly different from that in table 3.3. In particular, these findings indicate that the effects of concentration on all interstate wars using Gilpin's classifications (in table 3.3) are due to the impact of concentration on major-power wars, since there is no evidence that any feature of concentration is related to non-major-power wars in table 3.4. Whereas concentration had no influence on all interstate wars using Wallerstein's classifications, there is considerable evidence of a U-shaped relationship between concentration and interstate wars that do not involve a major power when these classifications are used in table 3.4. Further, *MOVE* is inversely related to the frequency of non-major-power wars.

This suggests that the relationship between concentration and major-power war is considerably different from that between concentration and non-major-power interstate war. Further, the effects of concentration on war seem to be quite sensitive to whose classifications of hegemony are analyzed. If we rely on Wallerstein's classifications, interstate wars that do not involve major powers occur most (least) frequently under those structural conditions in which major-power wars begin least (most) frequently. That is, whereas an inverted U-shaped relationship exists between concentration and the frequency of major-power wars, a U-shaped relationship exists between concentration and the incidence of interstate wars that do not involve major powers.[22] If we rely on Gilpin's classifications, however, aspects of polarity exert a much stronger effect on the incidence of non-major-power war than concentration. Further analysis of these relation-

---

[22] Moreover, the level of concentration that *maximizes* the incidence of major-power war is about .270; on average, the level of concentration that *minimizes* the frequency of non-major-power interstate wars is quite close to this value—about .295.

ships and their implications for this study will be conducted in the following chapter.

The results based on Gilpin's classifications of hegemony are quite robust with respect to whether Singer, Bremer, and Stuckey's estimates of concentration or estimates based on more recent data described above are used. However, contrary to the findings presented in table 3.4 based on Wallerstein's classifications of hegemony, there is little evidence that concentration is related to the incidence of non-major-power interstate wars when the estimates of concentration derived from more recent data are used.[23] And whereas the results in table 3.4 based on Wallerstein's classifications of hegemony indicate that the regression coefficients of *Hegemony*, *Polarity*, and *MOVE* are statistically significant, these regression coefficients have the opposite signs and are not statistically significant when the newer estimates of concentration are employed. Thus when Wallerstein's classifications of hegemony are adopted, the data used to measure concentration seem to influence the relationship between the distribution of power and the frequency of non-major-power wars.

A Further Examination of the Relationship Between Concentration and Major-Power War

The results of this chapter provide substantial evidence that certain (although not always the same) features of the distribution of power help to shape patterns of major-power wars, all interstate wars, and interstate wars that do not involve major powers. These relationships will be considered further in the following chapter. But since scholars of international relations have been preoccupied with explaining patterns of major-power wars, the relationship between concentration and wars of this sort form the basis of the remainder of this chapter.

To begin with, ordinary least squares was used to estimate the values of the parameters in equation 3.2 after excluding *Hegemony*, *Polarity*, and *Year* from the model, because the earlier findings in this chapter indicate that these variables exert little influence on the incidence of major-power war. The results in table 3.5 show that there is even stronger evidence of an inverted U-shaped relationship between concentration and the frequency of wars involving major powers than existed in table 3.2; and that the level of concentration at which the frequency of war is maximized (about .280) is virtually identical to that based on the earlier results in this chapter. These findings also demonstrate that both *delta CON* and *MOVE* con-

---

[23] Further, to the extent that concentration is related to the incidence of non-major-power interstate wars, this relationship seems to have an inverted U-shape. (This is also true of the corresponding analysis in chapter 4.)

TABLE 3.5

Regression of the Mean Number of Wars Involving Major Powers per Year for Each Five-Year Period (1825–1964) on CON, delta CON, MOVE, and CON², Two Data Sets[a]

Data Set	Intercept	CON	delta CON	MOVE	CON²	$\bar{R}^2$ [b]
Levy	−2.92***	23.06***	9.76**	16.35**	−42.93***	.22
	(−2.86)	(3.14)	(2.11)	(2.46)	(−3.24)	
Singer and Small	−3.09**	24.10***	7.54	16.11*	−44.16***	.15
	(−2.53)	(2.74)	(1.36)	(2.03)	(−2.78)	

[a] See table 3.2, note a.
[b] See table 3.2, note b.
* Significant at the .10 level. See table 3.2, note *.
** Significant at the .05 level. See table 3.2, note *.
*** Significant at the .01 level. See table 3.2, note *.

tinue to be directly related to the incidence of major-power war. Aside from their statistical significance, it is also important to note that the quantitative effects of these independent variables continue to be quite large. For example, if CON, delta CON, and CON² are each evaluated at their means, and if MOVE is allowed to vary from its lowest to its highest value, there is about a three-fold increase in the predicted mean number of wars per year. Finally, the fit of the model is somewhat better when *Hegemony, Polarity,* and *Year* are excluded from equation 3.2: table 3.5 shows that the model now explains about 20 percent of the variation in major-power war.[24]

Variations Over Time in the Relationship Between Concentration and Major-Power War

In this section, we turn to the issue of whether the relationship between concentration and the frequency of major-power war has changed over time. Singer, Bremer, and Stuckey found that balance-of-power explanations were supported for the nineteenth century, while power preponderance explanations were supported for the twentieth century. On the other hand, Bueno de Mesquita's analysis produced no significant results even when the data were split, while Thompson concluded that the power preponderance hypothesis was supported regardless of how the data were divided. The existence of intercentury differences would suggest that no

---

[24] This modest increase in the value of the adjusted coefficient of determination is expected, since, in any model, its value will increase if those variables whose *t*-statistics are less than 1.0 are deleted from the model (Maddala 1988:126). As table 3.2 shows, the *t*-statistics of the regression coefficients of *Hegemony, Polarity,* and *Year* are often less than 1.0.

TABLE 3.6
Results of Analysis-of-Variance Tests for
Equation Stability Between the Nineteenth
(1825–1890) and Twentieth (1895–1964)
Centuries, Two Data Sets[a]

Data Set	F-statistic
Levy	0.70
Singer and Small	2.25

[a] In the present case, the F-distribution has degrees of freedom equal to 5 and 18. Under these conditions, the F-statistic is statistically significant (at the .05 level) if it is greater than or equal to 2.77.

single explanation of the relationship between concentration and war will hold across time.

To determine whether the regression equation differed between the two centuries, analysis-of-variance tests of equation stability (Chow 1960; Maddala 1988:130) were conducted for each data set. The results (in table 3.6) indicate that in no case is the equation unstable from one century to the next.[25] Thus the earlier results using pooled data do not seem to mask any intercentury differences regarding the relationship between the distribution of power and the frequency of war.[26] The observed relationships do not appear to change over time.

Effects of the Number of Major Powers and the Inequality of Their Capabilities on Major-Power War

Another important issue regarding the effects of concentration on the incidence of major-power war concerns the influence of the components of concentration. It was noted in chapter 1 and at the outset of this chapter that concentration, as conventionally measured, is a function of the number of major powers in the international system and the relative inequality among them. It is useful to isolate the effects of these components on

[25] Some analysts argue that both predictive and analysis-of-variance tests should be used to determine whether an equation is stable. When predictive tests are conducted, there continues to be no evidence that the equations are unstable.

[26] Some analysts have objected to Singer, Bremer, and Stuckey's decision to include the period from 1895 to 1899 in the twentieth century. To determine whether the results of the F-tests are sensitive to whether or not this period is included in the twentieth century, the stability of the regression equations between the periods from 1825 to 1899 and from 1900 to 1964 was analyzed. For both data sets, there continued to be no evidence of instability between the nineteenth and twentieth centuries.

major-power war, since some analyses of war have emphasized the salience of one or both of these components.

In this section, I therefore begin by deriving a simple formula relating concentration to the number of major powers and the inequality of their capabilities. According to the Ray and Singer index (in equation 3.1),

$$CON_t = \sqrt{\frac{\sum_{i=1}^{N_t} (S_{it})^2 - 1/N_t}{1 - 1/N_t}}$$

Since the mean of S_{it} equals $1/N_t$:

$$(3.5) \qquad \sum_{i=1}^{N_t} (S_{it})^2 = N_t \sigma_t^2 + 1/N_t,$$

where σ_t^2 is the variance of S_{it}.[27] Thus,

$$(3.6) \qquad CON_t = \sqrt{\frac{N_t \sigma_t^2 + 1/N_t - 1/N_t}{1 - 1/N_t}} = \sqrt{\frac{N_t^2 \sigma_t^2}{N_t - 1}} = \frac{V_t}{\sqrt{N_t - 1}},$$

where V_t is the coefficient of variation (standard deviation divided by the mean) of S_{it}.

Equation 3.6, which does not seem to have appeared in the political science literature before, is a useful result. It enables us to unbundle the effects of the two components of concentration—the number of major powers (N) and the inequality of capabilities among them (V)—on the predicted number of wars beginning per year. (For simplicity, and because

[27] By the definition of the variance,

$$\sigma_t^2 = \frac{\sum_{i=1}^{N_t} (S_{it})^2}{N_t} - \bar{S}_t^2,$$

where $\bar{S}_t$ is the mean of S_{it}. Since $\bar{S}_t$ equals $1/N_t$,

$$\sigma_t^2 = \frac{\sum_{i=1}^{N_t} (S_{it})^2}{N_t} - (1/N_t)^2,$$

from which equation 3.5 directly follows.

TABLE 3.7

Predicted Number of Wars per Year, Based on the Number of Major Powers
and the Inequality of Capabilities Among Them, Using the Regression
Equations in Table 3.5 (and Evaluating *delta CON* and *MOVE*
at Their Mean Values), Two Data Sets

Number of Major Powers	Coefficient of Variation			
	Levy			
	.45	.50	.55	.60
5	.25	.31	.32	.28
6	.13	.24	.30	.33
7	—a	.15	.24	.30
	Singer and Small			
	.45	.50	.55	.60
5	.25	.33	.35	.32
6	.12	.24	.32	.35
7	—a	.14	.24	.31

a The predicted number of wars beginning per year is not computed because there are no
observations for which seven major powers exist and the coefficient of variation is approximately .45.

there is no danger of misunderstanding, the t subscript is dropped in this
and subsequent paragraphs.) To determine the effects of each of these
components, the predicted number of wars per year (in table 3.7) is derived
from the regression equations for major-power wars in table 3.5. Given the
value of N and V corresponding to each cell in table 3.7, we can compute
CON and CON^2, and hence the predicted number of wars per year in that
cell. (Both *delta CON* and *MOVE* are evaluated at their mean values for
the purposes of computing each predicted value.) The values of N and V
generally have fallen in the ranges specified in table 3.7. (It is very important to know what the relevant ranges are because the effects of changes in
N and V vary considerably, depending on their value.)

These results suggest at least three things. First, *within the relevant
range, if* N *is held constant, increases in* V *almost always tend to increase
the predicted number of wars per year, if* N *equals six or seven.* (See figure
3.1. Since the results based on Singer and Small's data are almost identical
to those based on Levy's data, only the latter are shown in figure 3.1.) Thus
balance-of-power explanations seem to be supported under these conditions. However, if N equals five (which has been the case since 1949),
increases in V seem to increase the frequency of war if V is less than about

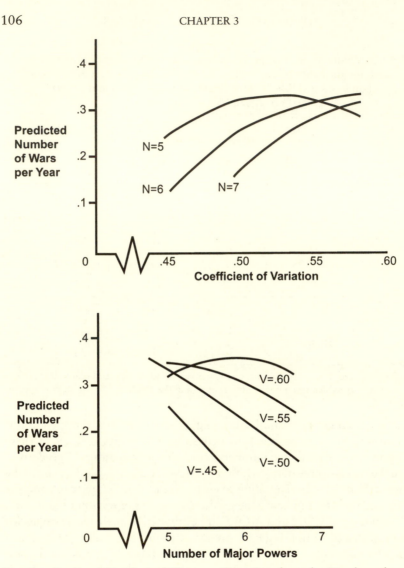

FIG. 3.1. Predicted Number of Wars per Year, Based on the Number of Major Powers (N) and the Coefficient of Variation (V), Using Levy's Data (*Source:* Table 3.7)

.55, but they seem to decrease it if V is greater than this level. Since values of V above and below this level are commonly observed, either possibility can occur. Thus if N equals five, there seems to be an inverted U-shaped relationship between V and the frequency of war.

Second, *holding constant the level of inequality (V), there tends to be an inverse relationship between the number of major powers and the pre-*

dicted number of wars beginning per year (see figure 3.1). This is the case for each level of inequality except .60 and, though these findings are clearly tentative, is in contrast with Levy's (1984) conclusion that no relationship exists between the number of major powers and the frequency of war. However, the apparent disagreement with Levy may be due to the fact that, unlike his study, V is held constant in the present analysis.

Third, *returning to the finding of an inverted U-shaped relationship between V and war, these results indicate that as the number of major powers increases, so too does the level of V at which the likelihood of war is maximized.* Specifically, the level of V that maximizes the incidence of war increases by about 10 percent when the number of major powers increases from five to six and by about 20 percent when the number of major powers increases from five to seven.

Table 3.6 estimates the effects that N and V have on the frequency of war via their effects on CON. In addition, N and V may influence the frequency of war directly and via their effects on variables other than CON. To see whether this is the case, both N and V were included as additional independent variables in equation 3.2 and the regressions were rerun. In no case was the coefficient of either N or V statistically significant, and in each case the regression coefficients of CON and CON^2 remained highly significant. Further, this continued to be the case when *Hegemony, Polarity,* and *Year* were excluded from equation 3.2. Hence, based on both data sets, *there was no evidence that either component of* CON *had a significant effect on war, except via their effects on* CON.

CONCLUSIONS

In this chapter, I have examined the effects of aspects of polarity and concentration on the frequency of major-power wars, all interstate wars, and non-major-power interstate wars. These findings indicate that both of these features of the system's structure are related to the outbreak of war. Given the emphasis that structural theories place on the distribution of power in shaping global outcomes, these results suggest that a neorealist approach to the study of war is likely to be useful. But these findings also indicate that the strength of the impacts of polarity and concentration on the frequency of war—and the nature of the relationships between these structural variables and the incidence of war—vary markedly depending upon which type of war (and often on the data set) that is examined.

First, there is substantial evidence of an inverted U-shaped relationship between concentration and the incidence of wars involving major powers, but little evidence that polarity is related to the incidence of wars of this sort. While both balance-of-power and power preponderance theories provide insights into the conditions under which major-power wars begin most frequently, neither explanation seems to capture fully the relationship between the distribution of power and the incidence of this type of war. It is therefore not surprising that previous empirical studies of these theories have yielded inconclusive and contradictory findings, and that little evidence was found in chapter 2 to support either explanation.

Second, all interstate wars tend to begin most frequently during periods of hegemony and multipolarity. Concentration also helps to explain the frequency of wars of this sort, but the strength and nature of its impact depends largely on whose classifications of hegemony are analyzed. When Gilpin's classifications are used, an inverted U-shaped relationship exists between concentration and war; when Wallerstein's classifications are used, no strong relationship exists between concentration and war. Further, as in chapter 2, the effects of (many) structural variables continue to depend on whose data set on war is analyzed.

Third, like all interstate wars, non-major-power interstate wars begin most frequently during periods of hegemony and multipolarity. These results also indicate that, like all interstate wars, the effects of concentration on wars of this sort depend heavily on whose classifications of hegemony are used. When Gilpin's classifications are examined, no strong relationship exists between concentration and war; when Wallerstein's classifications are analyzed, there is substantial evidence of a U-shaped relationship between concentration and the incidence of wars fought among non-major powers.

Fourth, given that the findings in this chapter indicated that the concentration of capabilities has a significant effect on the incidence of war, it seemed worthwhile to look more closely at the nature of these influences. I demonstrated that concentration can be expressed as a function of (1) the number of major powers; and (2) the relative inequality of capabilities among the major powers. Moreover, the influence of each of these components on the incidence of major-power war depends upon the level of the other. For example, the impact of increases in the number of major powers on the number of wars per year depends on the coefficient of variation of capabilities among the major powers. These results provide additional evidence that the actual relationship between concentration and war is much richer than either balance-of-power theory or power preponderance theory implies.

In sum, aspects of the distribution of power provide us with important insights into the conditions under which wars are likely to begin. If one recognizes the richness and complexity of the relevant relationships, it is possible to use these variables to explain a modest—but by no means negligible—amount of the observed variation over time in the frequency of war. However, it is also clear that, by themselves, structural variables offer an incomplete description of the conditions that give rise to war. As I argued in chapter 1, process-level variables may also be useful in this regard. The results in chapter 2 concerning the effects of trade (and the business cycle) on war suggested that this may be the case. In the following chapter, the models of war that were analyzed in this chapter are therefore supplemented with aspects of international trade.

As in any regression analysis of the sort conducted in this chapter, it is important to ensure that the statistical techniques are adequate. The purpose of this appendix is to present a series of diagnostic tests in order to determine if the appropriate techniques were used throughout this chapter. The three principal problems that might arise in these analyses are autocorrelation of the residuals, heteroskedasticity, and specification errors. To test for autocorrelation, Durbin-Watson statistics were computed. The results indicate that there is little evidence of first-order autocorrelation in tables 3.2, 3.3, and 3.5. Since there was evidence of first-order autocorrelation when interstate wars that do not involve major powers were examined, GLS estimates were presented in table 3.4.

To determine whether the residuals are heteroskedastic, the square of the residuals for each data set was regressed on each of the independent variables, the square of each of the independent variables, and their cross products (White 1980; Maddala 1988), and an F-test was conducted for each regression. In no case was the F-statistic statistically significant. Harry Kelejian and Wallace Oates (1989:242) argue that in small samples, the interaction terms should not be included if more than three independent variables are included in the model because the number of degrees of freedom becomes very small. When the regressions were rerun without the interaction terms, there continued to be no evidence of heteroskedasticity.

It is also important to consider the possibility that the use of OLS is inappropriate because the value of the dependent variable is truncated at zero. Gary King (1988; 1989) has pointed out that under these circumstances, estimates derived using OLS may be inefficient since the residuals may be heteroskedastic and may predict fewer than zero (in the present case) wars beginning per year. But as pointed out above, there is no evidence of heteroskedasticity in the present case, and so long as we stay within the normal range of the data (which, of course, should be done), the regression equations do not predict fewer than zero wars beginning per year. For example, in the analysis of major-power wars, there is only one observation in which this occurs; for 1946, when each independent variable is at its greatest level, the predicted value of War_t is slightly negative. However, it is important to note that none of the results in tables 3.2 and 3.5 is at all sensitive to whether or not this observation is included in the analysis.

A straightforward way of testing whether the truncation problem is of consequence (and if so, of dealing with it) is to use the well-known tobit model rather than ordinary least squares (Tobin 1958; Maddala 1983, chap. 6; Maddala 1988:283–89). To determine the extent to which the parameters in equation 3.2 are sensitive to whether OLS or tobit analysis is used for major-power wars, maximum likelihood estimates for each of the parameters in equation 3.2 were estimated using the tobit model. The results (in tables 3.8, 3.9, and 3.10) indicate that, while the size of the individual coefficients differ, there are few marked differences between the sign and the statistical significance of any of the maximum likelihood

TABLE 3.8

Tobit Analysis of the Mean Number of Wars Involving Major Powers per Year for Each Five-Year Period (1825–1964) on *Hegemony, Polarity, CON, delta CON, MOVE, CON²*, and *Year*, Two Data Sets[a]

| | Classifications of Hegemony | | | |
| | Gilpin | | Wallerstein | |
	Levy	Singer and Small	Levy	Singer and Small
Intercept	−21.93***	−14.93**	−19.78**	−12.86*
	(7.12)	(4.12)	(6.42)	(3.32)
Hegemony	0.32	0.19	0.27	0.19
	(1.41)	(1.11)	(0.81)	(0.48)
Polarity	0.66	0.19	0.52	0.07
	(2.23)	(0.24)	(1.60)	(0.03)
CON	66.82***	57.06***	46.76**	42.29**
	(11.18)	(9.31)	(4.19)	(4.11)
delta CON	9.58	17.45**	9.16	16.92**
	(1.63)	(5.51)	(1.40)	(5.08)
MOVE	15.47	20.65*	1.68	9.85
	(1.45)	(3.01)	(0.02)	(0.75)
CON²	−119.31***	−106.16***	−86.70**	−82.21**
	(10.78)	(9.46)	(4.35)	(4.59)
Year	0.006**	0.004	0.007*	0.004
	(4.45)	(1.94)	(2.96)	(1.18)
Log Likelihood	−4.69	−3.88	−4.99	−4.19

[a] The Chi-square statistic for each coefficient is reported in parentheses below the coefficient. Note that Chi-square (rather than t) statistics are used for each coefficient to test the null hypothesis that $B_i = 0$, $i = 1, \ldots 8$.

* Significant at the .10 level.
** Significant at the .05 level.
*** Significant at the .01 level.

TABLE 3.9

Tobit Analysis of the Mean Number of Interstate Wars per Year for Each Five-Year Period (1825–1964) on *Hegemony*, *Polarity*, CON, delta CON, MOVE, CON², and *Year*, Three Data Sets[a]

| | Gilpin's Classifications of Hegemony | | | Wallerstein's Classifications of Hegemony | | |
| | Small and Singer | Bueno de Mesquita | | Small and Singer | Bueno de Mesquita | |
		(Unadjusted)	(Adjusted)		(Unadjusted)	(Adjusted)
Intercept	−25.60***	−27.15*	−24.04***	−21.83***	−31.90**	−24.31***
	(11.82)	(3.71)	(9.03)	(7.07)	(4.91)	(8.15)
Hegemony	0.85***	1.45**	0.85***	0.63*	1.61***	0.82**
	(8.13)	(6.34)	(6.76)	(3.79)	(7.74)	(5.78)
Polarity	1.24***	1.33	0.77	0.89*	1.44*	0.69
	(7.22)	(2.29)	(2.39)	(3.59)	(2.95)	(1.91)
CON	37.29***	48.11*	51.98***	−3.75	−39.69	4.48
	(7.91)	(3.44)	(12.40)	(0.06)	(2.10)	(0.08)

delta CON	7.68	17.66	21.44**	8.25	13.06	19.40**
	(0.92)	(1.04)	(4.69)	(0.93)	(0.67)	(4.15)
MOVE	21.28	57.51**	32.44**	−15.99	−18.86	−9.56
	(2.43)	(4.61)	(4.52)	(1.22)	(0.58)	(0.42)
CON^2	−62.38***	−80.21*	−92.31***	1.97	60.52	−16.50
	(7.43)	(3.12)	(12.73)	(0.01)	(1.59)	(0.33)
Year	0.010***	0.009*	0.008***	0.012**	0.019**	0.013***
	(10.96)	(2.80)	(6.73)	(6.35)	(5.61)	(6.78)
Log Likelihood	−4.69	−19.67	−8.18	−6.55	−19.09	−8.62

[a] See table 3.8, note a.

* Significant at the .10 level.

** Significant at the .05 level.

*** Significant at the .01 level.

TABLE 3.10

Tobit Analysis of the Mean Number of Non-Major-Power Interstate Wars per Year for Each Five-Year Period (1825–1964) on Hegemony, Polarity, CON, delta CON, MOVE, CON^2, and Year, Three Data Sets[a]

	Gilpin's Classifications of Hegemony			Wallerstein's Classifications of Hegemony		
	Small and Singer	Bueno de Mesquita		Small and Singer	Bueno de Mesquita	
		(Unadjusted)	(Adjusted)		(Unadjusted)	(Adjusted)
Intercept	-19.18***	-27.09**	-24.36***	-17.11**	-21.68*	-17.94**
	(7.11)	(4.60)	(9.81)	(5.27)	(3.16)	(5.42)
Hegemony	0.76***	1.24***	0.87***	0.66**	1.03**	0.61*
	(7.80)	(7.21)	(9.72)	(4.71)	(4.31)	(3.72)
Polarity	1.16***	1.10	0.88**	1.04**	0.73	0.44
	(7.11)	(2.42)	(4.11)	(4.81)	(1.12)	(1.02)
CON	9.23	9.21	23.20**	-31.17**	-57.09**	-19.61
	(0.58)	(0.22)	(4.00)	(4.59)	(6.16)	(1.73)

delta CON	9.85	5.57	4.85	20.05	1.28	3.16
	(0.67)	(0.18)	(0.43)	(1.41)	(0.01)	(0.15)
MOVE	3.95	8.01	4.37	−33.87**	−49.18*	−37.38**
	(0.10)	(0.13)	(0.00)	(5.83)	(3.78)	(5.32)
CON^2	−13.49	−7.89	−35.87*	48.84*	98.00**	31.81
	(0.39)	(0.05)	(3.19)	(3.46)	(5.71)	(1.45)
Year	0.009***	0.012**	0.010***	0.011***	0.015**	0.011**
	(8.55)	(5.72)	(10.47)	(6.78)	(4.81)	(6.03)
Log Likelihood	−4.08	−10.17	−2.39	−5.42	−11.77	−2.39

[a] See table 3.8, note a.

* Significant at the .10 level.

** Significant at the .05 level.

*** Significant at the .01 level.

estimates in tables 3.8, 3.9, and 3.10 and the corresponding regression coefficients in tables 3.2, 3.3, and 3.4. Moreover, based on the tobit model, the level of concentration that maximizes the frequency of major-power war is about .275 when Singer and Small's data are analyzed and about .265 when Levy's data are analyzed; and, when Wallerstein's classifications of hegemony are used, the incidence of non-major-power interstate war is minimized when concentration is, on average, about .305. These values are almost exactly the same as the levels of concentration that maximize/minimize the incidence of war, based on the OLS estimates (in tables 3.2 and 3.4). (It should also be noted that tobit models yield much the same results as the OLS estimates in table 3.5; see Mansfield 1992b.)

Another possibility is that the relationship between concentration and war is misspecified. For example, the relationship may be cubic, rather than quadratic, or log CON and log CON^2 might be used in place of CON and CON^2 in tables 3.2, 3.3, 3.4, and 3.5.[28] However, there is no evidence that the relationship between concentration and war is cubic. When a cubic term (CON^3) is added to equation 3.2, the value of the adjusted coefficient of determination does not increase appreciably, and in no case is the cubic term statistically significant. There is also no evidence that the relationship is stronger or that the estimates are more precise if log CON and log CON^2 are used rather than CON and CON^2.

In the significance tests in tables 3.2, 3.3, 3.4, and 3.5, it is assumed that the error terms, e_t, are normally distributed. To check this assumption, a frequency distribution of the residuals was constructed. The distribution of the residuals is unimodal and appears to be roughly bell-shaped. Since the tests that are used are rather robust with respect to departures from normality, there seems to be no indication of substantial problems in this regard.[29]

[28] Research conducted by Ostrom and Aldrich (1978) indicates that when the size of the major-power system (as measured by the number of poles in the system) is analyzed, the addition of a cubic term helps to explain the outbreak of war involving major powers.

[29] The results in chapter 2 suggested that both Levy's and Singer and Small's data conform to the Poisson distribution (see also Levy 1983). There is, however, no reason why the marginal distribution of the data should be the same as the conditional distribution of the data (the distribution of the error term). Further, in chapter 2, annual data were analyzed, whereas, in this chapter, the mean number of wars beginning during five-year periods is analyzed.

Chapter 4

INTERNATIONAL TRADE AND THE ONSET OF WAR

THE BELIEF that commerce affects war is a theme that runs through many influential analyses of international relations. Interest in this topic is hardly new. But in recent years there has been a resurgence of interest within journalistic, policy-making, and academic circles concerning the nature and strength of this relationship. In chapter 2, the relationship between international trade and the onset of war was examined in a preliminary fashion. This chapter extends this earlier analysis of commerce and war in a number of ways.

First, it was noted in chapter 2 that the results presented there needed to be interpreted with some caution because other systemic factors that might influence the outbreak of war were not held constant. In chapter 3, substantial evidence was provided that certain aspects of the distribution of power help to explain patterns of war. In this chapter, a model of war that includes aspects of both the distribution of power and global trade is therefore developed and tested.

Adopting this strategy is necessary, given the objectives of this book. As pointed out in chapter 1, one purpose of this study is to evaluate the competing claims of structural theories and some leading alternative explanations. Neorealists (and others) argue that structural factors are more salient determinants of war than process-level variables, such as global commerce. Other scholars, however, have challenged this claim. Accounting for the effects of the distribution of power on any observed relationship between trade and war facilitates the evaluation of these competing views on war. It was also mentioned earlier that a related purpose of this study is to gauge the relative importance of international political and economic influences on global outcomes, such as the onset of war. This chapter's examination and comparison of the effects of both the distribution of power and trade on war will provide some of the first statistical results bearing on these central issues.

Second, the analysis of trade and war in chapter 2 centered on the effects of openness and closure. In this chapter, the analysis of trade is broadened by analyzing both openness and closure and another aspect of international trade, the ratio of global exports to total global production. Since these dimensions of global trade need not move in tandem, it is useful to examine both features of international commerce in a study of this sort. Third, this chapter examines whether, in addition to the distribution of power, certain process-level variables are responsible for any observed relationship between trade and war. In particular, the effects of the business cycle and international conflicts are considered, since a variety of studies have concluded that both of these factors influence patterns of international trade and the onset of war.

Defining and Measuring Trade

In chapter 2, the effects of openness and closure in the international trading system on the outbreak of war were analyzed. Stephen Krasner (1976) argues that whether the system is open or closed is determined by tariff levels, the ratio of trade to total economic activity, and regional trading patterns among the leading states in the system. Analyzing this variable is advantageous for present purposes because studies of international trade's influence on the onset of war have centered on both trade flows and trade instruments, such as tariffs; and Krasner's index captures both of these dimensions of global commerce.

However, this index also has a number of limitations. First, it is dichotomous. In addition to distinguishing between open or closed trading systems, it is important to examine the effects of various types of open and closed systems on patterns of warfare. Second, the components of this index need not move in tandem with one another. Tariff levels, trade flows, and regional trade patterns are likely to be at least loosely related: in fact, Krasner (1976:326–27) argues that this is the case during most of the nineteenth and twentieth centuries. But it is also clear that this need not be the case. For example, based on Krasner's analysis, increases in regional trade are associated with closure, while increases in total global trade (as a proportion of global output) are associated with openness. This leads us to expect that regional and global trade patterns should be inversely related. But if regional trading blocs are trade-creating (rather than trade-diverting), increases in regional trade may be associated with increases in the ratio of global trade to total economic output.

Moreover, many theories that are examined in this chapter focus primarily on the effects of trade barriers and trade flows and place little explicit emphasis on the influence of regional trade. Jacob Viner, for example, argues that "[w]hatever may be the merits or demerits on purely economic grounds and from a unilateral national point of view of trade barriers, they are undoubtedly the major economic contribution, directly and indirectly, to international conflict, tension, and war" (1951:259). This clearly points to the importance of trade barriers in accounting for the onset of war. But he also states that "[w]ar disrupts trade, and under free trade the proportion of the population whose everyday means of livelihood is directly or indirectly dependent on an uninterrupted continuance of foreign trade would be at a maximum; therefore, under free trade the proportion of the population with an obvious and vital vested economic interest in the avoidance of war would also be at a maximum" (261).

The extent to which trade will be forgone during war depends on the level of trade, rather than on trade barriers. Since openness and closure measures both trade flows and trade barriers (as well as regional trade patterns), it is useful to examine its effects in a study of this sort. But explanations of war often highlight the importance of trade levels and trade barriers, rather than regional trade. Further, it is clear that trade levels and trade barriers need not move in tandem. As a result, it would be useful to analyze separately the influence of these features of international commerce.

In addition to openness and closure, the impact of the level of total international exports as a percentage of global production on the incidence of war is therefore examined. Thomas Kuczynski's (1980) data are used for this purpose. For the reasons discussed above, it also would be useful to consider separately trade barriers. However, data limitations preclude such an analysis, since it is very difficult to obtain reliable data on effective levels of protection for the time period covered in this chapter. But since, as pointed out below, many of the topics that form the basis of this chapter concern the effects of trade flows on the outbreak of war, these limitations do not undermine the following analysis.

Previous Tests of the Effects of Trade on War

I argued in chapter 1 that the relationship between trade and war is of central importance to a variety of theoretical topics in the study of international relations. It is therefore surprising that so little empirical research has been conducted on the influence of commerce on war, and that virtually no attention has been devoted to this relationship in systemic analyses. Those studies that have been conducted on this topic generally have operated at either the dyadic or the national levels of analysis. They have examined the effects of trade flows on various aspects of war, and (not surprisingly) have arrived at somewhat different conclusions regarding the strength and nature of this relationship.

Much of the recent empirical literature on this topic has centered on the relationship between *dyadic* trade relations and *conflict* between members of the dyad in question. The findings of these studies are generally consistent with the commercial liberal explanation of war that was described in chapters 1 and 2. For example, Solomon Polachek's (1978; 1980) analyses of thirty dyads of states between 1958 and 1967 led him to conclude that higher levels of trade between states lead to lower levels of conflict. Similarly, Mark Gasiorowski and Solomon Polachek (1982) find that increased trade between the United States and members of the Warsaw Pact from 1967 to 1975 led to a decrease in tensions between them and was a contributing cause of détente. Further, Gasiorowski (1986) argues that increased trade between dyads of nations from 1960 to 1977 was associated with a decrease in conflict (although he also maintains that as the costs of severing commercial relations increase, so too does the level of conflict) (see also Pollins 1989a; 1989b).

Despite the importance of these studies, they do not address the concern of the present study—namely, the relationship between international trade and *war*. Wars are clearly one aspect of conflict. But conflict, as it is operationalized in these analyses, also includes a wide range of hostilities short of war; and trade may be related to lower salience disputes in one manner and to war in another manner.

Most empirical analyses of commerce and war have operated at the level of the nation-state. For example, Lewis Richardson (1960a) maintains that, in general, trade did not exert a strong influence on the onset of the "deadly quarrels" between 1820 and 1949, although he also points out that trade-related concerns were at least partially responsible for almost 25 percent of these events. However, his results indicate only that trade is sometimes related to war; they shed little light on the nature of this relationship. In addition, Nazli Choucri and Robert North (1975) analyze whether, from 1870 to 1914, variations in the per capita trade levels for each of six major powers contributed to fluctuations in their respective colonial acquisitions. They conclude that "[t]rade emerged as a weaker influence than might have been expected" (1975:188). Alternatively, William Domke, based on an analysis of the relationship between national trade and all interstate wars from 1870 to 1975, argues that "governments of nations that are more involved in foreign trade are less likely to make decisions for war" (1988:137), which is in keeping with predictions based on commercial liberal explanations.

Absent from the empirical literature on the effects of commerce on war has been any analysis at the systemic level. The only study of this sort was conducted over fifty years ago by A. Macfie (1938), who considered the relationship between fluctuations in what he referred to as the "trade cycle" and the onset of interstate wars involving European states from 1851 to 1914. He found that wars tended to begin during upswings in the trade cycle, a conclusion that is consistent with (neo)mercantilist explanations. However, Macfie was unable to measure trade directly in his study. Instead he examined the influence on war of unemployment, a measure that Macfie acknowledged was "unsatisfactory" for the purposes of gauging the effects of trade on war.

Because the focus of the present study is on the relationships among power, trade, and war at the level of the international system, the effects of systemic features of trade on the incidence of war will be examined. While empirical analyses at this level have been lacking, conceptual treatments of this topic have not. Chapters 1 and 2 provided a brief summary of a number of leading views concerning the relationship between commerce and war. In the following section, these views are discussed in greater depth. In particular, four leading hypotheses are outlined that link global commerce to the incidence of international war, and that will be tested in this chapter.

FOUR HYPOTHESES CONCERNING THE EFFECT ON WAR OF TRADE AND THE DISTRIBUTION OF POWER

As pointed out in chapter 1, scholars who have studied the influence of trade on war have drawn substantially different conclusions regarding both the importance of commerce and the nature of its effect. Some analysts suggest that the frequency of war is influenced by the distribution of power, but it is not affected (in any systematic fashion) by trade. This hypothesis is consistent with the position of those classical realists (for example, Herz 1951; Kissinger 1964; Morgenthau and Thompson 1985) who place little emphasis on economic factors in explaining outcomes in international relations (such as war).

This hypothesis is also in accord with the views of those observers, many structural theorists among them, who maintain that the strength of any bivariate relationship between trade and war is likely to be dramatically reduced when we account for the effects of political variables such as the distribution of power on both commerce and war. Indeed a variety of analysts (Kahler 1979-80; Wilkinson 1980, chap. 8; Buzan 1984; Gaddis 1986; Gilpin 1987; Levy 1989:260–62, 1991:149; Jervis 1991-92) argue that no generalizations can be made regarding the relationship between international trade and the onset of war. They maintain that wars often begin both when trade levels are relatively high and when trade levels are relatively low. The effects of trade on war depend on the structure of the international system. In their opinion, international political-military relations constitute a more salient source of warfare than do commercial relations. As Barry Buzan argues,

> Because of the dominance of military and political factors in determining the use of force, the impact of economic structure on international security is anyway subordinate. Within that subordinate position the choice between liberalism and mercantilism offers no decisive direction. Benign and malevolent features attend both options, but their effects are not strong enough to determine the basic character of international relations. In other words, the effect of either a liberal or a mercantilist economic structure is too heavily

influenced by the particularities of other historical conditions to have, by itself, a predictable impact on the stability of international relations. (1984:623)

Robert Gilpin agrees with this view, noting that

the major point to be made in these matters is that trade and other economic relations are not in themselves critical to the establishment of either cooperative or conflictual international relations. No generalizations on the relationship of economic interdependence and political behavior appear possible. . . . In general, the character of international relations and the question of peace and war are determined primarily by the larger configurations of power and strategic interest among both the great and small powers in the system. (1987:58)

Standing in contrast to these views are theories that posit a strong and systematic relationship between commerce and war. One set of these theories maintains that this relationship is inverse; another set argues that this relationship is direct. Support for either of these two positions, described below, would call into question structural and classical realist theories of war.

Commercial liberals assert that a higher density of trade among states reduces political tensions and the likelihood of war; when trade is depressed, the prospects of war are enhanced. They maintain that commerce provides a more efficient and less costly means than war for states to gain access to resources and markets. Further, trade relations foster dependence among the participants. And as this dependence is heightened through higher levels of trade, states are expected to become increasingly unwilling and unable to withstand the interruption of commerce that accompanies wars.

Since trade tends to enhance the welfare of all participants, liberals argue that the opportunity costs associated with severing ties between trade partners, and forgoing the gains from trade during wars, will deter states from engaging in hostilities. Hence, these scholars maintain that "a liberal economic order makes a substantial and positive contribution to the maintenance of international security" (Buzan 1984:598; Keynes [1935] 1964; Mitrany 1975; Mueller 1989). Alternatively, lower levels of trade engendered by mercantilist practices "ha[ve] been an incendiary force in a highly inflammable and explosive world" (Earle 1986:260).

Many liberals downplay the importance of the distribution of power in accounting for the onset of war. A related set of explanations suggests that both the distribution of power and international economic interactions help to shape the conditions under which wars are most likely to begin (Viner 1951; Keohane and Nye 1977, 1987; Rosecrance 1986; Nye 1988).

For example, interdependence theorists generally argue that higher levels of economic activity among states increase the (expected) costs associated with using armed force.[1] In this sense, their position is similar to that of liberals. But unlike liberals, interdependence theorists also suggest that the distribution of power may influence the frequency of war. As two leading exponents of this position argue, "adding the process level to the concept of structure in defining international systems enriches our ability to theorize. This emphasis on process as well as (rather than instead of) structure moves us toward a synthesis of, rather than a radical disjunction between, realism and liberalism" (Keohane and Nye 1987:747; 1977).

Contrary to the positions discussed above, mercantilists (and neomercantilists) and economic nationalists view trade as one of many arenas of conflict in the international system. They argue that trade relations help to shape power relations among commercial partners (Viner 1948; Hirschman [1945] 1980). Since the gains from trade are usually asymmetrically distributed across states engaged in international commerce, higher levels of trade can influence power relations (and hence the likelihood of war) by conferring disproportionately larger gains from trade on potential adversaries and rendering states vulnerable to both intended and unintended fluctuations in the international economy.

Reducing a state's trade is likely to precipitate a reduction in its dependence on foreign commerce, and hence to limit the possibility that trade will be used to undermine the state's power vis-à-vis its trading partners. Further, some analysts argue that since "close interdependence means closeness of contact and raises the prospect of at least occasional conflict . . . the [liberal] myth of interdependence . . . asserts a false belief about the conditions that may promote peace" (Waltz 1970:205, 222; 1979). (Neo)mercantilists and economic nationalists therefore suggest that higher levels of trade encourage more wars than lower levels of commerce.[2]

---

[1] There exists a well-known and important distinction between sensitivity interdependence and vulnerability interdependence. For discussions of the differences between these types of interdependence, see Waltz (1970; 1979), Keohane and Nye (1977; 1987), and Baldwin (1980). Consistent with much of the literature on the effects of trade on war, the focus of this study is on vulnerability interdependence (that is, the opportunity costs of forgoing an existing relationship).

[2] As a result, Alexander Hamilton, one of the foremost economic nationalists, proposed that the United States should seek to limit its foreign trade and should promote the development of domestic (infant) industries. Under these circumstances, "The aggregate strength of a nation . . . would be increased in every essential respect. The United States, by developing a diversified economy, would enjoy enhanced 'security from external danger, *less frequent interruption of their peace with foreign nations*, and what is more valuable, *an exemption from those broils and wars* between the [several] parts, if disunited, which their own rivalships, fomented by foreign intrigue . . . would inevitably produce'" (cited in Earle 1986:235; emphasis added).

In sum, liberal theories suggest that lower levels of trade and periods of closure should be associated with a higher frequency of war than higher levels of trade and periods of openness. So too do interdependence theorists. (Neo)mercantilist explanations imply that higher levels of trade and periods of openness should be related to a greater incidence of war than lower levels of trade and periods of closure.[3] However, many others, including those who advance purely structural explanations, argue that no systematic relationship exists between commerce and war.

A Model of the Effects on War of Trade and the Distribution of Power

Having outlined the hypotheses that will be tested in this chapter, it is important to describe the variables and the model that will be used for this purpose. Initial tests of the relationship between trade and war (in chapter 2) centered on the effects of openness and closure. As noted above, one purpose of the present chapter is to examine the effects on the incidence of war of both openness and closure and the level of international trade.

In addition to international trade, the impact on war of the distribution of power is also considered. This research strategy is necessary for both theoretical and empirical reasons. From a theoretical standpoint, in order to test the hypotheses described in the previous section, it is necessary to analyze the effects of trade on war in conjunction with the distribution of power. Many liberals discount the importance of the distribution of power in their explanations of war. Interdependence theorists and (neo)mercantilists emphasize the importance of both trade and power in this regard. And neorealists (and other structural theorists) often posit that one reason why commerce is not related to war in any systematic fashion is because the distribution of power helps to shape patterns of both trade and war. Only after holding constant the effects of the distribution of power is it possible to evaluate these competing hypotheses.

More generally, as I argued in chapter 1, this research strategy is essential in any analysis of structural and process-level variables. Since one purpose of this book is to compare the effects of structural and process-level factors on patterns of global outcomes, it is necessary to include both

---

[3] As Gilpin (1981; 1987) and Buzan (1984) note, there are two strands of thought among (neo)mercantilists. The so-called benign strand "sees a mercantilist system of large, inward-looking blocs, where protection is predominantly motivated by considerations of domestic welfare and internal political stability" (Buzan 1984:608). The so-called malevolent strand identifies protectionism as a means of enhancing a nation's power vis-à-vis other members of the international system. At least in the latter case, protectionism and other beggar-thy-neighbor policies are viewed as sources of conflict which may lead to war. For example, Keynes maintains that "mercantilists [have been] under no illusions as to the nationalistic character of their policies and their tendency to promote war" ([1935] 1964:348).

types of variables in the models that are used to explain the onset of war. This tack also permits the presentation of some preliminary results concerning the influence of international political and economic variables on outcomes, such as war, which is another purpose of this study.

From an empirical standpoint, the results in chapter 3 indicated that aspects of the distribution of power are often strongly related to the incidence of war. It makes little sense to exclude these structural features from the model if its purpose is to explain patterns of war.

The model of the distribution of power and war that was developed in chapter 3 is therefore extended by including in it the level of international trade and openness and closure. The extended model is as follows:

$$(4.1) \quad War_t = A + B_1 Hegemony_t + B_2 Polarity_t + B_3 CON_t$$
$$+ B_4 delta\ CON_t + B_5 MOVE_t + B_6 CON_t^2$$
$$+ B_7 Year_t + B_8 OC_t + B_9 Trade_{t-1} + e_t,$$

where War_t is the mean number of wars beginning per year in a five-year period starting in year t; $Hegemony_t$ is a dummy variable that equals one if a hegemon exists in year t, and zero if no hegemon exists in year t (based on both Gilpin's and Wallerstein's classifications); $Polarity_t$ is a dummy variable that equals one if year t is multipolar (before World War II), and zero if year t is bipolar (after World War II); CON_t is the level of the concentration of capabilities among the major powers in the international system in year t (the beginning of this five-year period); $delta\ CON_t$ is the average annual change in the concentration of capabilities during the five-year period from year $t - 5$ to year t; $MOVE_t$ is the average annual movement in shares of capabilities among major powers during the five-year period from year $t - 5$ to year t; $Year$ is t; OC_t is a dummy variable that equals one if the trading system is closed in year t, and zero if it is open in year t according to Krasner (1976);[4] $Trade_{t-1}$ is the ratio of total global exports to total production during year $t - 1$, based on data compiled by Kuczynski (1980);[5] and e_t is an error term.

[4] See chapter 2, footnote 20, for a description of the periods that Krasner classifies as open and closed.

[5] It should be noted that because the relationship between trade and war is being analyzed at a very high level of aggregation, it is not possible to test some liberal and (neo)mercantilist hypotheses. For example, Waltz argues that one reason why bipolar systems are less war-prone than their multipolar counterparts is that less interbloc trade will be conducted in systems characterized by two preponderant major powers than in systems characterized by more than two states of this sort. However, because this study examines aggregate global trade and not interbloc trade, Waltz's position cannot be adequately tested here.

It is also important to point out that *Trade* (as well as *OC*) is a static feature of global commerce. Since it is possible that dynamic features of trade might also influence the frequency of war, the change in *Trade* during each five-year period was also included in equation 4.1. However, there was little evidence that this variable influences *War*. As such, this chapter centers on the effects of static aspects of commerce.

All nonoverlapping five-year periods from 1850 to 1964 (for each data set) are included in this analysis, and 1855 is the initial year t that is considered. This time period is chosen because data on global trade could not be found prior to 1850 and the effect on *War* of *Trade* is lagged by one year. As in chapter 3, the present chapter focuses on explaining wars involving major powers, all interstate wars, and non-major-power interstate wars. Small and Singer's (interstate and major-power war), Bueno de Mesquita's (unadjusted and adjusted), and Levy's data sets continue to be used for this purpose.

It should be noted that, for each time series analyzed in this chapter, the disturbances are characterized by a first-order autoregressive process (AR[1]). As a result, generalized least-squares (GLS) models are utilized in each of the following analyses.

Estimates of the Parameters for Major-Power Wars

One of the central purposes of this study is to examine the systemic conditions under which major-power wars begin most frequently. To this end, GLS estimates of the parameters in equation 4.1 are shown in table 4.1 for wars involving major powers. These results demonstrate that the effect of international trade on the frequency of wars involving major powers depends largely on the aspect of commerce in question.

On the one hand, *there is substantial evidence that the level of international trade is inversely related to the incidence of major-power wars*; that is, wars involving major powers begin most (least) frequently after years during which the level of trade is relatively low (high). In addition to its statistical significance, *Trade* also has a large quantitative impact on the predicted frequency of war. If, for example, the system is nonhegemonic, bipolar, and open, and *CON*, *delta CON*, *MOVE*, *CON*², and *Year* are held constant at their mean values, the effect of increasing *Trade* from its lowest to its highest value is about a threefold reduction in the predicted frequency of major-power wars, based on Singer and Small's data set and Wallerstein's classifications of hegemony.[6] However, it is interesting to note that while the sign and statistical significance of the regression coefficient of *Trade* does not vary in table 4.1 across Singer and Small's and Levy's data sets, the size of the regression coefficient of *Trade* is about 50 percent larger when the former data are used than when the latter data are analyzed. Thus while both data sets produce substantial evidence of an inverse relationship between the level of global commerce and major-power

---

[6] However, in interpreting these results, it is important to recognize that these increases are so large because the predicted mean number of major-power wars beginning per year is usually quite small. Nonetheless, these results strongly suggest that features of global trade may exert a substantial impact on the incidence of major-power wars.

TABLE 4.1

Regression of the Mean Number of Wars Involving Major Powers per Year
for Each Five-Year Period (1855–1964) on *Hegemony, Polarity, CON,
delta CON, MOVE, CON², Year, OC,* and *Trade,* Two Data Sets[a]

	Classifications of Hegemony			
	Gilpin		Wallerstein	
	Levy	*Singer and Small*	*Levy*	*Singer and Small*
Intercept	−4.37	−1.95	−3.77	−4.87
	(−0.53)	(−0.21)	(−0.96)	(−1.10)
Hegemony	−0.08	−0.21	−0.17	−0.16
	(−0.27)	(−0.63)	(−0.96)	(−0.78)
Polarity	−0.14	−0.21	−0.18	−0.07
	(−0.33)	(−0.45)	(−0.91)	(−0.31)
CON	17.93**	14.39	25.35***	24.70***
	(1.91)	(1.34)	(3.20)	(2.73)
delta CON	13.35**	11.53*	13.41***	10.35*
	(2.96)	(2.17)	(3.31)	(2.15)
MOVE	6.35	−3.28	11.76	4.82
	(0.66)	(−0.30)	(1.39)	(0.50)
CON²	−38.51**	−33.37**	−50.65***	−49.59***
	(−2.59)	(−1.97)	(−3.71)	(−3.19)
Year	0.002	0.001	0.001	0.002
	(0.52)	(0.34)	(0.43)	(0.72)
OC	−0.08	−0.07	−0.10	−0.06
	(−0.89)	(−0.73)	(−1.39)	(−0.77)
Trade	−3.86**	−6.48***	−4.29**	−6.92***
	(−2.20)	(−3.50)	(−2.52)	(−3.60)
$\bar{R}^2$ [b]	.65	.74	.69	.74

[a] All coefficients are generalized least-squares estimates. The *t*-statistic of each regression coefficient is reported in parentheses below the coefficient.

[b] All values of R^2 are adjusted for degrees of freedom.

* Significant at the .10 level. One-tailed tests are conducted for the regression coefficients of CON and CON² because their signs are specified by the model. Two-tailed tests are conducted for all other regression coefficients.

** Significant at the .05 level. See note *.

*** Significant at the .01 level. See note *.

war, the magnitude of this effect seems to depend on whose data set is considered.

On the other hand, *whether the trading system is open or closed* (OC) *does not seem to be particularly important in this regard*. The regression coefficient of OC is neither statistically significant nor quantitatively large. But to the extent that OC is related to the incidence of war at all, major-power wars seem to begin more frequently when the system is open than when it is closed. These findings are consistent with the results in chapter 2, which also suggested that major-power wars tend to begin more frequently during periods of openness, but that this relationship is neither particularly strong nor pronounced.

Clearly, *Trade* seems to have a far greater effect on *War* than does OC. One explanation for this finding is that variations *within* open and closed systems are important for the purposes of explaining patterns in the incidence of wars involving major powers. Since OC is a dichotomous variable, it cannot capture these differences. Another possibility is that the components of openness and closure may be related in different ways to the frequency of major-power wars. Openness and closure is determined by (1) the level of global trade, (2) the level of global protectionism, and (3) regional trading patterns. These variables may not move in tandem and/or may not be related to war in the same ways. The fact that *Trade* is strongly related to the incidence of major-power war suggests that the first component of OC is also associated with war. But the fact that OC is very weakly related to war implies that the latter two components may either be unrelated to war or associated with it in a manner markedly different from that of the level of global trade.

Table 4.1 also indicates that the relationship between the distribution of power and the incidence of major-power war is virtually identical to that which was found in chapter 3. First, *there is considerable evidence of an inverted U-shaped relationship between concentration and the frequency of wars involving major powers*: the regression coefficient of CON is positive in all four cases (and statistically significant in three instances) and the regression coefficient of CON^2 is negative and statistically significant in all four instances. Second, both *delta CON* and *MOVE* tend to be directly associated with war, although the strength of *MOVE*'s effect is much weaker than in chapter 3. Third, *there continues to be no evidence that either* Hegemony *or* Polarity *is related to the frequency of major-power war*. While the regression coefficients of these variables were positive in chapter 3, table 4.1 shows that they are uniformly negative. But in no case can we have any confidence that the regression coefficient of either variable is different from zero.

Since OC, *Hegemony*, *Polarity*, and *MOVE* seem to have no noticeable effect on the incidence of major-power wars, it is useful to estimate the

TABLE 4.2

Regression of the Mean Number of Wars Involving
Major Powers per Year for Each Five-Year Period
(1855–1964) on CON, delta CON, CON[2],
Year, and Trade, Two Data Sets[a]

	Levy	Singer and Small
Intercept	−7.77***	−6.85***
	(−4.25)	(−3.86)
CON	16.55***	19.35***
	(3.49)	(4.09)
delta CON	11.79***	10.90**
	(3.33)	(2.79)
CON[2]	−35.64***	−41.17***
	(−4.26)	(−4.93)
Year	0.004***	0.003***
	(4.38)	(4.03)
Trade	−5.40***	−6.91***
	(−5.10)	(−6.73)
$\bar{R}^2$ [b]	.64	.78

[a] See table 4.1, note a.
[b] See table 4.1, note b.
** Significant at the .05 level. See table 4.1, note *.
*** Significant at the .01 level. See table 4.1, note *.

parameters of the remaining variables in equation 4.1 after excluding these variables. The results, shown in table 4.2, indicate that the direction and the magnitude of the effects of concentration and trade differ little from table 4.1. However, the t-statistic of each regression coefficient increases markedly when OC, Hegemony, Polarity, and MOVE are deleted from the model.[7] Further, unlike the results in table 4.1, there is evidence of an upward trend in the frequency of wars involving major powers.

ESTIMATES OF THE PARAMETERS FOR ALL INTERSTATE WARS

As pointed out in chapters 2 and 3, this study is not limited to explaining patterns of major-power wars. This study is also concerned with whether systemic factors help to explain patterns of all interstate wars, whether

[7] It should be noted that few changes occur in these results when OC, Hegemony, Polarity, and MOVE are included individually in the amended model.

systemic variables are related in the same way to major-power wars and all interstate wars, and whether the empirical results are sensitive to the particular data set that is used. GLS estimates of the parameters in equation 4.1 are shown in table 4.3 for the three data sets that include all interstate wars.

These findings indicate that *the effects of aspects of international trade on all interstate wars differ little from their influence on major-power wars, and that they do not vary markedly across the various data sets*. In particular, the regression coefficient of *Trade* is negative in all six cases, and it is statistically significant when Small and Singer's and Bueno de Mesquita's (adjusted) data are considered. And as in the case of major-power wars, the level of global commerce also has a substantial quantitative impact on the predicted frequency of all interstate wars. For those instances in which the regression coefficient of *Trade* is statistically significant, an increase of .02 in the ratio of total global exports to total production produces a decrease of more than .20 in the predicted mean number of wars per year, and hence one war per five-year period.

However, these results should be interpreted with some caution. As was the case in chapter 3, all the analyses in this chapter were conducted using both Singer, Bremer, and Stuckey's estimates of concentration and estimates based on more recent data on national capabilities that extend through 1970. While the findings based on the former estimates (in table 4.3) indicate that a strong, inverse relationship exists between the level of global trade and the incidence of all interstate wars, the findings based on the latter estimates of concentration indicate that this relationship is inverse when Gilpin's classifications are used, but direct when Wallerstein's classifications are used. Moreover, in no case are these results statistically significant. Thus unlike the findings for major-power wars, the relationship between trade and all interstate wars seems to depend on both which estimates of concentration and whose classifications of hegemony are analyzed.

Further, *whether the system is open or closed has little effect on the frequency of all interstate wars*. The regression coefficient of *OC* is negative in all six cases, which is consistent with the finding in chapter 2 that all interstate wars tend to begin more frequently during periods of openness than during periods of closure. However, each regression coefficient of *OC* is relatively small, and in no case is it statistically significant.

These results also indicate that, as in the previous chapter, the strength of the relationships between *Hegemony*, *Polarity*, and the incidence of all interstate wars seem to depend on whose classifications of hegemony, and whose war data, are analyzed. *Hegemony* and *Polarity* are directly related to war irrespective of whether Gilpin's or Wallerstein's data are used. But

TABLE 4.3

Regression of the Mean Number of All Interstate Wars per Year for Each Five-Year Period (1855–1964) on Hegemony, Polarity, CON, delta CON, MOVE, CON², Year, OC, and Trade, Three Data Sets[a]

	Gilpin's Classifications of Hegemony			Wallerstein's Classifications of Hegemony		
	Small and Singer	Bueno de Mesquita		Small and Singer	Bueno de Mesquita	
		(Unadjusted)	(Adjusted)		(Unadjusted)	(Adjusted)
Intercept	−21.71** (−2.24)	−17.80 (−0.57)	−28.55** (−2.80)	−13.40** (−2.77)	−23.05* (−1.89)	−20.42*** (−4.34)
Hegemony	0.36 (1.00)	0.62 (0.57)	0.53 (1.42)	0.05 (0.24)	1.29** (2.34)	0.33 (1.51)
Polarity	0.80 (1.66)	0.99 (0.65)	0.86 (1.70)	0.39 (1.56)	1.38** (2.22)	0.48* (1.98)
CON	9.60 (0.85)	15.29 (0.45)	25.48* (2.15)	−1.18 (−0.12)	−40.25 (−1.64)	1.73 (0.18)
delta CON	10.69* (1.92)	10.34 (0.64)	16.30** (2.84)	12.96** (2.47)	9.28 (0.73)	18.99*** (3.76)
MOVE	−17.32 (−1.50)	20.17 (0.59)	−7.08 (−0.59)	−26.03** (−2.49)	−22.00 (−0.84)	−25.98** (−2.56)

(continued)

TABLE 4.3 (Continued)

| | Gilpin's Classifications of Hegemony | | | Wallerstein's Classifications of Hegemony | | |
| | Small and Singer | Bueno de Mesquita | | Small and Singer | Bueno de Mesquita | |
		(Unadjusted)	(Adjusted)		(Unadjusted)	(Adjusted)
CON^2	−24.21	−28.69	−51.42**	−7.98	61.07	−14.27
	(−1.35)	(−0.53)	(−2.75)	(−0.47)	(1.44)	(−0.87)
Year	0.012**	0.009	0.014***	0.009**	0.015*	0.012***
	(2.94)	(0.64)	(3.25)	(3.05)	(2.11)	(4.27)
OC	−0.06	−0.31	−0.08	−0.12	−0.15	−0.11
	(−0.58)	(−0.92)	(−0.70)	(−1.42)	(−0.68)	(−1.32)
Trade	−11.84***	−7.79	−10.44***	−11.55***	−5.81	−9.64***
	(−6.00)	(−1.15)	(−4.94)	(−5.49)	(−1.11)	(−4.73)
$\bar{R}^2$ [b]	.81	.18	.79	.79	.53	.82

[a] See table 4.1, note a.
[b] See table 4.1, note b.
* Significant at the .10 level. Two-tailed tests are conducted for all regression coefficients.
** Significant at the .05 level. See note *.
*** Significant at the .01 level. See note *.

when Gilpin's classifications of hegemony are analyzed, there is no case in which either variable is statistically significant. When Wallerstein's classifications are considered, these variables are statistically significant in about half of the cases, although Bueno de Mesquita's (unadjusted) data are the only ones for which both *Hegemony* and *Polarity* exert a statistically significant effect on the incidence of all interstate wars. Indeed, aside from this case, there is only one instance in which either aspect of polarity has a non-zero impact on war, regardless of whose classifications of hegemony are considered.[8]

Whereas the results in chapter 3 indicated that an inverted U-shaped relationship existed between concentration and all interstate wars when Gilpin's data were analyzed, table 4.3 provides *little evidence that static features of concentration are associated with patterns of all interstate wars.* The regression coefficient of *CON* is positive and the regression coefficient of *CON²* is negative in each instance, but there is only one case (Bueno de Mesquita [adjusted]) in which they are both statistically significant. There also continues to be no evidence that static features of concentration are associated with all interstate wars when Wallerstein's data are used.

Turning to the effects of dynamic features of concentration on war, changes in concentration are directly related to the incidence of interstate wars: the regression coefficient of *delta CON* is positive in every case and, regardless of whose data on hegemony are analyzed, it is statistically significant in the cases of Small and Singer's and Bueno de Mesquita's (adjusted) data sets. But while there was weak evidence of a direct relationship between *MOVE* and all interstate wars in chapter 3, table 4.3 shows that there is considerable evidence that *MOVE* is inversely related to war when Wallerstein's classifications of hegemony are used.[9] Finally, there continues to be an upward trend in the incidence of all interstate wars beginning over time.[10]

In sum, these results indicate that the relationships between structural

---

[8] Findings concerning the effects of *Hegemony* and *Polarity* on the incidence of all interstate wars that are based on the newer estimates of concentration described earlier indicate that the regression coefficients of these variables are not statistically significant in any case, even when Wallerstein's classifications of hegemony are analyzed.

[9] However, based on the newer estimates of concentration described in chapter 3, there is weak evidence when both classifications of hegemony are used of a direct relationship between *MOVE* and the incidence of all interstate wars.

[10] There also continues to be no evidence that this upward trend is due to an increase in the number of states in the system over time. When the mean number of states in the system during each five-year period is included in equation 4.1, there is no evidence that this variable is statistically significant and the size and statistical significance of the remaining regression coefficients vary little from those in tables 4.1, 4.2, 4.3, and 4.4. It should be noted, however, that the strength of this upward trend in war over time is not as pronounced when the newer estimates of concentration described above are used.

features and war depend on whose data on war and hegemony are used, and that these relationships are rarely as strong as was the case in chapter 3. However, the effects of process-level variables and time are not particularly sensitive to the data on war and hegemony that are used. Trade and time are strongly related to the incidence of all interstate wars; whether the system is open or closed is not.

Estimates of the Parameters for Interstate Wars That Do Not Involve Major Powers

The results in chapter 3 indicated that the impact of structural variables on all interstate wars differed substantially from their influence on interstate wars that do not involve a major power. To the extent that analysts wish to explain patterns of the frequency of all interstate wars, the results in table 4.3 should be of interest. But to the extent that it is useful to distinguish between the systemic influences on major-power wars and interstate wars that do not involve a major power, this latter subset of wars should again be analyzed separately.

GLS estimates of the parameters of equation 4.1 are shown in table 4.4 for non-major-power interstate wars. They suggest that the relationship between aspects of international trade and the incidence of war is much the same, regardless of whether wars involving major powers or wars that do not involve a major power are considered. Of particular importance is the *evidence of an inverse relationship between the level of global commerce and the frequency of non-major-power wars*: table 4.4 shows that the regression coefficient of *Trade* is negative in each case and is statistically significant in five instances. Further, as in the previous two sections, this variable exerts a substantial quantitative impact on the incidence of war. In contrast, while the regression coefficient of *OC* is usually negative, there is little evidence that it has either a quantitatively large or statistically significant effect on the frequency of this type of war.

These results also indicate that, as was the case in chapter 3, *both* Hegemony *and* Polarity *are directly associated with the incidence of interstate wars that do not involve a major power*. But unlike the previous results (in chapter 3), there is much divergence among the present findings concerning the strength of these relationships, based on the data that are used. When Gilpin's classifications of hegemony are analyzed, the regression coefficients of both of these variables are statistically significant in the cases of Small and Singer's and Bueno de Mesquita's (adjusted) data. The quantitative effects of the variables also continue to be substantial. This is particularly true in the case of *Polarity*, whose regression coefficient is usually about 50 percent larger than that of *Hegemony*. But when Wallerstein's classifications of hegemony are examined, the relationships between

TABLE 4.4

Regression of the Mean Number of Non-Major-Power Interstate Wars per Year for Each Five-Year Period (1855–1964) on Hegemony, Polarity, CON, delta CON, MOVE, CON^2, Year, OC, and Trade, Three Data Sets[a]

	Gilpin's Classifications of Hegemony			Wallerstein's Classifications of Hegemory		
	Small and Singer	Bueno de Mesquita		Small and Singer	Bueno de Mesquita	
		(Unadjusted)	(Adjusted)		(Unadjusted)	(Adjusted)
Intercept	−19.07**	−13.48	−24.52***	−8.70**	−11.22*	−12.95***
	(−2.90)	(−1.02)	(−3.38)	(−2.39)	(−2.00)	(−3.25)
Hegemony	0.54**	0.32	0.64**	0.22	0.36	0.30
	(2.21)	(0.65)	(2.36)	(1.30)	(1.36)	(1.63)
Polarity	0.98**	0.49	0.90**	0.46**	0.40	0.34
	(2.94)	(0.74)	(2.47)	(2.50)	(1.40)	(1.66)
CON	−5.71	−31.19*	6.33	−26.36***	−51.14***	−18.88**
	(−0.73)	(−2.02)	(0.74)	(−3.53)	(−4.45)	(−2.32)
delta CON	−0.61	−2.28	−0.60	2.81	−1.14	3.12
	(−0.16)	(−0.30)	(−0.14)	(0.70)	(−0.18)	(0.72)
MOVE	−15.34*	−20.66	−11.31	−31.62***	−36.49**	−30.88***
	(−1.93)	(−1.31)	(−1.30)	(−4.01)	(−3.01)	(−3.58)

(continued)

TABLE 4.4 (Continued)

	Gilpin's Classifications of Hegemony			Wallerstein's Classifications of Hegemony		
	Small and Singer	Bueno de Mesquita		Small and Singer	Bueno de Mesquita	
		(Unadjusted)	(Adjusted)		(Unadjusted)	(Adjusted)
CON^2	10.44	54.05**	−9.23	42.43***	86.04***	29.92*
	(0.86)	(2.22)	(−0.69)	(3.30)	(4.35)	(2.14)
Year	0.011***	0.010	0.012***	0.007***	0.010***	0.009***
	(3.81)	(1.77)	(3.99)	(3.23)	(3.06)	(3.57)
OC	0.01	−0.15	−0.01	−0.06	−0.14	−0.08
	(0.17)	(−1.09)	(−0.10)	(−0.86)	(−1.39)	(−1.06)
Trade	−5.62***	−6.28**	−3.72**	−4.76**	−5.55**	−2.60
	(−4.32)	(−2.35)	(−2.54)	(−3.00)	(−2.27)	(−1.50)
$\bar{R}^2$ [b]	.81	.70	.70	.72	.75	.61

[a] See table 4.1, note a.
[b] See table 4.1, note b.
* Significant at the .10 level. See table 4.3, note *.
** Significant at the .05 level. See table 4.3, note *.
*** Significant at the .01 level. See table 4.3, note *.

Hegemony, *Polarity*, and *War* are much weaker. In fact, there is only one case in which the regression coefficient of either variable is statistically significant, and in almost every instance the size of the regression coefficient is smaller than in the corresponding case using Gilpin's data.

Turning to the effects of concentration, *there continues to be evidence of a U-shaped relationship between concentration and the frequency of non-major-power wars*. The regression coefficient of CON is negative and the regression coefficient of CON^2 is positive in five out of six cases, and these regression coefficients are statistically significant in four instances. The findings are consistent with those in chapter 3: indeed there is even more evidence of this type of relationship than existed in the previous chapter. This is largely due to the fact that, unlike the earlier results, the nature and strength of this relationship are not as dependent on which classifications of hegemony are used. In particular, the results in table 4.4 indicate that there is some evidence of a U-shaped relationship between concentration and the frequency of non-major-power wars when Gilpin's classifications of hegemony are analyzed. Like the results in chapter 3, however, this relationship continues to be stronger when Wallerstein's classifications are used than when Gilpin's classifications are considered.

It is interesting that either *Hegemony* and *Polarity* or CON (and CON^2)—but not both—are typically associated with non-major-power interstate wars. In the case of Gilpin's classifications, the regression coefficients of *Hegemony* and *Polarity* are relatively large and statistically significant, and the regression coefficients of CON and CON^2 are relatively small and not statistically significant, when Small and Singer's and Bueno de Mesquita's (adjusted) data are used. On the other hand, when Gilpin's classifications and Bueno de Mesquita's (unadjusted) data or when Wallerstein's classifications are used, the regression coefficients of CON and CON^2 are both large and statistically significant, and the regression coefficients of *Hegemony* and *Polarity* are typically small and not statistically significant. This suggests that structural features do impact non-major-power wars, but that which structural effects are most salient often depends on how hegemony is defined, measured, and operationalized, and whose data set of wars is utilized.

Dynamic features of concentration also continue to influence the frequency of non-major-power wars. In particular, *MOVE* is inversely related to war, although its statistical significance and the magnitude of its effect are considerably greater when Wallerstein's classifications of hegemony are analyzed than when Gilpin's classifications are used. But there is little evidence that changes in concentration are associated with the incidence of this type of war: the regression coefficient of *delta CON* is generally positive when Gilpin's data are considered and negative when Wallerstein's data are analyzed. Moreover, these regression coefficients are generally quite small, and in no case are they statistically significant.

The Stability-Instability Paradox

It is also important to note that table 4.4 provides evidence of three types suggesting that *the structural conditions that give rise to major-power wars reduce the frequency of non-major-power wars*. First, while the evidence that aspects of polarity are related to major-power wars is quite weak, wars of this sort seem to begin most frequently during periods of *nonhegemony*, whereas there is some evidence that non-major-power interstate wars break out disproportionately during periods of *hegemony*. There is also weak evidence that major-power wars begin most frequently during periods of *bipolarity*, whereas non-major-power wars begin most frequently during periods of *multipolarity*. Second, there is strong evidence of an *inverted U-shaped* relationship between concentration and major-power wars, while there is strong evidence of a *U-shaped* relationship between concentration and interstate wars that do not involve a major power. Third, both *delta CON* and *MOVE* appear to be *directly* related to the incidence of major-power wars (although changes in concentration appear to exert a stronger and larger impact than movement); and both *delta CON* and *MOVE* are generally *inversely* related to the frequency of non-major-power interstate wars (although the effect of *MOVE* is more pronounced than *delta CON*).

This finding seems to apply only to structural variables: the relationships between the level of international trade and war is inverse and strong regardless of whether major-power wars, all interstate wars, or non-major-power wars are examined. However, analyses based on the more recent data on national capabilities and estimates of concentration described in chapter 3 yield (1) some weak evidence of a direct relationship between trade and non-major-power wars; and (2) strong evidence of an inverse relationship between trade and major-power wars.[11] Thus, depending on the data used to measure concentration, the tendency for those systemic conditions that give rise to major-power wars to reduce the frequency of non-major-power wars may also apply to process-level variables.

One explanation for the tendency for the systemic conditions that deter the outbreak of major-power wars to encourage the onset of wars that do not involve major powers is the well-known stability-instability paradox that was described in chapter 2. The implication of this paradox for present

---

[11] It should also be noted that the effects of both polarity and concentration on non-major-power interstate wars are considerably weaker based on the estimates of concentration derived from the newer data than on Singer, Bremer, and Stuckey's estimates (in table 4.4).

purposes is that the same conditions that strengthen deterrence (and hence reduce the frequency of war) among the major powers may also foster conditions under which deterrence is reduced among smaller states.

I argued earlier that major powers are deterred from initiating wars when the level of concentration is both highest and lowest. If, under these conditions, major powers recognize that the expected costs of initiating a war are likely to be quite high relative to the expected benefits of doing so, they may view promoting proxy wars and minor-power wars involving their allies as a means to achieve their objectives and extend their influence. Actions of this sort by a major power are unlikely to be met with armed resistance from other major powers. Doing so could produce a series of conflicts that lead to the onset of a major-power war, the costs of which are likely to be quite high relative to the expected benefits of assisting a minor state. Even if it is not supported by a major-power patron, a minor power with a grievance against another small state may conclude that the time to strike is when the prospects of major-power intervention on behalf of its target are lowest. Under these circumstances, the prospective initiator faces a diminished risk that a large state will intervene and offset any advantage it may hold.

Conversely, when structural conditions undermine deterrence among the major powers (that is, when concentration is at an intermediate level), it is much more likely that a major power will intervene in a minor-power war, since it may view wars of this sort as a relatively quick and cheap way to improve its international position. Minor powers that fear that the involvement of major powers will make victory more difficult to attain may therefore be hesitant to initiate wars during periods characterized by inter-mediate levels of concentration.

THE EFFECTS OF THE BUSINESS CYCLE ON TRADE AND WAR

In chapter 2, the effects of Kondratieff cycles, one aspect of the business cycle, on the onset of war were analyzed. In this section, this relationship is considered further; and the relationship between short-term fluctuations in the business cycle and war is also examined. Aside from the possibility that the business cycle exerts a (process-level) impact on the incidence of war, it is also useful to analyze its effect because it may be responsible for the apparent effect of the level of international commerce. It is widely accepted that the business cycle influences the level of global trade, since increases in income are likely to give rise to increasing demand for imports and an increasing supply of exports. Indeed this point is central to many analyses of trade (Kindleberger 1966; Leamer and Stern 1970; Ethier 1983; Goldstein and Kahn 1984).

It is therefore possible that by causing global trade (as a percentage of total global production) to increase (decrease), while at the same time causing the frequency of war to decrease (increase), the business cycle is responsible for the relationship between trade and war that was observed above. Some scholars have suggested that this may be the case. For example, Gilpin argues that one

> factor determining the political effects of trade is the rate of economic growth in the system. Although it is true that the decline of protectionism and the enlargement of world markets stimulates economic growth, the corollary is also true; a rapid rate of economic growth leads to increasing trade and economic interdependence. By the same token, a slowdown in the rate of economic growth makes adjustment difficult, intensifies international trade competition, and exacerbates international political relations. (1987:57)

Other analysts have expressed more skepticism concerning the importance of the business cycle in this regard. For example, Viner reports that, with some exceptions, "I can find no distinct historical pattern of impact of mass unemployment or of the business cycle on the problem of war" (1951:262–63).

Initially, the impact on trade and war of the long cycles of economic activity that Kondratieff ([1926] 1979) identified, and that were examined in chapter 2, are considered. To determine whether the Kondratieff cycle is related to war, a dummy variable was included in equation 4.1, the value of which depended on whether each five-year period was in an upswing or a downswing of the cycle (based on data from Goldstein 1985; 1988). The results (using GLS and tobit models) indicate that the Kondratieff cycle is not associated with the frequency of wars involving major powers, which is consistent with the findings of Joshua Goldstein (1985; 1988). These findings are also in accord with the results in chapter 2, when Levy's data were analyzed. However, they suggest that the tendency (in chapter 2) for wars to begin more frequently during the upward phase of these cycles when Singer and Small's data are used is not as pronounced as it initially appeared. Further, there is no evidence that the Kondratieff cycle is associated with the frequency of either all interstate wars or non-major-power interstate wars. These results stand in contrast to the preliminary findings (in chapter 2), which indicated that, for Small and Singer's and Bueno de Mesquita's (adjusted and unadjusted) interstate war data, upswings are associated with a higher mean number of wars beginning per year than downswings.

Moreover, the sizes and significance levels of the regression coefficients in equation 4.1 are not influenced much by the addition of this variable to the model. This demonstrates that long waves in the business cycle diminish in importance when their effects are considered in the context of a more fully specified model of war than when simple analyses are conducted of the mean number of wars beginning per year during various phases of these waves (in chapter 2). These results also indicate that the Kondratieff cycle does not account for the effects of international trade on the frequency of any type of interstate war.

Next, the relationship between short-term fluctuations in the business cycle and war is examined. The relationship between this aspect of the business cycle and war has attracted very little attention. However, while the existence of the Kondratieff cycle remains the topic of heated debate, there is little doubt that these short-run fluctuations both exist and are likely to have a marked impact on commerce. As a result, it is useful to expand this analysis of the business cycle by including this variable in equation 4.1.

One way that economists have measured these fluctuations is by assuming that there is a long-term secular trend in output over time, and that the business cycle can be expressed in terms of the deviations from this trend (Lucas 1973, 1981; Zarnowitz 1985). For present purposes, data on global gross domestic product (GDP) adapted from Angus Maddison (1982:86, 170) are used to measure the international business cycle.[12] To estimate the trend in output over time, the logarithm of GDP in year $t - 1$ (the year in which *Trade* is measured in equation 4.1) was regressed on year $t - 1$ for each five-year period from 1855 to 1960 ($r^2 = .99$). The residuals from this regression were included as a measure of the business cycle in equation 4.1. The results indicate that in no case (using GLS and tobit models) is the coefficient of this variable statistically significant, and the addition of this variable to the model produced no major changes in the sizes or significance levels of the remaining coefficients. Hence, *there is little evidence that either long waves or short-term fluctuations in the business cycle are responsible for the strength of the observed relationship between trade and the frequency of any type of interstate war.*

The Effects of Political Conflict on Trade and War

Aside from features of the international economy, the observed relationship between trade and war may also be due to the effect of political conflict

---

[12] Maddison (1982:86) provides data on the annual change in the aggregate level of gross domestic product for sixteen leading countries from 1871 to 1981. These data are used to construct an index of the level of GDP by setting the level of GDP in 1870 equal to 100. The level of GDP is computed for each subsequent year t by multiplying the value of the index in the preceding year $t - 1$ by the change in GDP from years $t - 1$ to t. Maddison (1982:170) also provides data on the annual change in GDP for some of the sixteen states from 1850 to 1869. The (unweighted) average annual rate of change is determined for those states for which data are available, and the procedure described above is used to compute the level of GDP from 1855 to 1869. It is clear that if the rates of change in GDP among these sixteen states differ markedly from those of the remaining states in the system, this index may not reflect the level of global income. However, I am unaware of any more complete data on global income than those developed by Maddison.

(short of war) on both variables. Lower levels of trade may reflect the fact that states are curtailing commerce with those partners among which political relations are worsening. Since political conflicts may also be a harbinger of future wars, the inverse relationship between trade and war may be due to the effects of political disputes on both variables.

During periods in which political relations among trading partners are deteriorating or when states are engaged in conflicts, they may actively attempt to limit trade with one another in order to (1) reduce their dependence on potential antagonists; and (2) punish belligerent states. And when, for example, states engaged in economic warfare attempt to reduce their dependence on foreign markets, or limit exports that could be used to the advantage of potential adversaries in the event of war, decreases in commerce are particularly likely to lead to war (Mastanduno 1985). This is consistent with Brian Pollins's (1989a; 1989b) finding that (between dyads of nations) higher levels of conflict inhibit commercial flows.

Since there is also reason to believe that higher levels of conflict heighten the probability of war, one explanation for the observed relationship between trade and war may be that states which determine that war is becoming likelier (as the level of conflict increases) engage actively in economic statecraft vis-à-vis potential adversaries. This, in turn, exacerbates the conflict and enhances further the prospects of war. Unless trade with allies and neutrals increases (or levels of production decline) for those states anticipating war, the effect will be both a reduction in global (and national) trade and a high likelihood that war will break out in the near future.

Hence, the level of political conflict may account for the inverse relationship between trade and war. To determine whether this is the case, the number of interstate militarized disputes (short of war) that were in progress during year $t - 1$ was included in equation 4.1.[13] For the purposes of explaining the incidence of major-power wars, only those militarized disputes that involve at least one major power were included; for the purposes of explaining the incidence of all interstate wars, all interstate militarized disputes were included; and for the purposes of explaining the incidence of non-major-power interstate wars, only those interstate militarized disputes that do not involve a major power were included. It is clear that this procedure is quite crude. For one thing, the states that are engaged in militarized disputes may not be the ones that subsequently are engaged in

[13] Data developed by Gochman and Maoz (1984) and updated by the Correlates of War Project are used for this purpose. A number of studies have relied on conflict-events data in their analyses of the effects of political conflict on trade. But the present study focuses on interstate militarized disputes for this purpose because (1) none of the leading conflict-events data sets include data for the entire time period covered in this study; and (2) many of the political conflicts that are included in these data are extremely low-salience events. The effects of conflict on trade and war are likely to be most pronounced in the case of high-salience political conflicts, such as militarized disputes.

wars. Further, aggregating the number of disputes obviously provides only a very rough measure of systemic conflict. However, because I am unaware of any data on the level of *systemic* conflict, and since conflict data are rarely available for the entire period covered in this study, this analysis offers a useful, although clearly a tentative, first cut at the problem.

The results (using GLS and tobit models) indicate that there is no instance in which the coefficient of this variable is either statistically significant or particularly large. Moreover, there is little change in either the magnitude or the statistical significance of the remaining variables in equation 4.1. It is important to note that this continues to be the case when militarized disputes are measured in years $t - 2$ and t, as well as year $t - 1$. While their roughness is obvious, these results suggest that *political conflict short of war does not account for the observed relationship between trade and war*.

DOES THE DISTRIBUTION OF POWER ACCOUNT FOR THE RELATIONSHIP BETWEEN TRADE AND WAR?

The previous two sections indicated that the inverse relationship between global commerce and the frequency of war is not due to the omission of variables, such as the business cycle or political conflict, from the model. However, it is also possible that the earlier results in this chapter (in tables 4.1, 4.2, 4.3, and 4.4) are sensitive to the lag structure that was imposed on the variables in equation 4.1. This issue bears heavily on a number of conceptual topics addressed in this study.

I argued in chapter 1 that the extent to which structural variables condition the effects of process-level variables on systemic outcomes, such as war, is fundamental to the study of international relations. Structural explanations, particularly neorealist theories, suggest that the distribution of power largely accounts for whatever systematic effects that process-level factors exert on the outbreak of war. It could be argued that the earlier results in this chapter do not adequately address their position because, in equation 4.1, *Trade* is measured in year $t - 1$ and *Hegemony*, *Polarity*, and *CON* are measured in year t. Thus it is not possible to determine whether the distribution of power accounts for the observed influence of commerce on war. In order to attend to this possibility, equation 4.1 can be respecified as follows:

$$(4.2) \quad War_{t+1} = A + B_1 Hegemony_t + B_2 Polarity_t + B_3 CON_t \\ + B_4 delta\ CON_t + B_5 MOVE_t + B_6 CON_t^2 + B_7 Year_t \\ + B_8 Trade_t + e_t,$$

where *Trade* is measured in the same year (t) as each static feature of the distribution of power, and *War* is the mean number of major-power wars beginning per five-year period starting in year $t + 1$ (which avoids potential problems of simultaneity between *War* and *Trade*).[14] Based on this specification, 1850 is the initial year *t* that is considered. Note that *OC* is omitted from the model because the earlier results indicated that it had no discernable effect on *War*.

For present purposes, we focus on explaining the frequency of wars involving major powers. Many explanations, including structural theories, imply that, based on equation 4.2, *Trade* should have little influence on *War*: structural features should account for the effects of commerce on the incidence of war. But this does not appear to be the case. GLS estimates of the parameters in equation 4.2, shown in table 4.5, are much the same as the earlier findings (based on equation 4.1). Of particular importance is the fact that the regression coefficient of *Trade* is negative in all four cases and is statistically significant in three instances. Moreover, the level of global commerce continues to exert a quantitatively large effect on the frequency of major-power war, although the magnitude of this effect is marginally smaller than in tables 4.1 and 4.2.

These results also indicate that there is little difference in the strength of the effects of *Hegemony*, *Polarity*, and dynamic aspects of concentration on *War*. But it is interesting to note that the relationship between concentration and war is somewhat weaker when *Trade* is measured in the same year as *CON* than when it is lagged by one year, particularly when Levy's data are used. While there continues to be evidence of an inverted U-shaped relationship between concentration and the frequency of major-power wars, table 4.5 shows that the regression coefficients of *CON* and *CON*[2] are statistically significant when Singer and Small's data, but not when Levy's data, are analyzed.[15]

These results are clearly at odds with a strictly structural model, since *there is little evidence that the effect of the level of international trade on war is due to the influence of the distribution of power on both commerce and war*. However, it remains to be seen *why* the level of global trade is an

---

[14] See the appendix to chapter 5 for an analysis that treats *War* and *Trade* as jointly determined.

[15] As noted in the appendix to chapter 3, the degree of confidence that is placed in the results in the present chapter depends upon the extent to which a number of statistical conditions are satisfied. It was pointed out earlier that, since there was evidence of first-order autocorrelation in each time series, GLS models were utilized (the results of which are shown in tables 4.1, 4.2, 4.3, 4.4, and 4.5). It is also important to determine whether the error terms (e_t) in equations 4.1 and 4.2 have a common variance. As was the case in the previous chapter, there is no evidence of heteroskedasticity. And like chapter 3, the fact that the dependent variable is truncated at zero does not pose any noticeable problem. So long as we stay within the normal range of the data, the regression equation rarely predicts fewer than zero wars beginning per year; and estimates of the parameters in equations 4.1 and 4.2 that are derived from a tobit model differ little from the corresponding GLS estimates in tables 4.1, 4.2, 4.3, 4.4, and 4.5. Further, in every instance, the distribution of the residuals is unimodal and appears roughly bell-shaped. Hence, the error terms, e_t, appear to be normally distributed.

TABLE 4.5
Regression of the Mean Number of Wars Involving Major Powers per Year
for Each Five-Year Period (1850–1964) on *Hegemony, Polarity, CON,
delta CON, MOVE, CON^2, Year,* and *Trade,* Two Data Sets[a]

| | Classifications of Hegemony | | | |
| | Gilpin | | Wallerstein | |
	Levy	Singer and Small	Levy	Singer and Small
Intercept	−8.39	−7.23	−10.82*	−9.11*
	(−0.91)	(−0.92)	(−2.15)	(−1.87)
Hegemony	0.04	−0.07	0.23	−0.004
	(0.16)	(−0.28)	(1.15)	(−0.02)
Polarity	0.008	0.06	−0.18	−0.04
	(0.02)	(0.16)	(−0.67)	(−0.15)
CON	10.65	17.53*	5.50	19.36**
	(1.01)	(1.67)	(0.58)	(1.96)
delta CON	10.74*	13.77**	10.69*	13.25**
	(1.92)	(2.33)	(2.09)	(2.35)
MOVE	−4.44	0.21	−7.15	1.70
	(−0.42)	(0.02)	(−0.73)	(0.17)
CON^2	−21.91	−35.70**	−13.42	−38.35**
	(−1.25)	(−2.05)	(−0.80)	(−2.21)
Year	0.004	0.003	0.006*	0.004
	(0.94)	(0.90)	(1.91)	(1.40)
Trade	−3.64*	−4.86**	−2.60	−4.92**
	(−1.84)	(−2.72)	(−1.33)	(−2.55)
$\bar{R}^2$[b]	.21	.61	.31	.61

[a] See table 4.1, note a.
[b] See table 4.1, note b.
* Significant at the .10 level. See table 4.1, note *.
** Significant at the .05 level. See table 4.1, note *.

important statistical determinant of patterns of the outbreak of war. In the
following section, this issue is addressed.

THE NATURE OF THE LINKAGES BETWEEN TRADE AND WAR

There are a number of possible explanations for the inverse relationship
that exists between the level of global commerce and the frequency of war.

One reason why lower levels of trade increase the frequency of war may be that as global trade decreases (or even remains constant), competition over international market share becomes more intense, and this competition (by, among other things, decreasing the opportunity costs associated with the gains from trade) spills over onto the battlefield (Keynes [1935] 1964; Viner 1951; Choucri and North 1975; Gilpin 1975). Attempts to protect existing markets and cultivate (or expand) newer markets have created potentially explosive situations by lowering the opportunity costs of forgone trade associated with war.

Of course, the extent to which trade influences the opportunity costs of war depends on a number of factors. Of particular importance is the availability of substitutes for the commerce that will be forgone in the event of war. If a state can offset the loss of commerce with an adversary by increasing trade with a neutral state or an ally, or by quickly conquering an adversary, war may impose few trade-related costs (Milward 1977; Kaysen 1990). But if alternative trading partners are in short supply and commerce is deemed important, the trade-related costs of war are likely to be substantial.

A rational decision maker is expected to forgo war as a means of resolving trade-related conflicts unless the expected commercial benefits of waging war exceed the expected costs of doing so. However, this condition may have been met in cases in which decision makers believed that trade was an issue of national security, that macroeconomic policies could not be used to offset losses in international market share, and that their potential adversary(ies) was (were) either weak or unwilling to bear the costs of war. For example, these circumstances seemed to characterize the situation in Germany and Japan prior to World War II. International trade levels were quite low during the 1930s. Each of these states was heavily dependent on commerce for both economic development and national security. Under these circumstances, the expected trade-related costs of war were very small, and the expected economic and political benefits were perceived to be substantial. As Alan Milward argues, "The Japanese decision for war, like the German, was taken under the persuasion that in Japan's situation, given the correct timing and strategy, war would be economically beneficial" (1977:16).

Another point to note in this regard is that access to commercial routes is often necessary for states to engage in trade and "struggles over the principal arteries of commerce have been constant sources of interstate conflict" (Gilpin 1981:112; Viner 1951; Choucri and North 1975). States may prefer trade to war as a means of obtaining strategically important imports and securing export markets (Viner 1951; Keohane and Nye 1977, 1987; Baldwin 1985; Rosecrance 1986; Mueller 1989). As Viner argues, "Under universal free trade, the attractiveness of territorial expansion, in so far as this is based on economic considerations, would be very much reduced" (1951:261). If, however, the flow of strategically important imports is stemmed, few sources or substitutes for the traded goods exist, or declining exports threaten economic growth, states may initiate wars to achieve these aims (Choucri and North 1975; Gilpin 1977; Buzan 1984). Thus under certain circumstances, war may serve as a (more costly and hence less desirable) substitute for trade.[16]

This situation appears to have characterized German foreign policy during the 1930s. Milward (1977) argues that, during this period, decision makers in Germany often contended that it was necessary to create large areas (*Grossraume*) that were both economically and geographically unified so as to gain access to raw materials and other resources on which Germany depended. Initially, Germany pursued policies that called for the expansion of commerce in order to achieve this end. When this strategy failed, war was one alternative that was used for this purpose. As Milward notes,

> For a time it seemed that Germany might create her *Grossraumwirtschaft* and dominate international economic exchanges in Europe through peaceful means; a series of trade agreements was signed between Germany and the underdeveloped countries of south-eastern Europe after 1933. Germany was able to get better terms in bilateral trading from these lands than from more developed European economies . . . and German trade with south-eastern Europe increased in relation to the rest of German and world trade in the thirties. But German-Russian trade after 1933 became insignificant and it was clear that a re-ordering of Europe's frontiers to correspond with Germany's economic ambitions would ultimately have to involve large areas of Russian territory. South-eastern Europe, without Russia, could make only a very limited contribution to emancipating Germany from her worldwide network of imports. A war against Russia seemed to be the necessary vehicle for political and economic gain. (1977:10)

These explanations suggest that the relationship between international trade and war is inverse because, all other things being equal, states go to war when the opportunity costs of forgone trade are lowest; and this condition is most likely to obtain during periods when relatively little global trade is conducted. In this sense, trade and war may serve as substitutes for one another. The choice of which avenue nations pursue to secure resources, goods, and markets has depended in large measure on the expected opportunity costs of the alternative(s). To the extent that high levels of global trade reflect relatively free access on the part of nations to vital

---

[16] This viewpoint has been espoused by many neomercantilists (Aron 1981:245). Others have made the opposite argument: increasing national wealth (by trade or other means) may make a nation a more attractive target for aggression (Thompson 1979).

resources and markets, the growth of commerce may have reduced the incentives for states to initiate wars. It also appears that heightened competition over global market share has played a role in creating conditions that promote wars.

Particularly when states depend on trade for their economic development and national security, a smaller global market may lead to new, and exacerbate existing, tensions. Indeed this is probably one reason why trade is inversely related to smaller, as well as to major-power, wars. By virtue of their size, small states are heavily dependent on international commerce. Richard Rosecrance argues that their dependence is likely to increase in the future and, as a result, among "small and even weak states . . . the method of international development sustained by trade and exchange will begin to take precedence over the traditional method of expansion and war" (1986:15). The results of this chapter indicate that, whatever the effects of the dependence of smaller states on trade may be in the future, this factor seems to help to explain patterns of non-major-power wars during the course of the nineteenth and twentieth centuries.

IMPLICATIONS OF THE RESULTS FOR THE PRESENT STUDY

In this chapter, I have examined the relationships between aspects of both trade and the distribution of power, and the incidence of war. At this point, it is useful to consider briefly some of the implications of the results in this chapter for the issues that were raised in chapter 1.

First, as noted earlier, previous empirical analyses of war operating at the level of the international system have emphasized disproportionately the effects of the distribution of power. This is not surprising, since realism and neorealism have attracted such a wide range of adherents. However, as pointed out in chapter 1, one consequence of this tendency is that process-level factors have not been addressed adequately in studies of war. One purpose of this study is to make some progress in redressing this apparent imbalance by examining the effects of some process-level factors and comparing the strength of their impact with those of their structural counterparts.

The results in this chapter indicate that certain structural *and* certain process-level variables help to shape patterns of major-power wars, as well as all interstate and non-major-power wars. As a result, the tendency of previous studies of war to underemphasize the importance of process-level factors—particularly those associated with global trade flows—is problematic. Not only does the level of global trade (as a percentage of global production) have a marked impact on the incidence of each type of war considered in this chapter, but its effect is not due to the influence of structural factors on both commerce and war. These findings therefore stand in stark contrast to the expectations of neorealist, and many other structural, theories of international relations.

This is not to imply, however, that all process-level variables are strongly related to the incidence of war: openness and closure in the international trading system and features of the international business cycle seem to have little impact on patterns of the onset of each type of war considered in this chapter. These results also do not imply that structural variables are unimportant for the purposes of explaining the frequency of war. On the contrary, features of the distribution of power often are of considerable importance in this regard. But as in chapters 2 and 3, substantial variations exist in the nature and strength of these effects, depending on the structural variable and the type of war in question. In sum, the fact that both the distribution of power and the level of international trade influence the onset of war, and that the level of trade is inversely related to the incidence of war, is in accord with Robert Keohane and Joseph Nye's argument that "[n]eorealism is appropriate at the structural level of systemic theory; liberalism is most fruitful at the process level" (1987:747, 1977; Viner 1951; Nye 1988). These findings provide *strong support for the interdependence hypothesis*.

Second, these results also indicate that aspects of the international economy bear heavily on international political outcomes. This is not to suggest that all economic factors are equally useful in this regard, or that political factors can be dismissed in systemic analyses of war. On the contrary, the results in this, and the previous, chapter clearly demonstrate that features of the distribution of power have a marked influence on patterns of war. But I do argue that certain economic variables—particularly the level of trade—are strongly related to the frequency of war; and that by neglecting their impacts analysts are likely to overlook some important systemic determinants of patterns of major-power, all interstate, and non-major-power wars.

CONCLUSIONS

Central to any study of the relationships among power, trade, and war is the effect of commerce on war. The purpose of this chapter has been to analyze this relationship. First, the results of this chapter demonstrate that regardless of whether we focus on wars involving major powers, all interstate wars, or interstate wars that do not involve a major power, there is an inverse relationship between the level of international trade and the frequency of war: higher (lower) levels of commerce are associated with a lower (higher) incidence of war. Further, the level of trade appears to exert a large quantitative effect on war. In considerable measure, these results may reflect the fact that as trade levels increase, so too do the opportunity costs (associated with the forgone gains from trade) of war. However, not all features of international trade are of equal importance in this regard, since (unlike the preliminary results in chapter 2) there is no evidence that whether the system is open or closed is related to the onset of war.

Second, like the results in the previous two chapters, there continues to be evidence that aspects of the distribution of power help to explain patterns of warfare. But as in chapter 3, different structural features are related to the frequency of war in very different ways. On the one hand, there continues to be evidence of an inverted U-shaped relationship between the concentration of capabilities and the incidence of major-power wars. Polarity, on the other hand, continues to be of little importance for the purposes of explaining wars of this sort. On the other hand, aspects of polarity are of considerable use in explaining patterns in interstate wars that do not involve a major power: like the findings in chapter 3, multipolar and hegemonic systems are associated with the highest frequency of non-major-power interstate wars. The results in this chapter also indicate that a U-shaped relationship exists between concentration and the incidence of wars of this sort. However, the strength of the relationship between the distribution of power and the frequency of non-major-power wars continues to depend on which classifications of hegemony and data on war are utilized.

The fact that both commerce and the distribution of power are important elements in shaping the incidence of war sheds doubt on structural and classical realist and commercial liberal explanations of war. Based on the results of this chapter, it does not appear that the distribution of power accounts for the effects of trade on war. Nor does it seem that trade is substantially more important than the distribution of power in this regard. Instead these findings lend support to the interdependence hypothesis.

Many empirical studies of war neglect the effect of international trade. The findings of this chapter indicate that this omission is problematic because trade appears to be related strongly to war—and that this relationship is inverse. More generally, these results indicate that both structural and process-level variables, as well as both international political and economic factors, provide insights into the conditions under which wars begin most often.

Chapter 5

THE EFFECTS OF POWER AND WAR ON TRADE

THUS FAR, the analysis in this book has centered on identifying the systemic conditions under which wars begin most frequently. Since, as pointed out in chapter 1, the extent to which systemic factors influence patterns of international trade is also a central concern and a matter of considerable debate among scholars of international relations, the purpose of this chapter is to develop and test a systemic model of the level of international trade (as a percentage of global production). More specifically, this analysis will focus on the effects of aspects of the distribution of power, major-power war, and international economic factors on patterns of global commerce.

Many systemic analyses of the international political economy conclude that the distribution of power helps to shape patterns of commerce. It was noted in chapter 1 that much of this literature centers on the effects of hegemony. Indeed one of the most persistent and controversial topics among analysts of the international political economy concerns whether the existence of a hegemon facilitates the coordination of the international economy. Yet few quantitative analyses of this topic have been conducted. One purpose of this chapter is to assess statistically the influence of hegemony on trade.

I also argued at the outset of this book that, by virtue of their preoccupation with hegemony and its effects, scholars of the international political economy have generally given short shrift to the effects of concentration. This is both surprising and unfortunate, since the use of concentration is consistent with the arguments of many leading theories concerning the effects of the distribution of power on patterns of global commerce. In this chapter I indicate why this is the case, and why concentration provides insights into the relationship between the distribution of power and trade that hegemony is, by itself, unable to furnish.

Like most structural theories of war, theories of the international political economy generally posit that a monotonic relationship exists between the distribution of power and aspects of international trade. In chapter 1, I argued that there is reason to believe that the relationship between the concentration of capabilities and the level of international trade should be U-shaped. Another purpose of this chapter is to develop further and test this hypothesis.

One of the central purposes of this book is to compare the effects of structural and process-level factors on global outcomes. In addition to aspects of the distribution of power, the effects of war and some aspects of the global economy on the level of international trade are therefore analyzed. The impact of major-power war on trade is important not only because it may be a central process-level influence on trade, but also because it bears on issues raised earlier in this study concerning the extent to which analyses of war and analyses of the international political economy need to be further integrated.

Finally, as pointed out in chapter 1, another purpose of this study is to compare some international political and economic effects on war and trade. Assessing the importance of international economic influences on the level of global trade is important not only because they are potentially salient process-level effects on commerce, but also because much of the study of the international political economy is predicated on the argument that economic outcomes cannot be understood adequately with reference only to the effects of economic factors. Yet like previous studies of war, few studies have examined empirically the relative importance of international economic and political variables in analyses of commerce.

Hegemony and Trade

Throughout this book, it has been noted that some scholars emphasize the effects of hegemony in their analyses of war. However, interest in the effects of hegemony is hardly limited to analysts of war. Among scholars of the international political economy, few topics have generated as much attention during the previous two decades as the influence of hegemony on global economic outcomes. Much research in this area concerns the relationship between hegemony and aspects of international trade.

Hegemonic stability theorists agree that hegemony is associated with an open trading system, while the lack of a hegemon is associated with closure. Many of them also agree that because the creation and coordination of a liberal trading system take on features of a public good, its provision engenders collective action problems (Olson 1971). Without a state that is willing and able to act as a privileged group and unilaterally provide a liberal trading order, the establishment of a system characterized by free trade is unlikely.

Disagreements exist among them, however, regarding how much emphasis to place on the provision of collective goods in the global arena and why hegemons provide a liberal trading system. On the one hand, Charles Kindleberger (1973; 1981) suggests that hegemons provide public goods largely for altruistic reasons. He maintains that the central cause of the depression during the 1930s was the absence of a benevolent "stabilizer" to coordinate the international economy;[1] Great Britain was no longer able to assume this role as it had done in the nineteenth century, and the United States was not yet willing to assume the mantle of leadership. On the other hand, Robert Gilpin (1975; 1981; 1987), Stephen Krasner (1976), and David Lake (1988) argue that because the hegemon derives disproportionately greater gains from such a system, it has an incentive to create and sustain a liberal international economic order. They maintain that the periods of relatively free trade during much of the nineteenth century and after World War II can be explained best by the benefits that accrued to Great Britain and the United States from an open trading system.[2]

During the past decade, much has been written regarding the theoretical limitations of hegemonic stability theory. Many critics argue that systems need not be hegemonic in order to be open, and hence that no strong relationship exists between whether or not the system is hegemonic and international trade. Because the theory of collective action does not preclude the provision of public goods by small (or k) groups (Olson 1971), certain nonhegemonic systems can also lead to a liberal trading order. The existence of a hegemon may ameliorate collective action problems when public goods such as a trade regime are initially supplied; but hegemony is not necessary for either their provision or maintenance (McKeown 1983; Keohane 1984; Snidal 1985a). Others maintain that hegemony is unrelated to trade because hegemonic stability theory incorrectly identifies free trade as a public good. Since it does not meet the criterion of nonexcludability, a hegemon need not act as a privileged group to ensure its provision (Conybeare 1984, 1987; Russett 1985; Snidal 1985a).

Analysts also argue that hegemony is related to trade, but that the relationship is inverse rather than direct. They posit that nonhegemonic systems are likely to be relatively liberal because in the absence of a hegemon, no state possesses sufficient market power to influence world prices through the use of trade barriers. A hegemon, on the other hand, has the market power necessary to improve its terms of trade by imposing an optimal tariff, and the noncooperative aspects of international commerce

---

[1] In his original study on this topic, Kindleberger (1973) argues that a hegemon not only provides a source of countercyclical liquidity, stabilization of currencies, and a market for distressed goods but also serves as a lender of last resort and ensures an open international trading system. In a subsequent study (Kindleberger 1981), he indicates that hegemons also manage foreign exchange rates and coordinate domestic monetary policies.

[2] Hegemonic stability theorists often posit that hegemony is a necessary, though not a sufficient, condition for the development of a liberal international economic order. For example, Gilpin argues that in addition to hegemony, a "liberal ideology [and] common interests [among the states in the system] must exist for the emergence and expansion of the liberal market system" (1987:73; 1981, chap. 3).

provide it with the incentive to take advantage of this ability (Conybeare 1984, 1987).

However, the extent to which the critiques described in this section undercut hegemonic stability theory remains open to question. Joanne Gowa maintains that its critics "have not deprived hegemonic stability theory of its analytic base: hegemons can reject the prescriptions of standard trade theory [to impose optimal tariffs]; . . . open international markets [often] do present public-good problems; and privileged groups enjoy a stronger advantage than small-group advocates acknowledge" (1989a:322). Further, not all variants of this theory ascribe equal importance to the provision of public goods in the international political economy. Those analysts who place less weight on this aspect of hegemony are less susceptible to critiques that highlight either the absence of public goods in the international system or the ability of small groups to provide these goods. This suggests that the debate over the analytic underpinnings of hegemonic stability theory remains far from resolved. Also unresolved is the issue of what (if any) empirical relationship exists between hegemony and international trade.

EMPIRICAL EVIDENCE AND ISSUES REGARDING HEGEMONIC STABILITY THEORY

In addition to the analytic critiques discussed above, hegemonic stability theory has also been challenged on empirical grounds. First, some analysts argue that the relationship between hegemony and an open international trading system is weak. For example, John Conybeare (1983) found little cross-sectional or longitudinal evidence that hegemony is associated with national tariff levels, based on data in 1902 and 1971. Similarly, Timothy McKeown (1991) concludes that no strong relationship exists between variables related to hegemony and national import levels (as a percentage of national income) of the advanced industrialized states from 1880 to 1987.

Second, others concede that hegemony may be associated with a relatively open trading system, but challenge the causal linkages between hegemony and commerce. For example, Timothy McKeown (1983), Arthur Stein (1984), Giulio Gallarotti (1985), and Susan Strange (1987) maintain that a variety of international political and economic factors provide more satisfactory explanations than British hegemony for the existence of a liberal trading system during the nineteenth century. And Robert Keohane (1980) argues that while the empirical record from 1966 to 1977 is consistent with the predictions of hegemonic stability theory, the causal relationship between American hegemony and trade in manufactured goods is weak.[3]

Third, hegemonic stability theorists have been criticized for failing to measure adequately the distribution of power. This, in the opinion of some observers, leads them to choose incorrectly the cases of hegemony that they hold up as support for the theory. For example, Bruce Russett (1985) concludes that the theory mistakenly attributes hegemonic status to Great Britain during the nineteenth century and that, contrary to the position of many (critics and) adherents of the theory, American control over outcomes in the international political economy has not declined since the early 1970s (McKeown 1983; Keohane 1984; Strange 1987, 1988; Nye 1990).

Three fundamental disagreements over the definition, measurement, and operationalization of hegemony underlie much of the controversy surrounding the empirical relationship between hegemony and trade. First, there is disagreement over the scope of hegemony—that is, over what range of international relations a state must wield preponderant power to be considered a hegemon (Russett 1985; Nye 1990). Some argue that hegemony is characterized by a situation in which a single state dominates and orders both economic and political relations (for example, Gilpin 1975, 1981, 1987; Wallerstein 1983; Russett 1985; Kennedy 1987), while others maintain that hegemony is characterized by a situation in which a single state dominates and orders international economic relations and possesses sufficient political power to ward off military threats to the international system (for example, Krasner 1976; Keohane 1984; Lake 1988).[4]

---

[3] Gilpin also notes the inability of hegemonic stability theory "to demonstrate a close association between power and outcome" (1987:91). Further, Lake argues that because hegemonic stability theory "lacks a conception of process, or an explanation of how the constraints or interests derived from the international economic structure are transformed into decisions or political strategies within particular countries . . . the causal link between the system-level international economic structure and national-level policy is open to question" (1983:539–40; see also Nye 1990).

[4] In addition, some scholars (particularly those who study war rather than the international political economy) place less emphasis on economic power, and define hegemony as a preponderance of military power (Organski 1958; Modelski 1978; Doran and Parsons 1980; Organski and Kugler 1980; Levy 1985a; Modelski and Thompson 1988). Still others differentiate between economic and political/military hegemony (for example, Goldstein 1988). Hence, the types of power that are emphasized in the definition and operationalization of hegemony appear to be determined, in large measure, by the issue area being studied.

Further, some scholars of the international political economy argue that dimensions of hegemony other than political and economic power must also be considered. For example, Russett (1985) and Nye (1990) highlight the importance of cultural aspects of hegemony, and Ikenberry and Kupchan (1990) argue that hegemons exercise control by socializing elites in secondary states. Despite their potential importance, these dimensions of hegemony are not

Second, scholars disagree about the domain of a hegemon—that is, about the range of actors over which a state must wield preponderant power to be considered a hegemon.[5] Though hegemonic stability theory purports to explain *systemic* outcomes, as Stephan Haggard and Beth Simmons point out, "The relevant 'structure' is usually defined [by hegemonic stability theorists] as the distribution of power within the international capitalist system rather than within the world political system as a whole" (1987:503; see also Keohane 1984; Stein 1984; Grieco 1988; Nye 1990).

Finally, there is no consensus regarding the inequality of power that is necessary for hegemony to obtain. While analysts agree that hegemons are more powerful than the other actors in the system, most have been conspicuously silent on the fundamental issue of *how much more powerful* they need to be in order to meet the requirements for hegemony (McKeown 1983; Russett 1985; Frey 1986). A related problem is that analysts tend to treat as homogeneous all nonhegemonic distributions of power. However, as pointed out in chapter 1, the starkness of the dichotomy between hegemony and nonhegemony may mask the differential effects of various nonhegemonic distributions of power on outcomes in the international political economy (Lake 1988:38).

These disagreements over the definition, operationalization, and measurement of hegemony appear to influence substantially the empirical relationship between hegemony and trade. For example, Conybeare's (1983) and McKeown's (1991) statistical results indicate that hegemony is largely unrelated to trade, while my own findings suggest that hegemony is directly related to the level of global commerce when Gilpin's data on hegemony are used, but inversely related to it when Immanuel Wallerstein's data are used (Mansfield 1989). Moreover, even if it had an unambiguous effect on the international trading system and no disagreements existed regarding how to define, operationalize, and measure it, hegemony is only one aspect of the distribution of power. Various other features of this distribution, not only hegemony, may have effects on trade; and it is important to analyze the effects of hegemony in conjunction with these other features of the distribution of power before assessing the extent to which hegemony can explain outcomes in the international political economy.

---

considered in the present analysis due to the difficulty of operationalizing and measuring them.

[5] For a more complete discussion of the importance of specifying the scope and domain of power in analyses of international relations, see Baldwin (1979).

ANALYZING THE EFFECTS OF HEGEMONY
AND CONCENTRATION ON TRADE

I argued in chapter 1 that, for the purposes of testing theories of the distribution of power and trade, focusing on both hegemony and the concentration of capabilities among the major powers is likely to be advantageous. Indeed one reason why this is likely to be a useful strategy is that the importance of both variables has been emphasized in studies of the international political economy, but I am unaware of any previous efforts to analyze and compare the effects of *both* of these variables on trade. In addition, it is important to determine whether the same structural variables that help to explain the incidence of war also account for patterns of global commerce: earlier findings (in chapters 3 and 4) indicated that both concentration and hegemony are related to certain (although not necessarily the same) types of war.

Moreover, as I argued in chapters 1 and 3, hegemony and concentration measure different features of the distribution of power. Despite disagreements over how to operationalize it, most analysts agree that hegemony obtains when a sufficiently "large" relative power disparity exists between the *two* most powerful states (and, by extension, between the largest state and every other state) in the international system. But whether the relative power disparity between the two most powerful states has or has not reached a particular threshold provides us with no information concerning how the remaining states in the system stand in relation to one another. Alternatively, concentration is a continuous measure of the distribution of power that captures the aggregate inequality of capabilities among all the major powers. Hence, concentration is a measure of how *all* the major powers stand in relation to one another. Since they capture different aspects of the system's structure, examining both the concentration of capabilities and hegemony provides a richer typology of the distribution of power than is gained by considering only one of these variables.

This section has presented a case for comparing the effects of hegemony and concentration on patterns of trade. However, it is necessary to examine further the theoretical importance of concentration for the following analysis of the level of global trade, since, although the features of the distribution of power that it measures have been highlighted in previous research on this topic, concentration rarely has been considered in studies of the international political economy. The following section addresses this issue. A number of hypotheses regarding the influence of concentration, and its components, on the level of international trade are then described.

Concentration and Theories of the International Political Economy

There are a variety of reasons to analyze the effects of concentration in systemic studies of trade. First, as noted above, many explanations of the international political economy posit that collective action problems characterize the establishment and coordination of an open international trading system. Hegemonic stability theorists have largely ignored the importance of group size in overcoming collective action problems, while small-group theorists often have neglected the impact of relative inequality among "group members" in this regard. But Mancur Olson argues that "*in small groups marked by considerable degrees of inequality*—that is, in groups of members of unequal 'size' or extent of interest in the collective good—there is the greatest likelihood that a collective good will be provided" (1971:34; emphasis added). Thus each set of scholars focuses on one important aspect of the theory of collective action, while giving short shrift to a second dimension.

In chapter 3, I demonstrated that the level of concentration is a function of (1) the number of major powers in the international system (N); and (2) the relative inequality of capabilities among the major powers (V). (See equation 3.6.) The preceding discussion indicates that both of these variables may influence outcomes in the international political economy. Focusing on concentration, in addition to hegemony, therefore provides a way to help resolve some of the debates between hegemonic stability and small-group theorists, since we can compare the relative importance of both group size and relative inequality, as well as hegemony, on the level of international trade. Further, there has been considerable interest in the effect of the interaction between the size of groups providing collective goods and the relative inequality among members of groups on outcomes in the international political economy (Russett and Sullivan 1971; Snidal 1985a, 1985b). But despite long-standing calls for empirical research on this topic (for example, Russett and Sullivan 1971), few studies of this sort have been conducted. By focusing on concentration, it will be possible to assess empirically the influence of some aspects of the interaction between the number of major powers and the power inequalities among them on international trade.[6]

---

[6] The only study (that I am aware of) that analyzes the relationship between concentration and trade is McKeown (1991). However, his analysis differs from the present study in a number of important ways. First, he uses a different set of capabilities and major powers to measure concentration than is used here. Second, his model is specified differently than the model in this chapter. He examines the effects on the ratio of imports to GNP (for industrial capitalist countries) of: (1) the concentration of capabilities; (2) the percentage of global imports that the largest importer accounts for ($TCON1$); (3) the percentage of international

It is also useful to consider concentration in analyses of trade because distinguishing only between hegemonic and nonhegemonic systems implies that the relationship between the distribution of capabilities and trade is characterized by a step function. Little international economic coordination is possible in the absence of a hegemon; and high degrees of coordination are possible only in the presence of a hegemon. But Olson (1971) and others imply that a continuous relationship exists between the degree of relative inequality in a group and the amount of a collective good that is provided. The theory of collective action therefore suggests that there may be considerable variations among different nonhegemonic systems in the degree of international economic coordination. If we rely only on hegemony to measure the distribution of power, it is not possible to account for these potential variations.

Second, as noted above, a variety of scholars argue that the market power of the leading states in the global system influences commerce. The Hirschman-Herfindahl (or some related) index is generally used to measure market power. Conybeare, for example, points out that, for the purposes of measuring a hegemon's market power, "[a] Herfindahl index would be the best index of hegemony, since it would discriminate between situations where a country faced a large number of small powers or a small number of medium-sized countries" (1987:287 n. 4). It was pointed out in chapter 3 that CON is closely related to the Hirschman-Herfindahl index (HH). But while concentration is a measure of market power, it is important to reiterate that neither it nor the Hirschman-Herfindahl index is technically a measure of hegemony, since they both measure the distribution of power among all major powers—not just the relative strength of the most powerful state. It is precisely for this reason that concentration is a more comprehensive measure of aggregate market power than hegemony, and thus ought to be considered in a study of this sort. Hegemons are not uniquely able to impose optimal tariffs: large nonhegemonic states may also possess considerable market power vis-à-vis the remaining states in the system (Lake 1988:38).

Hence, the starkness of the distinction between hegemony and nonhegemony is likely to mask the extent to which collective goods will be provided and the market power of the leading states in the international system. This problem has not been lost on hegemonic stability theorists (as well as some of their critics). Lake, for example, argues that "[t]he theory of hegemonic stability, perhaps due to its focus on the absence or presence of

imports that Great Britain, the United States, France, (West) Germany, and Japan account for ($TCON5$); (4) the ratio of $TCON1$ to $TCON5$; (5) the ratios of the nominal income of Great Britain and the United States, respectively, to that of the other leading states in the system; (6) time; (7) the growth of nominal income; and (8) a lagged dependent variable.

hegemony, has failed to develop the analytic tools necessary to comprehend adequately the interests and policies of all countries within the international economy" (1983:521). And Keohane points out that "[c]oncern for the incentives facing the hegemon should also alert us to *the frequently neglected incentives facing other countries in the system*" (1984:39; emphasis added). Supplementing the traditional focus on hegemony with concentration may help to remedy this problem.

Third, concentration possesses a number of properties that are particularly desirable for analyzing the problem at hand. For example, it is measured by using economic and military (as well as demographic) capabilities, the same general indices of power that hegemonic stability theorists emphasize. Analyzing the effects of both hegemony and concentration on trade thus facilitates the comparison of different features of the distribution of power, holding constant the variables used to measure power.

The use of concentration also provides insights into a number of aspects of the relationship between the distribution of power and trade that hegemony is unable to provide. On the one hand, while it is a theory of the international political economy, hegemonic stability theory is generally used to explain international relations among only the advanced industrialized countries. On the other hand, concentration measures the distribution of power among all the major powers and, as a result, is closer than hegemony to a global measure of this distribution. Further, concentration is a continuous measure, which allows us to examine the effects of different nonhegemonic distributions of power on trade and mitigates the problem of how to distinguish between hegemonic and nonhegemonic distributions of power.

Relative Inequality and Trade

The previous section outlined some salient reasons to consider the impact of concentration in this analysis of trade. In this and the following sections, some hypotheses are described linking concentration and its components (N and V) to patterns of global trade flows. As pointed out earlier, the concentration of capabilities is a function of both the number of major powers and the relative inequality among them. Because of their effects via concentration and for other reasons, each of these variables is likely to influence global trade, when the other is held constant.

Many theories of the international political economy focus primarily on the influence of the relative inequality of power in the system and place less emphasis on the size of the group. Most prominent among these explanations is hegemonic stability theory. Hegemonic stability theory (and the theory of collective action) suggests that the effect of relative inequality on trade is direct. All other things being equal, greater relative inequality enhances the prospects for solving collective action problems (Olson 1971); as V approaches its highest level, the amount of a collective good that is provided will approach an optimal level. Lake (1988), for example, finds empirical support for this hypothesis. He measures the structure of the system by the relative inequality of power among a fixed group of major powers, and concludes that higher levels of inequality are associated with greater openness.[7]

Alternatively, the relationship between relative inequality and trade may be inverse. The argument that Conybeare advances rests on the premise that, all other things being equal, "the gains from . . . tariff[s] . . . are likely to be directly proportional to the countries' relative sizes" (1987:26). When the relative inequality among the major powers is low, no major power possesses sufficient market power to influence its terms of trade. Hence, states have little economic incentive to impose tariffs or other trade barriers that would be expected to reduce global trade. As relative inequality reaches higher levels, so too does the relative market power of the largest state(s) in the system. Since the largest state(s) has an incentive to exploit its (their) market power by imposing an optimal tariff,[8] relative inequality may be inversely related to the level of global trade (Conybeare 1984, 1987).[9]

Group Size and Trade

Another set of theories of the international political economy centers largely on the impact of group size and focuses less on the relative inequality among the states that comprise the group. Small-group theorists, for example, maintain that, all other things being equal, smaller groups are better able than larger groups to provide collective goods in international relations (Schelling 1978:211–43; Hardin 1982; Keohane 1984; Lipson 1984; Axelrod and Keohane 1985; Oye 1985). Thus, N may be inversely related to international trade, when V is held constant.

Other scholars, however, imply that the number of major powers is directly associated with trade. Kenneth Waltz (1970; 1979) argues that as the number of major powers declines, each major power is likely to be larger and more economically self-sufficient. Since states in an anarchic

---

[7] In particular, Lake focuses on the United States, the United Kingdom, Germany, and France. Japan is also considered, beginning in 1950 (1988:33). For a critique of hegemonic stability theory that also centers on the effects of inequality, see Russett (1985).

[8] For a fuller discussion of this issue, see Johnson (1953–54), Ethier (1983), Conybeare (1984; 1987), and Gowa (1989a).

[9] The extent to which this is the case is an empirical question beyond the scope of this study. However, it is an assumption that is made often and one that seems reasonable for the purposes of a first cut at the problem.

system seek to reduce their dependence on one another, trade among major powers (which comprises a large portion of global trade) may be lowest (highest) when few (many) major powers exist, because major powers in these systems are best able to forgo commerce with (and limit their dependence on) one another. The number of major powers may also be directly related to trade if, as the size of the major-power subsystem decreases, the market power of each state increases vis-à-vis the remaining states in the system. Under these circumstances, fewer major powers may be associated with higher overall tariff levels, and hence lower levels of global trade.

A U-Shaped Relationship Between Concentration and Trade

It is also likely that V and N influence trade via their effects on concentration, as well as through other channels. As mentioned in chapter 1, with regard to their influence via concentration, I posit that the relationship between CON and trade is curvilinear. Specifically, holding N constant, I hypothesize that this relationship is U-shaped.

It was pointed out earlier that this hypothesis rests on the assumption that the demographic, economic, and military capabilities that are used to measure concentration are rough proxies for a state's market power.[10] Based on well-known arguments concerning optimal protection, I hypothesize that when market power is dispersed (and, hence, when the level of concentration is low), the level of tariffs and other protectionist instruments will be relatively low. Since, under these circumstances, states cannot influence their terms of trade, the use of trade barriers will only serve to impose welfare losses on those states that do so. And since there is reason to expect that the level of protectionism should be at least loosely related to the level of international trade, this suggests that lower levels of concentration will give rise to relatively high levels of global commerce.

As V increases and N decreases (and the level of concentration increases), the market power of the dominant states rises. Since, under these circumstances, large states can use tariffs (and other protectionist instruments) to improve their terms of trade, these states have an economic incentive to impose an optimal tariff. All other things being equal, less international commerce is expected to be conducted under these circumstances.[11]

However, this need not imply that the relationship between concentration and trade is always inverse. Beyond some level of concentration at which trade is minimized, increases in the level of concentration may tend

[10] See footnote 9, above.

[11] Of course, this assumes that larger states will not band together to deter each other from imposing optimal tariffs. Under these circumstances, the level of protectionism may remain relatively low.

to increase commerce. Recent work by Gowa (1989a; 1989b) suggests why this may be the case. States with little market power have few economic incentives to impose trade barriers; and as market power increases, so too does the economic incentive to impose an optimal tariff. But when concentration is highest, a rational, nonmyopic state with substantial market power may forgo the use of such an instrument in order to maintain its monopoly power in the international economy. And, even "[c]ritics [of hegemonic stability theory] acknowledge that hegemons which pursue political as well as economic goals may prefer free trade for political reasons" (Gowa 1989a:311 n. 12; see also Conybeare 1984, 1987). For example, a hegemon interested in enhancing its political power may promote free trade in an effort to foster the dependence of smaller states (Hirschman [1945] 1980). A hegemon may also make commercial concessions and expand its trade with certain states in order to induce political concessions from these trading partners (McKeown 1983; Conybeare 1984).

This suggests that there is some level of concentration at which trade is minimized; but beyond this point, powerful states may abstain from the use of trade barriers for both political and economic reasons. Indeed the level of global protectionism may be lowest (and hence the level of trade may be greatest) both when concentration is lowest *and* highest. And the level of international trade may be minimized when concentration lies somewhere between its highest and lowest levels.[12] Hence, I hypothesize that a U-shaped (that is, quadratic) relationship exists between concentration and trade, since this is the simplest functional form of the relationship in which both of the extreme levels of concentration are associated with the highest levels of trade.

WARFARE AND TRADE

Studies of the relationship between international politics and global trade often focus on the effects of the distribution of power. However, many observers argue that process-level features of the international system also influence commerce. It was pointed out in chapter 1 that, among these features, the impact of war has been of particular interest (Kindleberger 1966; Leamer and Stern 1970:15; Krasner 1976; Stein 1984; Strange 1988). Because one purpose of this book is to assess and compare the effects of structural and process-level variables on patterns of global out-

---

[12] Of course, only the range of variation of concentration found in the data is considered. For example, if the world consisted entirely of two countries, one with few inhabitants, few resources, and little capital, and the other with the remainder of the world's population, resources, and capital, one would expect practically all trade to be intranational, and the level of international trade to be relatively small, even though the level of concentration might be quite high.

comes, the relationships between the incidence of wars between and involv-ing major powers, respectively, and the level of international trade, are examined.

The effect of war on the level of commerce is also of interest because it is important to determine whether the relationship between trade and war (in chapter 4) is multidirectional. Though I am not aware of any empirical research on the effect of war on trade at the systemic level, Brian Pollins (1989a; 1989b) found that among dyads of nations during the period after World War II, higher levels of conflict led to lower levels of trade. However, as mentioned in the previous chapter, the vast majority of the conflict-events data that Pollins (and others) used were not wars. Further, results at the dyadic level may diverge from those at the systemic level. It is therefore worthwhile to examine this relationship further.

In this chapter I focus on the contemporaneous effect of war on com-merce. If, as Strange maintains, "[n]othing . . . has such a dampening effect on international trade as war" (1988:167; Stein 1984; Rosecrance 1986), the incidence of war should be inversely related to trade. Wars may reduce commerce since many resources that would otherwise have been exported by the antagonists are consumed in the war effort. Trade may also decline during wars if the combatants previously imported goods that are not essential to the war effort and are forgone during hostilities. Finally, wars may reduce commerce by disrupting commercial transportation.

On the other hand, the relationship between war and trade may be direct. Nations that depend heavily on commerce in order to obtain the resources necessary to wage war may increase trade with allies or neutral states during war. If this increase more than offsets decreases in commerce among adversaries, trade may be greater during wars than in the absence of hostilities.[13]

ECONOMIC DETERMINANTS OF GLOBAL TRADE

I also argued in chapter 1 that in order to assess fully the influence of political factors on commerce, it is necessary to account for the impact of economic factors in this regard. Moreover, in addition to war, economic variables may be important process-level determinants of global trade flows. And since some hegemonic stability theorists and many of their critics have argued that more attention needs to be paid to the effects of global market conditions (beyond the scope of the hegemon) in political analyses of international economic outcomes (Krasner 1976; Cowhey and Long 1983; Gowa 1984; Stein 1984; Gallarotti 1985; Cassing, McKeown, and Ochs 1986; Gilpin 1987; Strange 1987; McKeown 1991), it is impor-tant to include variables of this sort in the model of trade.

---

[13] For an excellent discussion of the effects of war on foreign trade, see Milward (1977).

Economists have tried in various ways to analyze what determines the amount of trade that is conducted, but they have focused primarily on the determinants of national and bilateral commerce rather than on total global trade. This chapter focuses on explaining the percentage of global output that is exported. Unfortunately, there has been a relative dearth of economic analyses of this topic (that I am aware of). However, a number of economic variables appear likely to influence the value of the ratio of global exports to total production.

First, the level of trade barriers throughout the system is likely to influence the value of the ratio of global exports to total production. All other things being equal, greater restrictions on trade are expected to reduce the level of international commerce. Second, technological advances are likely to influence the percentage of international output that is exported (Kindleberger 1966). For example, technological improvements that decrease transportation costs or improve communications would be expected to increase the value of the ratio of global trade to output. Further, technological advances often give rise to new products; international trade is likely to increase more quickly than output if demand for these products increases rapidly among consumers who are unable to obtain these goods domestically. Third, the discovery of natural resources may increase the percentage of global output that is exported (Kindleberger 1966), particularly if these resources are in great demand, have few substitutes, and are not distributed uniformly throughout the world.

Unfortunately, data on global levels of protectionism,[14] technological advances, and the discovery of natural resources do not seem to be available during the period covered in this study. However, data on global income (the fourth feature of the international economy that may influence the percentage of global output that is exported) do exist, and I will therefore focus on the effect of this variable in the following analysis. It is expected that global income is directly related to the value of the ratio of international trade to total production for the following reasons. First, some analysts conclude that the business cycle has a large political influence on tariff levels (Krasner 1976; Gallarotti 1985; Cassing, McKeown, and Ochs 1986; McKeown 1991). They argue that during periods of prosperity, tariff levels are likely to be lower (and, hence, trade levels are likely to be greater) than during depressions.

Second, one determinant of the level of international trade is the income elasticity of demand. If, for example, the income elasticity of demand for manufactured and capital goods (which historically have comprised a par-

---

[14] It should be noted, however, that to the extent that V and N predict the level of global protectionism and that this variable, in turn, predicts the level of global trade, the level of global protectionism is endogenized. Under these circumstances, lack of data on this variable does not pose a problem.

ticularly large percentage of global trade)[15] is greater than unity, higher
levels of global income are likely to be directly associated with higher levels
of international trade as a percentage of total production.[16]

Third, it is widely recognized that trade has increased more quickly than
output over time (Kindleberger 1966; Kuczynski 1980; Maddison 1982;
Deardorff and Stern 1987). Since it is also clear that there has been an
increase in global income over time (Maddison 1982), global income
should capture whatever secular trend exists in the value of the ratio of
global exports to total production.[17] Increases in global income may be
highly correlated with—and thus a good proxy for—decreases in transportation costs, improvements in communications, and the development
of new products, all of which would be expected to increase the percentage
of total output that is exported.

Finally, to the extent that intra-industry trade comprises a large portion
of global trade, higher levels of global income may lead to higher levels of
global trade as a percentage of total output. As Jagdish Bhagwati argues,
"[I]ntra-industry trade in similar products . . . is an important characteristic of trade among industrialized countries. This alone could imply a
higher rather than a lower ratio of trade to gross national product as
incomes increase and consumption gets increasingly more diversified in
terms of variety within broad industry groups while the trading countries
continue to specialize in production of similar goods with differentiated
characteristics" (1988:5–6).

The Statistical Model of Trade

I therefore assume that trade is a function of the distribution of power, the
incidence of warfare, and global income. The independent variables are
defined and discussed below. The complete model is:

$$(5.1)\quad Trade_t = A + B_1 Hegemony_{t-j} + B_2 Warfare_t + B_3 GDP_{t-1} +$$
$$B_4 CON_{t-j} + B_5 CON^2_{t-j} + B_6 N_{t-j} + B_7 V_{t-j} + B_8 delta\ CON_{t-j} +$$
$$B_9 MOVE_{t-j} + e_t,$$

where $Trade_t$ is the annual level of global exports as a percentage of total
production in year t;[18] $Hegemony_t$ is a dummy variable that equals one if a

---

[15] See Kindleberger (1966:89).

[16] Of course, as aggregate GDP increases, the supply curves for imports may shift and this
may be of consequence too.

[17] Time and global income are not both included as independent variables because they are
highly collinear ($r^2 = .82$).

[18] As in chapter 4, data provided by Kuczynski (1980:312) are used for this purpose. Since
for the world as a whole exports must equal imports, this variable will provide an estimate of

hegemon exists and zero if a hegemon does not exist in year t; CON_t is the concentration of capabilities in year t; N_t is the number of major powers in year t; V_t is the coefficient of variation of the shares of the total capabilities that each major power possesses in year t; *delta* CON_t is the average annual change in concentration in the five-year period from years $t - 5$ to t; $MOVE_t$ is the average annual movement in capabilities from years $t - 5$ to t; *Warfare*$_t$ is the number of wars between major powers being conducted during year t; GDP_{t-1} is the total global gross domestic product in year $t - 1$; and e_t is an error term.

This model is estimated for the period from 1850 to 1965, since data on *Trade* are not available prior to 1850. Because data on *CON*, *delta CON*, *MOVE*, CON^2, *N*, and *V* are available only at five-year intervals (1850, 1855, ... 1960), these are the values of $t - j$ that are used. Since the effects of these variables are expected to occur with a lag, it is assumed in equation 5.1 that there is a lag of j years.[19] In estimating this model, three values of j are used—one, three, and five years.[20]

The independent variables are defined as follows:

Hegemony. Because analyses in previous chapters of the effects of hegemony on the frequency of war indicated that the impact of this variable may depend on whose classifications are chosen, both Gilpin's and Wallerstein's classifications of hegemony are used in the following analysis of trade.

CON. This variable is defined and discussed in chapter 3. Singer, Bremer, and Stuckey's estimates of the annual level of *CON* (every five years) continue to be used in this analysis.

---

aggregate international commerce. It should be pointed out that hegemonic stability theorists do not agree as to whether the focus of this theory should be the explanation of trade (and other) outcomes in the international political economy or policy instruments and outcomes (such as tariffs, quotas, and subsidies) (Lake 1991; McKeown 1991).

This study focuses on the former and, in particular, on the level of international trade, since there is little data on tariff levels and other policy instruments for much of the period analyzed in this study and because many noted experts argue that "international trade [is] the most important constituent of international economic relations" (Hirschman [1945] 1980:xvi). It is clear, however, that trade flows and trade policy need not move in tandem. As a consequence, the results of this chapter may not apply uniformly to all variants of hegemonic stability theory.

[19] The effects of hegemony and concentration are lagged because "the core propositions in . . . [hegemonic stability] theor[y] state that a change in the distribution of power at time t causes a change in international outcomes at time $t + 1$" (Hart 1986:15).

[20] To illustrate this procedure, consider the data for 1900. In this case, *CON*, CON^2, *N*, *V*, and *Hegemony* are measured in 1900; and *delta CON* and *MOVE* are measured from 1895 to 1900. *Trade* is measured in 1901, 1903, and 1905 (one-year, three-year, and five-year lags); *Warfare* is measured in the same year as *Trade*; and *GDP* is measured in 1900 (when *Trade* is lagged by one year), 1902 (when *Trade* is lagged by three years), and 1904 (when *Trade* is lagged by five years).

N. This variable is the number of major powers in the system, which are described in chapter 2 (see Singer, Bremer, and Stuckey 1972; Small and Singer 1982).

V. This variable is the coefficient of variation of S_{it}. Equation 3.6 shows that V_t and N_t determine the level of concentration. As I argued above, there is reason to believe that both relative inequality and group size may have effects on *Trade* other than those via concentration. Hence, V_t and N_t, as well as CON_t (and CON_t^2), are included in equation 5.1.

delta CON. This variable is defined in chapter 3. Hegemonic stability theory suggests that a direct relationship exists between the change in concentration and trade. However, if in systems comprised of small states, nations abstain from protectionist measures while, in highly concentrated systems, dominant states have incentives to use such measures, the relationship may be inverse.

MOVE. This variable is also defined in chapter 3. The regression coefficient of this variable will indicate the extent to which commercial relations are sensitive to stability in the relative share of capabilities held by each major power.

Warfare. Since they would be expected to have the most pronounced impact on global trade, I will focus initially on the effects of wars between major powers on trade, using Levy's (1983) data set. However, since much of the previous analysis has centered on wars involving major powers, the influence of these events on the level of global commerce will also be examined. The coefficient of this variable will indicate whether (and if so, the extent to which) international trade is sensitive to the number of wars between—and involving—major powers being conducted in the year that *Trade* is measured.

GDP. For the reasons mentioned above, a direct relationship is expected to exist between total global gross domestic product (the measure of global income used in the present study) and *Trade*. The data for this variable are adapted from data compiled by Maddison (1982:86, 170) and are described in chapter 4.[21]

ESTIMATES OF THE EFFECTS OF THE DISTRIBUTION OF POWER ON TRADE

Ordinary least-squares regressions are used to estimate the parameters of equation 5.1.[22] The results (in table 5.1) indicate that this equation fits

[21] The data on global income are expressed in real terms and are adapted from Maddison (1982). See chapter 4, footnote 12, for a fuller explanation.

[22] As in the earlier regression analyses in this book, two problems that might arise in the present analysis are autocorrelation of the residuals and heteroskedasticity. Durbin-Watson statistics indicate that there is no clear evidence that the disturbances are characterized by an

TABLE 5.1

Regression of the Level of Global Exports as a Percentage of Total Production on *Hegemony* (Gilpin's and Wallerstein's Classifications), *Warfare*, GDP, CON, CON², N, V, delta CON, and MOVE, Using One-Year, Three-Year, and Five-Year Lags, 1850–1965 [a]

| | Classifications of Hegemony | | | | | |
| | Gilpin | | | Wallerstein | | |
Length of lag	One-year	Three-year	Five-year	One-year	Three-year	Five-year
Intercept	1.88***	1.47***	1.62***	1.45**	1.07**	1.66***
	(4.31)	(4.68)	(5.22)	(2.44)	(2.29)	(3.78)
Hegemony	0.0317	0.0327**	0.0345**	-0.0105	-0.0057	0.0173
	(1.56)	(2.30)	(2.55)	(-0.48)	(-0.36)	(1.11)
Warfare	-0.0024	-0.0410***	-0.0349***	-0.0007	-0.0460***	-0.0367***
	(-0.25)	(-4.29)	(-5.32)	(-0.07)	(-4.13)	(-4.74)
GDP	0.00008***	0.00006***	0.00005***	0.00008***	0.00006***	0.00006***
	(3.10)	(3.92)	(3.79)	(2.66)	(3.10)	(3.52)
CON	-13.77***	-10.39***	-11.33***	-9.60**	-6.47**	-10.93***
	(-3.97)	(-4.10)	(-4.60)	(-2.08)	(-1.77)	(-3.21)
CON²	13.96***	10.76***	12.38***	10.85**	7.92**	13.21***
	(4.09)	(4.43)	(5.22)	(2.25)	(2.09)	(3.74)

(continued)

TABLE 5.1 (Continued)

| | Classifications of Hegemony | | | | | |
| | Gilpin | | | Wallerstein | | |
Length of lag	One-year	Three-year	Five-year	One-year	Three-year	Five-year
N	-0.132*** (-3.13)	-0.098*** (-3.17)	-0.103*** (-3.38)	-0.080 (-1.72)	-0.047 (-1.27)	-0.081** (-2.31)
V	2.93*** (3.29)	2.17*** (3.29)	2.17*** (3.42)	1.71 (1.75)	0.97 (1.24)	1.65** (2.27)
delta CON	-0.66 (-1.00)	-1.22** (-2.70)	-0.74 (-1.68)	-0.79 (-1.13)	-1.37** (-2.59)	-0.83 (-1.61)
MOVE	-1.61 (-1.17)	-1.84* (-2.12)	-1.23 (-1.41)	-2.95** (-2.52)	-3.08*** (-3.87)	-2.68*** (-3.34)
$\bar{R}^2$ [b]	.54	.79	.81	.46	.70	.74

[a] The t-statistic for each regression coefficient is reported in parentheses below the coefficient.
[b] All values of R^2 are adjusted for degrees of freedom.
* Significant at the .10 level. One-tailed tests are conducted for the regression coefficients of CON, CON², and GDP because their signs are specified by the model. Two-tailed tests are conducted for all other regression coefficients.
** Significant at the .05 level. See note *.
*** Significant at the .01 level. See note *.

better when CON, CON^2, N, V, and *Hegemony* are lagged by three or five years rather than one year, which implies that *Trade* does not respond immediately to the distribution of capabilities. Regardless of whether Wallerstein's or Gilpin's periods of hegemony are used, the regression coefficients of the variables other than *Hegemony* are much the same, and (when lags of three and five years are used) the value of $\bar{R}^2$ is quite high—about .75. Thus *this simple model seems to explain about three-quarters of the variation in the ratio of global exports to total output.*

Although the overall explanatory power of the model is not very sensitive to which classification of hegemony is used, the same cannot be said for the effect on *Trade* of *Hegemony* itself. Instead, as in the earlier analyses of the relationship between hegemony and the frequency of war, the influence of hegemony varies markedly depending on whose classifications are analyzed. *When Gilpin's data are used,* Hegemony *is directly related to* Trade, *and the regression coefficient of* Hegemony *is statistically significant in two out of three cases.*[23] Hegemony also has a relatively large quantitative effect on *Trade*. The existence of a hegemon is associated with an increase of about .034 in the ratio of global trade to output (which is substantial given that the ratio has varied by only about .124 during the period covered in this study). Further, if the other variables in equation 5.1 are held constant at their mean values, the percentage of output that is exported is about 25 percent greater when a hegemon exists than when a hegemon does not exist. *But, when Wallerstein's data are used, the effect of hegemony on commerce is much weaker.* The sign of the regression coefficient of *Hegemony* depends upon the length of the lag, and in no case is it statistically significant.

On the other hand, variables related to the concentration of capabilities appear to have both strong and consistent effects on *Trade*. The results indicate that the number of major powers and the relative inequality

---

AR(1) process. As noted in chapters 3 and 4, for small samples, methods that correct for first-order autocorrelation will provide better estimates than OLS when $|\hat{\rho}| \geq .30$.

The only instance in which $|\hat{\rho}| \geq .30$ is when Gilpin's data on hegemony and a one-year lag are used. To correct for first-order autocorrelation in this case, GLS models were used. While these results do not differ markedly from those in table 5.1, the t-statistic of each coefficient is larger for the GLS estimate than for the OLS estimate. Of particular interest is the increase in the value of the t-statistic of *Hegemony* from 1.56 ($p = .14$) to 1.91 ($p = .08$).

To test for heteroskedasticity, the squares of the residuals were regressed on each of the independent variables and their squares, and an F-test of the regression was conducted. In no case was there any evidence of heteroskedasticity. It should also be pointed out that there is little evidence of multicollinearity among the independent variables in equation 5.1, since the estimated coefficients are generally statistically significant and tend to remain stable when variables are omitted from the model.

[23] When a GLS model is used, the regression coefficient of *Hegemony* is also statistically significant (at the .10 level) using Gilpin's data and a one-year lag. See footnote 22, above.

among them each influence *Trade* via concentration, as well as through other channels. The regression coefficient of N is negative and the regression coefficient of V is positive in all six cases; and both regression coefficients are statistically significant in four instances (although the results tend to be much stronger when Gilpin's data on *Hegemony* are used).

It should be noted that, when Gilpin's classifications of hegemony are analyzed, the nature and strength of these results are quite robust with respect to whether the analysis is based on Singer, Bremer, and Stuckey's estimates of concentration or the estimates described in chapter 3 that extend through 1970 and are derived from newer data on national capabilities. However, when Wallerstein's classifications of hegemony are analyzed, the effects of concentration and its components (N and V) on trade are much weaker when the newer data on national capabilities are used to derive estimates of concentration than when Singer, Bremer, and Stuckey's data are used. Thus the strength of the relationships between concentration and its components, on the one hand, and trade, on the other hand, is relatively insensitive to which classifications of hegemony are used based on Singer, Bremer, and Stuckey's data; but it is quite sensitive to which classifications of hegemony are used based on the newer estimates of concentration.

Returning to the results in table 5.1, it is important to assess the quantitative impacts of both N and V on *Trade*. In order to assess the effect of each of these variables, it is necessary to consider both its direct effect on *Trade*, as well as its indirect effect via concentration, holding constant the other variable. This can be accomplished by rewriting equation 5.1, using equation 3.6:

$$(5.2) \quad Trade_t = A + B_1 Hegemony_{t-j} + B_2 Warfare_t + B_3 GDP_{t-1} +$$
$$B_4 (V/\sqrt{N-1})_{t-j} + B_5 (V^2/(N-1))_{t-j} + B_6 N_{t-j} + B_7 V_{t-j} +$$
$$B_8 delta\ CON_{t-j} + B_9 MOVE_{t-j} + e_t.$$

Table 5.2 shows the predicted level of *Trade*, given the value of N and V, holding constant *Warfare*, *GDP*, *delta CON*, and *MOVE* at their mean values, for periods of both hegemony and nonhegemony.[24] The results indicate that, *regardless of the level at which* V *is held constant*, N *is directly related to the predicted level of* Trade. Further, when N equals five or six, *there is a U-shaped relationship between* V *and the predicted level of* Trade, since the highest levels of *Trade* (in table 5.2) obtain both when V equals .45 and when it equals .65.

---

[24] The values of *Trade* in table 5.2 were estimated using Gilpin's data and a three-year lag because this is the only specification of equation 5.2 in which all the regression coefficients are statistically significant (see table 5.1). The values of N and V in table 5.2 correspond roughly to the range of values that they take on during the period covered in this study.

TABLE 5.2

Predicted Level of Global Exports as a Percentage of Total Output, Based on
the Number of Major Powers and the Inequality of Capabilities Among Them,
Using the Regression Equation in Table 5.1 with Gilpin's Data and
a Three-Year Lag (and Evaluating *Warfare, GDP, delta CON,*
and *MOVE* at Their Mean Values)

Number of Major Powers	Coefficient of Variation				
	Periods of Hegemony				
	.45	.50	.55	.60	.65
5	.20	.18	.17	.17	.19
6	.24	.22	.21	.21	.22
7	—[a]	.23	.22	.22	—[a]
	Periods of Nonhegemony				
	.45	.50	.55	.60	.65
5	.17	.14	.13	.14	.16
6	.21	.18	.17	.17	.19
7	—[a]	.20	.19	.19	—[a]

[a] The predicted level of *Trade* is not computed because there are no observations for which
seven major powers exist and the coefficient of variation is approximately .45 or .65.

As I hypothesized, holding N constant, *there is a quadratic relationship
between CON and* Trade: in every case, the regression coefficient of CON
is negative and statistically significant and the regression coefficient of
CON^2 is positive and statistically significant. If V is expressed in terms of N
and CON, and the derivative of equation 5.2 is taken with respect to CON
and the result set equal to zero, the level of concentration that minimizes
the level of global commerce, according to equation 5.2, is determined. The
level of CON that minimizes *Trade,* however, depends upon the value of N.
In fact, this level becomes progressively lower as the number of major
powers increases. If N equals five, *Trade* is minimized when CON is approximately .282 using Gilpin's data, and when it is about .287 using
Wallerstein's data. If N equals six, *Trade* is minimized when CON is
approximately .259 using Gilpin's data, and when it is about .271 using
Wallerstein's data. And if N equals seven, *Trade* is minimized when CON is
approximately .238 using Gilpin's data, and when it is about .256 using
Wallerstein's data.

In addition to static features of concentration, dynamic features of concentration also seem to influence *Trade.* The regression coefficient of *delta*

CON is negative in each instance. And although it is statistically significant in only two cases, decreases in concentration seem to be associated with higher levels of global commerce. Further, there is also evidence that greater movement in the shares of capabilities among the major powers discourages international trade, while stability in the shares of capabilities among the major powers produces higher levels of commerce, since the regression coefficient of *MOVE* is negative in every instance and statistically significant in four cases.

ESTIMATES OF THE EFFECTS OF WAR AND GLOBAL INCOME ON TRADE

With regard to the effect of war on trade, *less trade is conducted during years in which wars between major powers are waged.* Not only is the regression coefficient of *Warfare* negative in every case and statistically significant in four of them, but it is large enough that this effect is quantitatively, as well as statistically, significant. When three-year and five-year lags are used, a change from no war to one war decreases *Trade* by about .040.

It is interesting to note that, like wars between major powers, *wars involving major powers also reduce the level of global trade* and the regression coefficient of *Warfare* continues to be statistically significant when three-year and five-year lags are utilized. But the magnitude of the effect on *Trade* of wars involving major powers is, on average, approximately .020, or about half of that for wars between major powers. This is not surprising. Wars involving major powers include both wars between major powers and wars that involve only one major power; and those wars that involve a single major power would not be expected to disrupt as many leading economies or to interrupt the transportation of goods and raw materials to the same degree as wars in which major powers confront one another. (It is also important to point out that the sign, size, and *t*-statistics of the remaining variables in equation 5.1 do not depend on whether wars involving or between major powers are examined.)

While the contemporaneous incidence of wars that are being conducted among major powers exerts a strong and sizable impact on *Trade*, the same is not the case for other features of major-power war. For example, the issue of whether the termination of war between major powers influences *Trade* in subsequent years was also examined.[25] When this variable[26] is intro-

[25] After wars are concluded, it may take time for nations to reallocate resources from sectors of the economy that are vital for fighting a war to commercial sectors, and trade with former adversaries may not be quickly reestablished. As a result, the relationship between the termination of war and trade may be inverse. On the other hand, the relationship may be direct if states rely on trade to help repair and revitalize their war-torn economies.

[26] A variable, $Warfare_o$, is defined, the value of which is determined by the number of wars between major powers ending in the five years prior to the year in which *Trade* is measured.

duced into equation 5.1, there is little evidence that it has a non-zero effect on *Trade*. This indicates that the influence of war on trade subsides rather quickly after hostilities end.

Finally, as expected, *there is strong evidence of a direct relationship between global gross domestic product and trade*: the regression coefficient of *GDP* is positive and statistically significant in all six cases. Further, like the political variables in this model, *GDP* has a strong quantitative effect on *Trade*. For example, when a three-year lag and Gilpin's classifications of hegemony are used, a change in *GDP* from its lowest to its highest level produces about a 40 percent increase in the level of *Trade* during periods of hegemony, and about a 50 percent increase in *Trade* during periods of nonhegemony (holding constant the political variables in the model at their mean levels). This suggests that, not surprisingly, international economic conditions strongly affect the level of global commerce.

In addition to examining the influence of *GDP* on *Trade*, it is also possible to consider separately the effects on *Trade* of the secular trend in *GDP* over time and the deviations from that trend. And it is useful to do so in order to determine whether the observed relationship between *GDP* and *Trade* is due solely to an upward trend in both variables, or whether the business cycle also has an independent effect on the level of global commerce. To this end, *GDP* was replaced in equation 5.1 with (1) the year in which *Trade* is measured (*Year*); and (2) the residuals from a regression of the logarithm of *GDP* in year $t - 1$ on year $t - 1$ for each five-year period from 1850 to 1965 (*Cycle*).[27] The results indicate that the respective influences of these variables on *Trade* are largely consistent with that of *GDP*. As expected, there is substantial evidence of an upward trend over time in *Trade*: the regression coefficient of *Year* is positive and statistically significant in every case. And higher levels of trade are conducted in years following upswings in the business cycle: the regression coefficient of *Cycle* is positive in five out of six cases, and is statistically significant in three of these five instances. Hence, both time and the business cycle have individual effects on *Trade* which are much the same as their combined influence on *Trade* via *GDP*.

Have the Effects on Trade of the Distribution of Power, War, and GDP Changed Over Time?

The final empirical issue that is addressed in this chapter is whether the effects on trade of the distribution of capabilities, war, and GDP have changed over time. In particular, the stability of the model between the periods prior to and subsequent to World War II is examined.

[27] See chapter 4. A one-year lag is used to avoid problems of simultaneity between *GDP* and *Trade*.

TABLE 5.3
F-Statistics Based on (Chow) Predictive Tests for
Equation Stability Between the Period Prior to
World War II (1850–1938) and the Period
Subsequent to World War II (1946–1965)[a]

Length of lag	Classifications of Hegemony	
	Gilpin	Wallerstein
One-year	0.66	2.24
Three-year	1.06	2.93
Five-year	1.13	2.94

[a] In the present case, the *F*-distribution has degrees of freedom equal to 4 (the number of observations in the period subsequent to World War II) and 9 (the number of observations in the period prior to World War II minus the number of independent variables in the model minus one). Under these conditions, the *F*-statistic is statistically significant (at the .05 level) if it is greater than or equal to 3.63.

As noted earlier, many analysts argue that the multipolar system that existed prior to World War II gave way to a bipolar system after the war (for example, Snyder and Diesing 1977; Waltz 1979). Further, Waltz (1970; 1979) maintains that the polarity of the system influences the level of global interdependence (measured, in part, by aspects of international trade). While they measure different features of the international distribution of power, polarity and the level of concentration should be loosely related. It may therefore be the case that the relationship between concentration and trade changed too after World War II. Further, the direct relationship between *GDP* and *Trade* almost certainly reflects (among other things) technological advances in transportation and communications. If the rate of technological change in these areas was higher after World War II than in the prewar period, one might expect that this would result in a change in the relationship between *GDP* and *Trade*.

McKeown (1991:163) concludes that his model of trade is unstable between the period prior to and after World War II. To determine whether the model of trade that is used in this chapter is stable across this period of time, predictive tests of equation stability were conducted.[28] The results (in table 5.3) indicate that, unlike McKeown's results, there is no evidence that

---

[28] This is the appropriate test (rather than, for example, an analysis-of-variance test) because the number of observations after World War II (four) does not exceed $k + 1$ (ten) (where k is the number of independent variables in the model). See Maddala (1988:134–36).

any of the models are unstable between the periods prior to and subsequent to World War II.[29] Thus it is appropriate to pool the data, as was done in table 5.1.

IMPLICATIONS OF THE RESULTS FOR HEGEMONIC STABILITY THEORY

The results of this chapter have a number of important implications for theories of the international political economy. Debates surrounding the merits of hegemonic stability theory have been at the forefront of research on the international political economy for some time. One reason why these debates remain unresolved is that scholars do not agree on how to define, measure, and operationalize hegemony, and thus no consensus exists regarding its influence on international relations. My findings clearly illustrate this problem. The extent to which the empirical relationship between hegemony and trade depends upon which data set (Gilpin's or Wallerstein's) is used is both marked and troubling. Indeed differences of this sort are not limited to analyses of global commerce: the results in chapters 2, 3, and 4 demonstrated that, in certain cases, these classifications are also related to the incidence of war in markedly different manners.

The primary difference between Gilpin's and Wallerstein's data (for the periods covered in this chapter) lies in the dating of the conclusion of British hegemony: Wallerstein dates its conclusion in 1873; Gilpin dates its conclusion in 1914. Since trade levels were relatively high in the last decade of the nineteenth century and the portion of the twentieth century prior to World War I, it is not surprising that this disagreement produces substantial differences in the observed relationship between hegemony and trade.

Defining and Measuring Hegemony

Central to the observed variation in the relationship between hegemony and trade is whether, as Gilpin argues, Great Britain was a hegemon in decline during the approximately forty years prior to World War I (1975:79–85; 1981:127–44) or whether, as Wallerstein argues, Great Britain had ceased being a hegemon during this era. The resolution of this

---

[29] It should be noted that the apparent disagreement between these findings and McKeown's results is probably due to differences in the specifications of the two models. (See footnote 6, above.) In addition, a number of points should be made concerning predictive tests of this sort. First, because the number of observations after World War II is less than $k + 1$, it may be more appropriate to think of these tests as tests of unbiasedness in prediction (in other words, tests of whether or not the prediction error has a mean equal to zero), rather than stability. Second, predictive tests of stability assume that the variance-of-error terms for both periods is equal. Finally, although these tests indicate that the model is stable over time, this does not deny the fact that the effects of some of the individual coefficients may have changed over time. See Maddala (1988:136) for a fuller explanation of these points.

issue hinges in part on which material bases of power are used to measure hegemony. For example, based on an analysis of GNP, military expenditures, and manufacturing production, Russett concludes that

> the United Kingdom was *never*, even at its peak in the 19th century, the dominant power as measured by either GNP or military expenditures. . . . Only in manufacturing production, and then only rather briefly, did it lead the world. . . . These data should encourage a cautious interpretation of Britain's "hegemonic" power. Britain's commercial power, reflected in trade or financial indicators, is not evident in other very important indicators of power base. (1985:211; emphasis in original)

On the other hand, Gilpin focuses on naval, technological, and commercial power; and based on the preponderance of British power in these areas, he argues that Great Britain was hegemonic throughout the nineteenth century (1975:79–84; 1981:127–44; 1987). In terms of land-based military capabilities and other capabilities that are often used to measure national power, however, Gilpin points out that Great Britain was not hegemonic. He maintains that, during the *Pax Britannica*, "the four major powers on the continent were kept in check by their own rivalries and by Britain, which, having no direct interests at stake on the continent, could play a *balancing* and mediating role" (1981:135, emphasis added; 1975:82–83). Gilpin therefore seems to argue that, at least in the political-military sphere, British hegemony existed only *outside of Europe*, where its naval superiority could be employed; within Europe, where land-based military capabilities were central elements of national power, stability was due to a rough balance of power rather than to British preponderance.

This characterization of British hegemony stands in contrast to that of Wallerstein, who argues that Great Britain was preponderant along economic, political-military, cultural, and diplomatic lines during portions of the nineteenth century (1983:101). Many analysts dispute the view that Great Britain was preponderant in each of the issue areas mentioned by Wallerstein. But there is considerable evidence that, at least until the turn of the twentieth century, Great Britain was the world's superior naval (Modelski 1978; Kennedy 1983, 1987; Friedberg 1988; Thompson 1988) and commercial (Krasner 1976; Friedberg 1988; Lake 1988) power; and that, in these respects, it was in (marked) decline during the latter quarter of the nineteenth century. It also appears to be the case that British political hegemony did not extend to the continent at any point during the nineteenth century. As Paul Schroeder argues, during this period, "Britain enjoyed command of the seas, and for a long while was preeminent in empire, industry, and commerce. But so far as continental Europe is concerned, what Lord Salisbury said was always true and well-known: 'We are fish'" (1986:9). He further points out that "Europe accepted British naval and colonial supremacy, choosing to live with it and, so far as strictly European politics was concerned, to ignore it" (1986:14).

From this standpoint, there seems to be support for the position advanced by Gilpin that Britain was a declining naval and commercial hegemon during the period in dispute. It is clear that a comprehensive analysis of hegemony, British or otherwise, will need to address the problems discussed above concerning exactly how much power a state must wield in order to be considered a hegemon, and that the issues of how to define the scope and domain of hegemony remain unresolved. But this cursory discussion of this topic does suggest that, *based on the criteria that Gilpin presents*, Britain was hegemonic during (at least most) of the period from 1874 to 1914. To the extent that this is the case and that even a declining hegemon is likely to foster a more liberal trading system than the total absence of such a state, the results in this chapter suggest that hegemony has been associated with higher levels of trade, which is consistent with the hegemonic stability thesis.

This discussion also suggests one reason why the findings in chapters 3 and 4 yielded no evidence that hegemony was associated with the frequency of major-power wars. Many of these wars were fought on the European continent; and Great Britain was not a "land-based" hegemon. In these cases, it was therefore unable to perform the deterrent function that many power preponderance theorists emphasize.

Concentration and Trade

The findings of this chapter also indicate that, regardless of whether or not the relative inequality between the two largest major powers (hegemony) is associated with trade, more attention should be devoted to the effects of the distribution of capabilities among all the major powers. For example, there is substantial evidence that the relative inequality of power among the major powers (V) is related to trade and that this relationship is U-shaped. Further, such a relationship also exists between concentration and trade. To the extent that market power is a function of the inequalities of power among the leading states in the system, this finding is entirely consistent with the hypothesis advanced above that the level of protection is likely to be greatest when intermediate levels of inequality obtain among the major powers. High levels of trade may obtain when the level of relative inequality (and concentration) is low because, under these conditions, market power is diffused among the states in the system. As the level of relative inequality (and concentration) increases, so too does the market power of the largest states in the system. This may lead these states to impose an optimal tariff, which would be expected to decrease global trade. But when market power is highest, states may choose to forgo the use of optimal tariffs for both economic and political reasons.

There is some evidence to support this explanation for the observed relationship between concentration (and relative inequality) and trade. For example, it was noted above that the level of concentration that minimizes the level of international trade depends on the number of major powers that exists. Given the number of major powers that existed during the 1930s (seven), the level of concentration that minimizes trade during the period from 1850 to 1965 based on the results using Gilpin's classification (.239) was quite closely approximated by those levels which obtained during the early 1930s (from .228 to .241). Moreover, Conybeare suggests that one reason for the especially pervasive protectionism during this period was that economic incentives for the use of trade barriers existed among the major powers. As he concludes, "[T]he 1930s provide us with [an] example of the predatory opportunities available to large powers" (1985:169).[30]

It is important to note that the finding of a U-shaped relationship between concentration and trade, and relative inequality and trade, is not completely inconsistent with the position of most hegemonic stability theorists. Since they are concerned primarily with the influence of power inequalities on global economic outcomes, the fact that higher levels of relative inequality are associated with higher levels of trade is consistent with their position. This finding is not consistent with the argument that when relative inequality is highest, the largest states in the system are likely to depart from liberal trade practices. One reason why the results in this chapter are at odds with the predictions of the latter argument may be that, as Gilpin points out, this position assumes

> that the maximization of economic gain is the highest priority of the hegemon. The possibility of retaliation and of negative effects on relations with friendly states and political allies and the ideological commitment to liberalism inhibit the hegemon's use of this strategy. Yet the hegemon is increasingly tempted to take advantage of its position as its power declines, as has occurred with the United States in the 1980s. (1987:89)

To the extent that declining hegemony is associated with intermediate levels of relative inequality (and of concentration), the findings in this

---

[30] Another reason why a U-shaped relationship exists between concentration and trade may be that intermediate levels of concentration are associated with high levels of intraregional trade. If intraregional trade tends to be trade-diverting (Krasner 1976; Pomfret 1988; Bhagwati 1991), high levels of intraregional trade would be expected to reduce the level of global trade. For a discussion of this issue, see Mansfield (1993b).

chapter are in accord with Gilpin's view. However, they are also in keeping with the hypothesis that, as concentration changes from low to intermediate levels, states are increasingly likely to impose optimal tariffs as their market power increases. This would explain why low, as well as high, levels of V (and CON) are associated with the highest levels of trade. And this finding is at odds with the predictions of (most variants of) hegemonic stability theory, since this explanation seems to argue that all non-hegemonic periods will experience lower levels of trade than their hegemonic counterparts. In sum, these results are partially in accord with both hegemonic stability theorists and some alternative explanations. But the relationship between the distribution of power and trade is much richer than either view hypothesizes.

Interestingly, the existence of a U-shaped relationship between relative inequality and trade is consistent with at least one variant of hegemonic stability theory. Krasner argues that while a preponderant state will favor an open trading system because it augments this state's political power, systems comprised of many small, highly developed states may also produce an open system because the opportunity costs of closure for states in such a system are quite large.[31] However, "a system comprised of a few very large, but unequally developed states . . . is likely to lead to a closed system" because openness would create only moderate increases in these states' income and would engender social instability and political vulnerability (Krasner 1976:321–22). Thus Krasner suggests that the system is likely to be open when relative inequality is both highest and lowest. The findings of this chapter are in accord with his position.

These results also suggest that critics of hegemonic stability theory are correct in arguing that shifts toward a more uniform distribution of capabilities need not be associated with closure; and that the prognosis offered by some observers that the decline in American power will undermine the liberal international economic order may be overly pessimistic. If, all other things being equal, V is greater than the level that minimizes trade and is reduced, these fears may be warranted. But if, for example, Germany and Japan have become (or are becoming) major powers, the combination of a decrease in relative inequality and an increase in the number of major powers may improve the prospects for freer trade.

The influence of dynamic features of the distribution of capabilities on trade is also apparent in the case of the effects of movement in the shares of capabilities among major powers. The fact that $MOVE$ is inversely related to $Trade$ indicates that one precondition for the expansion of trade may be a relatively stable structure of the international system. When large shifts

---

[31] The magnitudes of these opportunity costs are due to the benefits that small states derive from an open system and the difficulty of existing under conditions of autarky.

occur in the distribution of power, states whose relative capabilities are declining may feel that trade relations with states whose relative capabilities are growing will, as Gilpin maintains, "become a source for increasing the political power of the strong over the weak" (1987:57). Under these circumstances, weaker states may be hesitant to engage in commerce, thereby leading to lower levels of global trade.

IMPLICATIONS OF THE RESULTS FOR SMALL-GROUP THEORIES

In addition to their implications for hegemonic stability theory, the results of this chapter also have implications for small-group theories of the international political economy. When the total effects of N (both via CON and other channels) are considered, the number of major powers is directly related to *Trade*, which is at odds with the predictions of small-group theories. It could be argued that, since the number of major powers does not exceed eight during the period covered in this study, even a large number of major powers constitutes a k-group. Under these circumstances, small groups may be able to provide an open international trading system. Even if this is the case, however, small-group theory remains mute on why the value of k should be directly, rather than inversely, related to the level of trade. Indeed one of the major shortcomings of small-group theory is that it fails to specify precisely *how small* a small group is.

Another reason why the results of this chapter are not consistent with the expectations of small-group theories may be that these theories draw their analytical foundation from the theory of collective action, and an open trading system is not a collective good. As such, neither a small group nor high levels of inequality are required for its provision. There is considerable evidence to support the position that many of the benefits derived from an open international economic order are quite excludable. The most obvious example of this is the Soviet Union and its allies, which were systematically excluded from the benefits of free trade with the advanced industrialized countries during the Cold War.

One explanation for the direct relationship between group size and trade is that as N increases, the market power of each major power declines. As a result, the ability of any major power to impose an optimal tariff may be lowest as N approaches its maximum. These results may also reflect the fact that, all other things being equal, the fewer the number of major powers, the better able each major power is to provide for its own economic needs without engaging in commerce. And since there are security externalities associated with trade (Gowa 1989b; Gowa and Mansfield 1993), states may attempt to reduce their dependence on potential adversaries once they are self-sufficient enough to do so.

A related explanation for this finding inheres in the trade-offs between

relative and absolute gains among states engaged in foreign trade. Neorealists argue that cooperation in the international political economy is inhib-
ited by concerns over how the gains from trade will be divided, since the
distribution of these gains may influence the distribution of power among
the participants in commerce (Waltz 1979; Gilpin 1987; Grieco 1988).
However, Duncan Snidal (1991) suggests that, under certain circumstances, the salience of concerns over relative gains is reduced as the number of major powers in the system increases. Hence, the direct relationship
between N and $Trade$ may reflect the tendency for states to worry less
about the security implications of commerce, and therefore to become
increasingly willing to engage in foreign trade, as N increases.

ADDITIONAL IMPLICATIONS OF THE RESULTS

The results of this chapter provide clear evidence that structural variables
are strongly related to patterns of international trade, although the nature
of their effects often are more complex than is commonly recognized.
However, these findings also highlight the importance of examining
process-level features in systemic analyses of commerce. In particular, Stein
and others are correct in arguing that among the "real dangers to a relatively liberal trading order are wars that destroy political relationships and
disrupt economic ones or major sustained downturns—real depressions in
the global economy" (1984:385). The importance of these factors has not
been lost on hegemonic stability theorists. A number of them highlight
explicitly the effects of economic fluctuations and war on patterns of trade
(Krasner 1976; Gilpin 1987). But while some studies have concluded that
"[u]ltimately, structure and process must be integrated in a theory of political economy" (Lake 1983:540), little progress has been made on this
front.

The results of this chapter also indicate that, as in the earlier analysis of
warfare, aspects of both global politics and economics help to account for
patterns of international trade. Clearly, economic factors exert a strong
influence on the level of global commerce. As a result, political scientists
should be wary of using models of international trade that do not account
for the effects of these factors. However, my findings indicate that neglecting political factors in analyses of trade is also likely to be a hazardous
strategy. The simple model used in this chapter includes both political and
economic variables, and it provides a remarkably good fit; in fact, it often
explains about three-quarters of the variation in the level of international
trade. Since economic models of trade often neglect the influence of international politics,[32] the strength of these results indicates that economists

---

[32] For some exceptions, see Roemer (1977) and Green and Lutz (1978).

might benefit from examining more carefully the effects of international politics in their analyses of trade.[33]

Moreover, although political variables other than the distribution of capabilities have received scant attention in systemic analyses of trade, the contemporaneous incidence of war between major powers also determines the amount of commerce that is conducted. As might be expected, less trade is conducted during wars between major powers than in the absence of such wars. There is also evidence that the relationship between trade and wars involving major powers is multidirectional. The findings in chapter 4 indicated that the level of international commerce influences strongly wars of this sort. The findings in this chapter indicate that wars involving major powers also exert a marked impact on the level of global trade (although the magnitude of this effect is less than that of wars between major powers). These results suggest that analysts of the international political economy and analysts of war could benefit from an expanded dialogue, since a series of interesting and important relationships exist between trade and war and because aspects of the distribution of power influence patterns of both of these variables.

Conclusions

The purpose of this chapter has been to examine the effects of the distribution of power and war on trade. Because it was found in the previous chapter that the level of global commerce is strongly related to the incidence of war, analyses of war should consider the systemic conditions that give rise to fluctuations in trade. But aside from their implications for the study of war, analyses of commerce are of great importance in their own right; indeed they are central to the study of international economics and the international political economy.

The results of this chapter indicate that systemic features of both power and war have a significant impact on the level of global trade. First, while the distribution of power is of considerable importance in this regard, various features of the distribution of capabilities are related to the level of global trade in very different ways. Because much of the literature on the international political economy has focused exclusively on the effects of hegemony, studies of this topic have failed to uncover central aspects of the relationship between the distribution of power and international commerce. Under certain circumstances, hegemony is related to the level of global trade; and the direction of this relationship is often in accord with the prediction of hegemonic stability theory. But whether or not there is a statistically significant relationship between hegemony and the level of

---

[33] On this point, see Cohen (1990) and Odell (1990).

global trade depends on how hegemony is defined, measured, and operationalized.

Second, there is substantial evidence that features of the concentration of capabilities are related strongly to the level of global commerce, though the relationship is more complex and richer than is usually thought. Previous studies have analyzed only whether a monotonic relationship exists between the distribution of power and trade (perhaps because they have focused primarily on the effects of hegemony, which is often operationalized as a dichotomous variable). But it is important to recognize that the level of concentration depends on both the number of major powers and the relative inequality of their capabilities. Holding constant the number of major powers, there is a U-shaped relationship between the relative inequality among the major powers in the international system and the level of trade. Holding constant relative inequality, there is a direct relationship between the number of major powers and the level of trade.

Third, the contemporaneous incidence of warfare exerts a substantial impact on the level of trade. Less trade is conducted when major-power wars are being waged than during periods in which no such wars are being waged. In combination with the results of the previous chapter, this suggests that a multidirectional relationship exists between trade and war.

Finally, economic factors, such as global gross domestic product, are also important determinants of patterns of international commerce. Not surprisingly, the level of trade is directly associated with the level of global income. As I argued at the outset of this study, one limitation of previous studies of the international political economy is that they have generally failed to consider explicitly the effects of both economic and political variables on outcomes, such as trade. But it is only by comparing the effects of these types of variables that we can assess the relative importance of political factors on economic outcomes. The results in this chapter strongly support the position that both political and economic effects shape patterns of international trade.

Appendix: A Simultaneous Equations Model of the Relationship Between Trade and War

Almost all the models of war and trade in this book have been constructed by lagging the effects of the relevant exogenous variables. This specification is consistent both with my argument and with the vast majority of systemic theories that underlie this study. In this appendix, we determine whether the findings obtained earlier would have been significantly different if we had assumed that simultaneous relationships exist between the level of international trade and the incidence of wars involving major powers.

To address this issue, two structural equations are specified, one for war and the other for trade. These equations are as follows:

$$(5.3) \quad War_t = A_1 + B_1 CON_t + B_2 delta\ CON_t + B_3 CON_t^2$$
$$+ B_4 Year_t + C_1 Trade_t + e_{1t}$$

$$(5.4) \quad Trade_t = A_2 + B_5 CON_t + B_6 MOVE_t + B_7 CON_t^2 + B_8 N_t$$
$$+ B_9 V_t + B_{10} GDP_{t-1} + B_{11} Hegemony_t + C_2 War_t + e_{2t}$$

In these equations, A_1 and A_2 are the parameters of the intercepts; $B_1 - B_{11}$ are the parameters of the predetermined variables; C_1 and C_2 are the parameters of the endogenous variables (*Trade* and *War*, respectively); and e_{1t} and e_{2t} are error terms. Further, War_t is the mean number of wars involving major powers during the period from years t to $t + 5$; $Trade_t$ is the annual level of global exports as a percentage of total production in year t; CON_t is the concentration of capabilities in year t; N_t is the number of major powers in year t; V_t is the coefficient of variation of the shares of the total capabilities that each major power possesses in year t; *delta* CON_t is the average annual change in concentration in the five-year period from years $t - 5$ to t; $MOVE_t$ is the average annual movement in capabilities from years $t - 5$ to t; GDP_{t-1} is the total global gross domestic product in year $t - 1$; *Year* is t; and $Hegemony_t$ is a dummy variable that equals one if a hegemon exists and zero if a hegemon does not exist in year t.

It is important to note that, although these equations correspond to equations that were analyzed in this and the previous chapter, they are specified differently from the earlier ones. More specifically, it is clear that the lag structures in equations 5.3 and 5.4 differ from those in the equations that were analyzed in this and the previous chapter, since all the static variables are measured at time t, except for *GDP*. Further, while equation 5.3 includes the same variables that were analyzed in table 4.2, *delta CON* has been dropped from equation 5.1 in equation 5.4. This specification of equation 5.4 is chosen because the results in table 5.1 indicated that, regardless of whose classifications of hegemony were analyzed, *delta CON* was weakly related to *Trade* when the lag between them was short (one year). This suggests that, to the extent that it influences trade, changes in concentration take some time to impact the level of global commerce. It therefore seems reasonable to exclude this variable from an equation in which its effect on trade would be measured with no lag. Further, results derived from the newer estimates of concentration described above provide no evidence that the change in concentration has a statistically significant effect on the level of global trade, regardless of the length of the lag or the classifications of hegemony that are used. As a result, *delta CON* is not included in equation 5.4.

It is well known that estimating simultaneous equations models using OLS will generate biased and inconsistent estimates of the parameters (Hanushek and Jackson 1977; Berry 1984; Kmenta 1986; Maddala 1988). One alternative method that is widely used and that avoids these problems is two-stage least squares. As a result, this method is used to estimate the parameters in equations 5.3 and 5.4 for the period from 1850 to 1965. It should be noted that both Gilpin's and Wallerstein's classifications of hegemony continue to be used; but because the results differ relatively little depending on whether Levy's or Singer and Small's data on major-power wars are considered, only the former compilation is used for the purposes of measuring War_t.

ESTIMATES OF THE PARAMETERS OF EQUATION 5.3

The results of this analysis are presented in table 5.4. The estimates of the parameters of equation 5.3 indicate that there is considerable evidence that the nature and strength of the effects of trade on war are virtually identical to those when the effects of trade on war are lagged (in chapter 4). More specifically, the results in table 5.4 indicate that the level of international trade is inversely related to the incidence of major-power war, since the coefficient of *Trade* is negative and statistically significant. It is also interesting to note that the size of the coefficient of *Trade* in table 5.4 is quite similar to its size in table 4.2 where the effects of *Trade* are lagged.

In addition, the effects of the concentration of capabilities and time on war, based on equation 5.3, are entirely consistent with the results in chapter 4. There continues to be considerable evidence of an inverted U-shaped relationship between concentration and the frequency of wars involving major powers. The coefficient of *CON* continues to be positive and statistically significant, and the coefficient of CON^2 continues to be negative and statistically significant. There also continues to be evidence

TABLE 5.4
Two-Stage Least-Squares Estimates of Simultaneous Equations Models of *War* and *Trade*, 1850–1965[a]

	Classifications of Hegemony			
	Gilpin		Wallerstein	
	Equation 5.3	Equation 5.4	Equation 5.3	Equation 5.4
Intercept	−7.10*** (−3.16)	1.40*** (4.11)	−7.28*** (−3.23)	0.93** (2.52)
Warfare	—	−0.0507 (−1.53)	—	−0.0519 (−1.57)
Trade	−5.14*** (−3.40)	—	−5.70*** (−3.64)	—
Hegemony	—	0.0176 (1.29)	—	−0.0129 (−1.06)
CON	10.85** (1.89)	−9.57*** (−3.46)	10.08* (1.74)	−5.33** (−1.87)
CON²	−24.26** (−2.46)	9.24*** (3.45)	−23.33** (−2.36)	5.50** (1.85)
N	—	−0.091** (−2.87)	—	−0.046 (−1.60)
V	—	2.03*** (2.97)	—	0.96 (1.61)
delta CON	9.07** (2.58)	—	9.27** (2.62)	—
MOVE	—	−1.12 (−1.35)	—	−1.74** (−2.70)
Year	0.0038*** (3.23)	—	0.0040*** (3.38)	—
GDP	—	0.00009*** (5.72)	—	0.00008*** (4.83)
$\bar{R}^2$ [b]	.48	.81	.50	.80

[a] The *t*-statistics for each coefficient are reported in parentheses below the coefficient.

[b] All values of R^2 are adjusted for degrees of freedom.

* Significant at the .10 level. One-tailed tests are conducted for the coefficients of CON, CON², and GDP because their signs are specified by the model. Two-tailed tests are conducted for all other coefficients.

** Significant at the .05 level. See note *.

*** Significant at the .01 level. See note *.

that increases in concentration promote the onset of major-power war, since the coefficient of *delta CON* is positive and statistically significant in both instances. Further, the coefficient of *Year* continues to be positive and statistically significant, which continues to suggest a secular increase in the frequency of major-power war over time.

It is also interesting that the magnitude of the effects of these variables on the incidence of war varies little depending on whether or not the relationship between trade and war is lagged or simultaneous. As in the case of *Trade*, the sizes of the coefficients of *delta CON* and *Year* are quite similar to those in table 4.2. And the level of concentration that maximizes the predicted frequency of war based on the results in table 5.4 is virtually identical to the level of concentration based on the findings in table 4.2.

Estimates of the Parameters of Equation 5.4

The estimates of the parameters of equation 5.4 indicate that the relationship between *War* and *Trade* is inverse, which is consistent with the earlier findings in this chapter concerning the contemporaneous effects of wars between and involving major power (*Warfare*) on the level of global commerce. But unlike the earlier results based on the effects of *Warfare*, the coefficient of *War* is not statistically significant.

There are a number of possible explanations for this difference. Most important is the fact that war is measured differently in equation 5.4 than in the earlier model of trade (equation 5.1). *War* in equation 5.4 is defined as the mean number of wars involving major powers beginning from years t to $t + 5$. *Warfare* in equation 5.1 is defined as the number of wars between major powers being waged in year t. Wars that begin during the period from years $t + 1$ to $t + 5$ would not be expected to influence *Trade* to the same extent as those beginning in year t, unless in year t states anticipate the onset of war in the near future (from years $t + 1$ to $t + 5$) and alter their trade patterns accordingly. Another possible explanation for the difference between the results in this appendix and the earlier findings in this chapter may be that wars involving major powers exert less impact on global trade than do wars between major powers. In this chapter, both types of wars were examined. As noted above, both the number of wars involving major powers and between major powers being waged at time t were strongly related to trade; but the quantitative impact and the statistical significance of *Warfare* were noticeably smaller when wars involving, rather than between, major powers were analyzed.

Turning to the remaining variables in equation 5.4, there appears to be relatively little difference in their estimated effects on *Trade*, depending on whether it is assumed that they exert lagged or simultaneous influences. There continues to be strong evidence of a U-shaped relationship between concentration and the level of international trade when a system of simultaneous equations is used. Regardless of whether Gilpin's or Wallerstein's classifications of hegemony are used, the coefficient of CON is positive and statistically significant, and the coefficient of CON^2 is negative and statistically significant. In addition, like the earlier results in this chapter based on a model in which their effects on commerce were lagged, the coefficient of N is negative; the coefficient of V is positive; and both variables tend to have larger and stronger effects on the level of global trade when Gilpin's, rather than Wallerstein's, classifications of hegemony are used. Further, the coefficient of $MOVE$ is negative in both cases, but it tends to exert a larger and more significant impact on trade when Wallerstein's, rather than Gilpin's, classifications are used. This finding is also consistent with the earlier results in this chapter.

There also continues to be evidence that the effects of hegemony on trade depend on whose classifications are used. The results in table 5.4 show that when Gilpin's classifications of hegemony are used, hegemony is associated with higher levels of trade; when Wallerstein's classifications are used, hegemony is associated with lower levels of trade. However, it is interesting to note that neither coefficient is statistically significant and that the size of the coefficient based on Gilpin's classifications is about half of its size in table 5.1 (where the effect of hegemony on trade is lagged).

The earlier findings in this chapter indicated that, based on Gilpin's data, the strength of the relationship between hegemony and trade increased as did the length of the lag between the times in which these variables were measured. In fact, the relationship between hegemony and trade was not statistically significant when a one-year lag was used. The results in table 5.4 are consistent with these earlier findings. In sum, unlike concentration and its components (N and V), hegemony seems to have a significant effect only when it is assumed that it has a lagged effect on trade.[34]

There continues to be evidence that global income exerts a direct and strong influence on the level of trade. Like the results in table 5.1, the findings in table 5.4 indicate that the coefficient of GDP is positive and statistically significant, regardless of whether Gilpin's or Wallerstein's classifications of hegemony are analyzed.

IMPLICATIONS OF THE RESULTS

This appendix indicates that the nature and strength of the relationships among the distribution of power, the level of international trade, and the incidence of major-power war are much the same, regardless of whether we assume that the effects of war and trade occur simultaneously or with a lag. Indeed the robustness of these results is striking.

---

[34] See footnote 19, above.

Chapter 6

THE DETERMINANTS AND DYNAMICS OF CONCENTRATION

MUCH OF THIS BOOK has been devoted to assessing structural explanations of international relations. At the outset of this study, it was pointed out that controversies surrounding these explanations often center on the importance of the distribution of power in shaping global outcomes, the nature of the relationship between the distribution of power and patterns of international relations, and the ability of existing structural theories to account for structural change. Thus far, the first two issues have been analyzed. This chapter addresses the third topic.

Since aspects of the distribution of power are strongly related to patterns of war and trade, an understanding of the factors that determine the structure of the international system and changes in this structure may provide insights into the conditions under which wars tend to begin and trade levels vary. More generally, it was noted in chapter 1 that neorealist (and other structural) theories have been criticized for failing to provide adequate explanations of structural change (Ruggie 1983; Keohane 1986; Keohane and Nye 1987). Despite a number of prominent efforts to explain dynamic features of the system's structure (for example, Organski 1958; Russett 1968b; Wallerstein 1974; Modelski 1978; Organski and Kugler 1980; Gilpin 1981; Kennedy 1987; Doran 1991), this topic has received short shrift in analyses of international relations. Moreover, virtually all these studies have focused on hegemony and hegemonic change. But while the results in this book indicate that, under certain circumstances, hegemony (and other aspects of polarity) helps to shape patterns of war and trade, I have argued that concentration is often more strongly related to these outcomes.

The purpose of this chapter is therefore to explain the level of concentration and changes in concentration over time. This analysis of structural change is rooted in views expressed by neorealists and others that changes in the distribution of power are guided by strategic interdependence among the leading states in the system. Since states exist in an anarchic environment, they must either react to increases in the power of others or face the possibility that the ensuing imbalance of power will degrade their national security. This suggests that the leading states have a strong incentive to increase their capabilities at a roughly proportionate rate, and that periods that are not characterized by proportionate growth are especially likely to witness the onset of wars between major powers.

The view that growth in national capabilities should be characterized by this type of process is very similar to one leading explanation of structural change in markets and industries. As noted in chapter 1, neorealists often point to conceptual similarities between firms and states and between industries and international systems. It is therefore appropriate to analyze whether microeconomic models of structural change can be applied fruit-fully to the study of international relations. Very little research has been conducted on this topic. However, it is of considerable importance: to the extent that such models are useful in this regard, it may be possible to fashion a neorealist model of structural change.

Has There Been a Trend in the Concentration of Capabilities?

At the outset of this chapter, it is useful to examine whether there has been any pattern in the level of concentration of capabilities among the major powers. Since Singer, Bremer, and Stuckey's estimates of concentration have been used in earlier chapters, and because these data are provided only for the period from 1820 to 1960, this is the era on which the present section will focus. In subsequent sections, the newer data on national capabilities discussed in chapter 3 will be used to analyze the period from 1820 to 1980.

If a trend exists in the level of concentration over time, it may be possible to use this trend to help predict future values of concentration, and hence patterns of war and trade. To determine if any trend exists, Singer, Bremer, and Stuckey's estimates of concentration were regressed on their corre-sponding years (from 1820 to 1960). The results indicate that there has been a mild increase in concentration over time. However, although the regression coefficient of time is both positive and statistically significant (at the .10 level), it is quite small (.0004), and time explains only about 10 percent of the variation in concentration. It also appears that much of the upward drift in concentration is due to its marked increase after the con-clusion of World War II. In fact, there exists no trend in concentration prior to World War II. (From 1820 to 1938, the regression coefficient of time equals $-.0001$ and is not statistically significant.)

There are a number of possible explanations for the upward trend in the level of concentration over time, and the increase in concentration after World War II. First, many studies have found that major-power war is one of the most salient determinants of structural change (Waltz 1979; Gilpin 1981; Thompson 1988; Thompson and Rasler 1988). It may be that wars involving all the major powers lead to increases in the level of concentra-tion. In fact, this seems to be the case: the two highest levels of concentration during the period from 1820 to 1960 obtained in 1920 and 1946, the first years in which concentration was measured after World Wars I and II, respectively. However, explanations of structural change that are based solely on the conclusion of "systemic" wars provide few insights into why concentration decreased rapidly after 1920 (until the conclusion of World War II), while it remained at a relatively high level after 1946 (at least until 1960).

Second, since concentration is an equally weighted aggregation of economic, demographic, and military capabilities among the major powers in the system, the concentration of one (or a number) of these components may be responsible for the level of, and changes in, systemic concentration. Jeffrey Hart suggests that this may be the case, noting that "[a]lthough there is a reasonably high level of correlation among different indicators of military and generalized capabilities, there is enough variation across the different indicators, especially at the high end of the scales, to pose problems for putting forth an overall index of capabilities" (1985:26). To determine whether there are differences among patterns of the concentration of individual capabilities, military expenditures, military personnel, and national population—three of the four demographic and military components of Singer, Bremer, and Stuckey's index—as well as gross national product (GNP), are examined separately to see how they changed over time. These capabilities were chosen because, although there is considerable disagreement regarding the most important indices of national power, they have received a disproportionate amount of attention among analysts of international relations.[1]

Table 6.1 presents Singer, Bremer, and Stuckey's estimates of concentration and estimates of the concentration of GNP, military expenditures, military personnel, and national population for selected years during the nineteenth and twentieth centuries.[2] Figures 6.1, 6.2, 6.3, and 6.4 show that these four capabilities exhibit quite different behaviors over time. The

---

[1] On the importance of GNP as a measure of national power, see Davis (1954), Organski (1958), Hitch and McKean (1965), Alcock and Newcombe (1970), Organski and Kugler (1980), Kugler and Domke (1986), and Kugler and Arbetman (1989). See also Doran (1991:47), who argues that national population, military expenditures, military personnel, and GNP are the most important indices of a state's international "size."

[2] The years in table 6.1 are chosen because they are ones for which data on GNP are available. The data on GNP from 1830 to 1937 are taken from Bairoch (1976) for all European states, from Mitchell (1982) for Japan, and from Mitchell (1983) for the United States. Data for 1950 and 1960 are taken from Summers and Heston (1984). Exchange-rate data are taken from Liesner (1984) for Japan and the World Bank (1983) for China. The GNP price deflator was then used to compute all figures in 1960 U.S. dollars. This figure was chosen because all of Bairoch's figures are in 1960 U.S. dollars. All data on military expenditures, military personnel, and population were taken from the Correlates of War Project's "National Material Capabilities Data" (1991).

TABLE 6.1

Levels of Concentration (CON) Provided by Singer, Bremer, and Stuckey, and
Derived for GNP, Military Expenditures, Military Personnel, and Population
Based on the Ray and Singer Index, 1830–1960

Year	CON	GNP	Military Expenditures	Military Personnel	Population
1830	.242	.071	.226	.395	.230
1840	.232	.063	.265	.279	.226
1850	.260	.059	.213	.311	.230
1860	.280	.105	.221	.260	.242
1870	.233	.137	.314	.235	.210
1880	.226	.140	.187	.259	.228
1890	.203	.145	.160	.199	.251
1900	.202	.270	.296	.216	.202
1913	.208	.320	.119	.240	.235
1925	.247	.428	.221	.169	.219
1937*	.217	.359	.248	.259	.237
1950	.293	.409	.434	.472	.479
1960	.303	.348	.459	.279	.497

* CON is measured in 1938.

concentration of GNP among the major powers has increased steadily
from 1830 to 1960. (The regression coefficient of time equals .0034 and is
statistically significant.) On the other hand, there is little trend in the
concentration of population until 1950, when it rises markedly due (in
large measure) to China's entrance into the major-power subsystem. For
military expenditures and personnel, there are no perceptible trends during
the period from 1830 to 1960, although the concentration of both capabilities also increased markedly after World War II.

To better understand the relationship between CON and these four
capabilities, Singer, Bremer, and Stuckey's estimates were correlated with
the concentration of each of these components. The results indicate that the
correlation between the concentration of GNP and the aggregate level of
concentration (CON) is virtually zero.[3] The correlation between the con-

[3] Interestingly, these results are at odds with the conclusions of Kugler and Arbetman that
"[the COW index and GNP] are equally serviceable in cross-temporal analysis" (1989:57; see

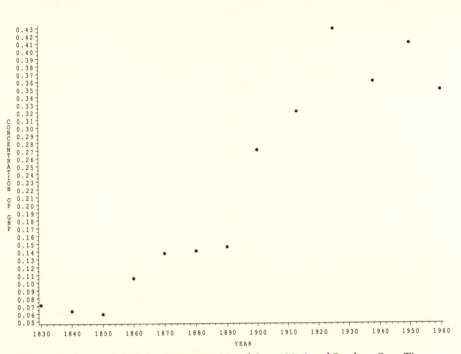

FIG. 6.1. Scatterplot of the Concentration of Gross National Product Over Time, 1830–1960

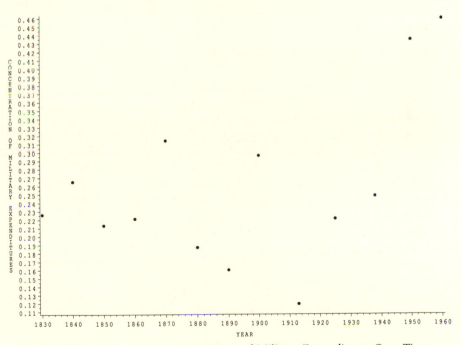

FIG. 6.2. Scatterplot of the Concentration of Military Expenditures Over Time, 1830–1960

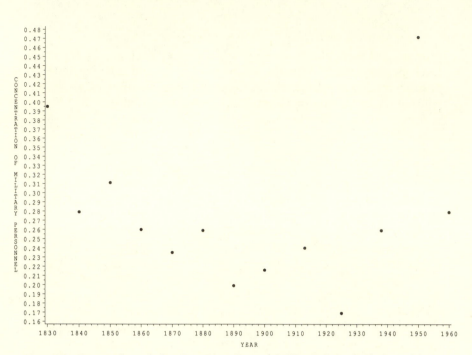

FIG. 6.3. Scatterplot of the Concentration of Military Personnel Over Time, 1830–1960

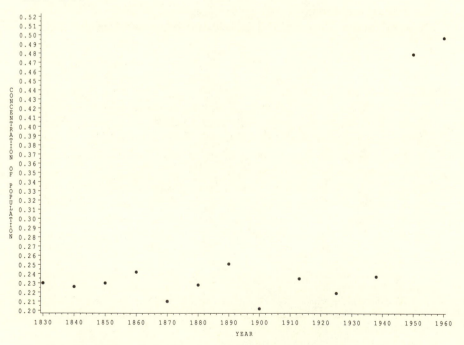

FIG. 6.4. Scatterplot of the Concentration of National Population Over Time, 1830–1960

centration of both military expenditures and personnel and the aggregate level of concentration is modest (adjusted r^2 = .41 and .22, respectively); and the correlation between the concentration of population and the aggregate level of concentration is somewhat higher (adjusted r^2 = .52). Taken together, the concentration of GNP, population, military expenditures, and military personnel explains about 45 percent of the variation in the aggregate level of concentration.

Third, while changes over time in the concentration of the components of CON appear to be partially responsible for changes over time in the level of concentration, changes in CON may also be due to changes in the composition of the major-power subsystem. For example, the marked rise in the concentration of population after World War II seems to reflect China's entrance into the subsystem and Italy's and Japan's exit from it. If the concentration of population in 1950 is recomputed after excluding China (which joined the ranks of the major powers in 1949) and including Italy and Japan (which exited the major-power subsystem in 1943 and 1945, respectively), the concentration of population is much lower (about .250) than in table 6.1. The introduction of the United States and Japan as major powers in 1900 also influences the level of concentration. When the concentration of each of the four capabilities is recomputed for 1900 without these two states, the levels of concentration of population (about .270) and military expenditures (about .340) increase, while those of military personnel (about .180) and GNP (about .160) decrease.[4] This also suggests that concentration depends in part on the entrance and exit of states to and from the major-power subsystem.

Fourth, and related to whether the entrance and exit of major powers influences concentration, is the issue of whether or not the level of concentration is sensitive to which group of states is considered for the purposes of measuring it. While structural explanations usually define the distribution of power in terms of the major powers, some scholars have examined structural change based on a broader set of states (Russett 1968b). In order to ascertain whether the determinants and dynamics of structure vary, depending on whether the distribution of power is defined in terms of the major powers or a broader group of states, the analysis in this chapter centers both on the major powers and on the largest twelve states in the system (until 1913 and the largest fifteen states thereafter).[5] It should be

---

also Organski and Kugler 1980:38). One reason for the divergence in these results is that they calculate the agreement between the *percentage share* among each major power for GNP and the COW index. Further, their analysis is confined to the period from 1850 to 1980 and relies on a constant set of major powers during this time (which is different than Singer, Bremer, and Stuckey's method of computing concentration).

[4] See Doran (1991:56) on this point.

[5] While the decision to use the largest fifteen states is somewhat arbitrary, this set is likely to include all the most influential states in the system. Further, data limitations preclude an

noted that the composition of this group is not constant: the largest twelve (or fifteen) states varies by capability and over time.

A preliminary test of the extent to which measures of the system's structure are sensitive to whether major powers or a broader group of states is considered was conducted by regressing the level of concentration among the major powers on the level of concentration among the largest twelve states (until 1913 and the largest fifteen states thereafter) for each of the following capabilities: GNP, national population, military expenditures, and military personnel. The results indicate that, for military personnel, military expenditures, and GNP, the level of concentration among the largest twelve to fifteen states explains between 70 and 90 percent of the variation in the level of concentration among the major powers. Further, there exists a strong and direct relationship between the level of concentration based on the larger group of states and the level based on major powers: in each case, the regression coefficient was positive, large, and statistically significant (at the .001 level). Only in the case of national population were the results weak. These findings indicate that, although changes on the margin in the composition of the major-power subsystem may influence the level of concentration, the level of concentration among the major powers is highly correlated with that among the largest dozen (or so) states.

In sum, the results in this section indicate that: (1) major-power war may influence concentration; (2) the concentration of different capabilities exhibits different patterns over time; (3) the composition of the major-power subsystem influences the level of concentration of each capability; and (4) the level of concentration among the major powers tends to be highly correlated with that among a broader set of twelve or fifteen states. In the remainder of this chapter, the composition of the system is held constant, and a model of the change over time in the concentration of population, GNP, military personnel, and military expenditures is developed and tested.

GIBRAT'S LAW

The fact that neorealists and others have been widely criticized for failing to provide a systematic explanation for changes in the distribution of capabilities suggests the need for a more fully articulated, dynamic explanation of growth in national capabilities. In the previous section, some salient aspects of the changes in concentration over time were described. However, it is not enough to *describe* the change in concentration; in order

---

analysis of GNP based on a larger group of states. These limitations also preclude analyzing more than twelve states during the period from 1820 to 1913.

to explain structural change within a neorealist framework, dynamic models are needed that *explain* the change in concentration.

The analogies that neorealists draw between the structure of industries and that of the international system suggest that microeconomic models of structural change might be of some use in this regard. As noted above, *CON* is closely related to the Hirschman-Herfindahl index (*HH*), which is one of the most widely used measures of industry structure. A variety of studies have found that changes in the value of this index (and other measures of industry structure) can be modeled as stochastic processes. These findings are consistent with the predictions of Gibrat's law (or the law of proportionate effect), which holds that, during a given period of time, the rates of growth among firms in a given industry are independent of their sizes at the outset of the period (Hart and Prais 1956; Simon and Bonini 1958; Mansfield 1962; Ijiri and Simon 1964, 1977; Hannah and Kay 1977; Scherer 1979; Waterson 1984). It predicts, for example, that the probability that the largest firm in a given industry will grow by 10 percent in any given period of time is the same as the probability of a 10 percent increase in size for a smaller firm in that same industry during the same period.

Further, a number of studies conclude that Gibrat's law accounts for observed changes in industrial concentration over time (Hart and Prais 1956; Prais 1974). Because *CON* is closely related to *HH*, it is useful to determine whether Gibrat's law also characterizes the growth in national capabilities during the nineteenth and twentieth centuries. In other words, the following analysis will focus on whether, during a given interval of time, "the factors that bring about growth and decline in each period are unrelated to the initial size" (Hannah and Kay 1977:99) of states at the beginning of that interval.

In addition to the analogies that neorealists draw between the structure of industries and that of the international system, and the similarities between economic and political measures of structure, it is useful to apply this model to analyses of international relations because it is consistent with some neorealist arguments concerning the dynamics of the distribution of capabilities. Gibrat's law is a very general and simple model of the rate of growth. As such, it does not specify the underlying mechanisms that account for growth. But Gibrat's law is consistent with explanations of the growth of firms that emphasize the strategic interactions among firms. For example, a situation in which firms react to an increase in output by a competitor by increasing their output proportionately in order to avoid losing market share would conform to the predictions of Gibrat's law. So, too, would a situation in which strategic interdependence guides the growth of capabilities among the leading states in the system, because the failure of states to match increases in capabilities on the part of potential antagonists would engender power disparities that might undermine their security (Waltz 1979; Gilpin 1981; Posen 1984; Walt 1987). As Robert Gilpin argues,

> the oligopolistic condition of international relations stimulates, and may compel, a state to increase its power; at the least, it necessitates that the prudent state prevent relative increases in the powers of competitor states. If a state fails to take advantage of opportunities to grow and expand, it risks the possibility that a competitor will seize the opportunity and increase its relative power. The competitor might, in fact, be able to gain control over the system and eliminate its oligopolistic rivals. (1981:87–88)

This, in turn, suggests that, on average, the rate of growth of capabilities among the leading states will be much the same. And this hypothesis is consistent with predictions based on Gibrat's law.

More generally, a number of seminal studies of international relations have implied that structural change might be modeled by Gibrat's law. Kenneth Waltz, for example, notes that

> [s]urveying the rise and fall of nations over the centuries, one can only conclude that national rankings change slowly. War aside, the economic and other bases of power change little more rapidly in one major nation than they do in another. Differences in . . . growth rates are neither large enough nor steady enough to alter standings except in the long run. (1979:177)

Waltz's position seems quite consistent with the expectations of Gibrat's law: it suggests that during any relatively short period of time, the rate of growth of capabilities among the largest states in the system should not be correlated with the amounts of capabilities that these states possess at the beginning of the period, except when events such as wars impose exogenous influences on capability growth. Further, Gilpin also implies that the rate of growth may conform to Gibrat's law. He maintains that

> there are certain benefits of large size, such as a greater resource base and economies of scale. On the other hand, increasing scale tends to stimulate centrifugal forces and fragmentation on the part of groups that believe they can maximize their own gains through breaking off [from the state]. . . . This limits economies of scale in political organization and constitutes an important limitation on the aggregation of political and economic power on the part of expanding states. (1981:152)

Gilpin's argument is in accord with Gibrat's law, which assumes that, above some minimum size, states (and firms) experience roughly constant returns to scale (Simon and Bonini 1958:609). In fact, Gilpin refers to a previous study (Russett 1968b) that relied on Gibrat's law to explain structural dynamics in the international system as evidence to support this argument.

Despite the fact that neorealists often suggest that structural change should occur in accord with Gibrat's law, it is important to reiterate that these arguments do not lead to the expectation that Gibrat's law will hold during periods surrounding systemic wars. It should also be noted that conformity to Gibrat's law does not imply that states grow at exactly the same rate; it only suggests that they will do so on average. Indeed, in the long-term, stochastic growth processes can produce wide variations in the distribution of capabilities.[6]

PREVIOUS EMPIRICAL STUDIES

This is not the first test of Gibrat's law in international relations. In a landmark article over twenty-five years ago, Bruce Russett asked whether "large nations have any particular advantages of scale, so that big states are likely to grow faster than small ones (and, hence, become proportionately bigger), or, on the contrary, do big countries face diseconomies of scale so that they typically grow at slower rates than smaller ones" (1968b:306)? If either of these questions are answered in the affirmative, the validity of Gibrat's law would be called into question. Russett analyzed the "distribution of nations by population size," although he acknowledged that this was a limited proxy for national power, and found that Gibrat's law held quite well. However, he also suggested that "a study of the distribution of power more generally would cover other variables" in addition to population (1968b:305).[7] In fact, some economists have examined whether Gibrat's law explains the rate of growth of some economic capabilities that political scientists have used to measure the distribution of power. For example, Boyan Jovanovic and Saul Lach (1990) find that the rate of change in per capita GNP for all states from 1960 to 1985 conforms to Gibrat's law.

But despite calls for further research on this topic (Zinnes 1976; Hart 1985), few studies have examined whether Gibrat's law explains the rate of growth of many of the capabilities that political scientists often use to measure the structure of the international system. One important exception, however, is Manus Midlarsky (1988:117–22), who examines the change in concentration from 1820 to 1945, using Singer, Bremer, and Stuckey's data. He concludes that the rate of change in the concentration of capabilities is closely approximated by Gibrat's law. But because the findings in the first section of this chapter indicated that different components of concentration may grow at different rates, it is important to determine

---

[6] For example, Scherer (1979:145–47) simulated the growth of firms over time when the rate of growth is stochastic and found that random growth can lead to wide variations in the concentration of firms in an industry.

[7] Russett's analysis centered on population in 1938, 1957, and 1967, and on GNP in 1957.

whether growth among the separate components conform to Gibrat's law. And it is also useful to consider whether the rate of capability growth depends upon the particular subset of states that is analyzed. In the remainder of this chapter, these issues are examined.

DOES GIBRAT'S LAW HOLD FOR POPULATION, GNP, MILITARY EXPENDITURES, AND MILITARY PERSONNEL?

If Gibrat's law holds,

$$(6.1) \qquad\qquad Y_i^{t+1} = Y_i^t U_i^t$$

where Y_i^t is the capability of the ith state at time t, and U_i^t is a random variable which equals one plus the proportional change in the ith state's capability between times t and $t + 1$ and whose probability distribution is independent of Y_i^t. Thus,

$$(6.2) \qquad\qquad \log Y_i^{t+1} = A + \log Y_i^t + z_i^t$$

where A is the mean value of $\log U_i^t$ and z_i^t is an error term.[8] Consequently, Gibrat's law can be tested by regressing $\log Y_i^{t+1}$ on $\log Y_i^t$. If this law holds, the slope of the regression line should be approximately 1.00.

Throughout this book, the structure of the global system has been defined in terms of the distribution of power among the major powers. This is entirely appropriate, since structural theories generally center on the behavior of major powers. However, as noted above, some analysts argue that the structure of the system is determined by the distribution of power among a broader group of states. For this reason, and to determine whether different processes characterize the rates of growth among major and nonmajor powers, the largest twelve states for which data are available (for each capability) until 1913 and the largest fifteen nations thereafter are initially examined. Following this analysis, an analysis of Gibrat's law based only on major powers will be conducted.

To test whether Gibrat's law holds for national population, military expenditures, military personnel, and GNP, the logarithm of each capability for each state was computed for each year at the beginning of every decade from 1820 to 1980.[9] The logarithm for each country in each decade

---

[8] Note that because "we assume a random walk of the [states] already in the system at the beginning of the time interval under consideration, with zero mean change in size," it is appropriate to use the log-normal distribution (Simon and Bonini 1958:611). If, on the other hand, the introduction of new states into the sample was allowed between the beginning and end of each interval, the Yule distribution should be used (Simon and Bonini 1958).

[9] Ten-year periods were used in all but four instances: 1900–1913, 1913–1925, 1925–1937, and 1937–1950. This procedure is consistent with that used in the previous three chapters.

TABLE 6.2

Regression Coefficients for the Logarithm of Population, Military Personnel, Military Expenditures, and GNP for Each State in the Final Year of Each Ten-Year Period Regressed on the Logarithm of the Same Capability and State in the First Year of Each Period (Using the Largest Twelve States Until 1913 and the Largest Fifteen States Thereafter), 1820–1980

Period	Population	Military Personnel	Military Expenditures	GNP
1820–1830	0.99	0.99	0.90	—
1830–1840	0.98	1.05	1.02	0.98
1840–1850	0.98	1.08	1.01	1.00
1850–1860	0.94	0.85	0.95	1.00
1860–1870	0.94	0.87*	0.99	1.05
1870–1880	0.99	1.03	0.80*	1.02
1880–1890	0.99	0.90	1.05	1.02
1890–1900	0.99	0.96	1.19	1.04
1900–1913	1.01	1.01	0.84	1.02
1913–1925	1.00	0.47	0.66	0.85
1925–1937	0.97	0.94	1.31	1.02
1937–1950	0.99	0.81	0.82	0.99
1950–1960	0.98	1.01	1.21*	0.99
1960–1970	1.01	1.04	0.97	0.96
1970–1980	0.99	0.95	0.87	0.97
Mean slope	0.98	0.93	0.97	0.99
Standard error of the mean slope	0.02	0.04	0.04	0.02

* Significant at the .05 level.

was then regressed on the logarithm for that country a decade earlier for each of the four component indices.

The results, shown in table 6.2, indicate that in only three out of fifty-nine cases is the null hypothesis that Gibrat's law holds rejected. By chance alone, one would expect about this number of rejections. Further, when the mean slope is derived for each of the capability indices across all decades, Gibrat's law again holds extremely well. For GNP, the mean is 0.99, almost

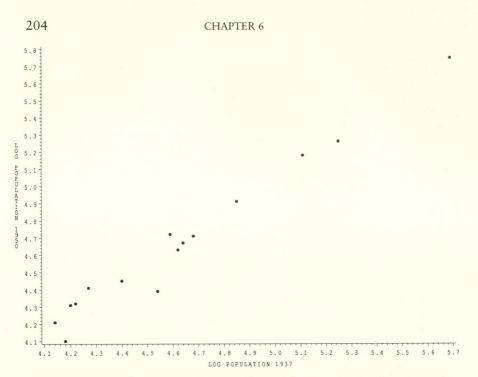

FIG. 6.5. Relationship Between the Logarithms of the Gross National Products of the Fifteen Largest States in 1937 and the Logarithms of Their Gross National Products in 1950

exactly what Gibrat's law predicts.[10] For population, the mean is 0.98; for military expenditures, the mean is 0.97; and for military personnel, it is 0.93. In three of the four cases, the mean is within one standard error of 1.00. For each of the four component indices, figures 6.5, 6.6, 6.7, and 6.8 show the relationship between the beginning-of-period and end-of-period logarithms for the case in which the regression coefficient is closest to its mean value.

These findings indicate that, as Russett and Gilpin argue, large states do not have any particular advantages or disadvantages of scale that make it likely that their capabilities will grow at a faster or slower rate than their smaller counterparts. Instead there is substantial evidence for the hypothesis that *among the largest states, size is not correlated with the rate of growth*. It is clear that the mechanisms underlying the fit of Gibrat's law are likely to vary across population, GNP, military expenditures, and military

[10] Russett was skeptical of data he collected for GNP; however, he did find that for 1957 (the only year he tested) that Gibrat's law seemed to hold. The results in this chapter, based on more reliable data, seem to corroborate his findings.

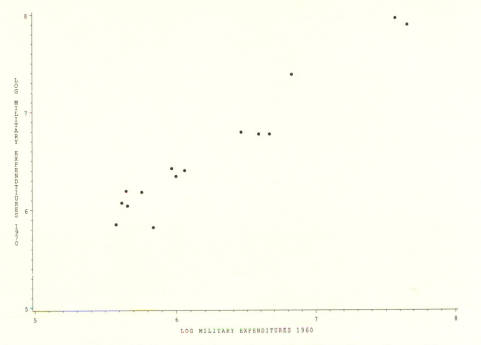

FIG. 6.6. Relationship Between the Logarithms of the Military Expenditures of the Fifteen Largest States in 1960 and the Logarithms of Their Military Expenditures in 1970

personnel. But, particularly for military capabilities, these results suggest that strategic interdependence may guide growth. It is interesting to note, however, that, contrary to the neorealist hypothesis, this is the case even during periods surrounding systemic wars.

INTERTEMPORAL CORRELATION AMONG THE RESIDUALS

The results of the previous section indicated that Gibrat's law appears to hold. In this (and the following) section, further analysis is conducted to determine whether any of the underlying assumptions of the strongest form of Gibrat's law are violated. The initial assumption that is considered is that, for each nation, the residuals of the regressions (estimated in the preceding section) for each capability and interval are independent of the residuals of the regressions for the same capability in the following interval. In the following section, the assumption that the residuals are homoskedastic is considered.

One assumption of Gibrat's law is that there is no correlation among the

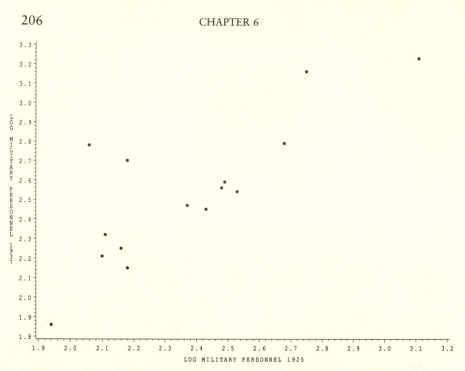

FIG. 6.7. Relationship Between the Logarithms of the Military Personnel of the Fifteen Largest States in 1925 and the Logarithms of Their Military Personnel in 1937

residuals; whether or not a nation grows more or less rapidly than the OLS estimate predicts in one interval is independent of whether or not it grows more rapidly than the OLS estimate predicts in the subsequent interval.[11] To test whether this assumption is violated, the value of the residual for each nation in every ten-year interval (from 1820 to 1980) was correlated with the value of the residual for the same country in the subsequent interval. This analysis was conducted for each of the four capabilities.

The results (presented in table 6.3) indicate that, *for population, there is positive correlation among the residuals*. The regression coefficient is positive in thirteen out of fourteen cases, and it is positive and statistically significant in eight cases. The positive relationship among the residuals may reflect the tendency for nations whose populations grow very quickly

[11] Positive correlations among the residuals would indicate that nations that grow more (less) rapidly than the OLS estimate predicts for a given capability in one interval, continue to grow more (less) rapidly in the subsequent interval. Negative correlations would indicate that nations that grow more (less) rapidly than the OLS estimate predicts in one interval, grow less (more) rapidly in the subsequent interval.

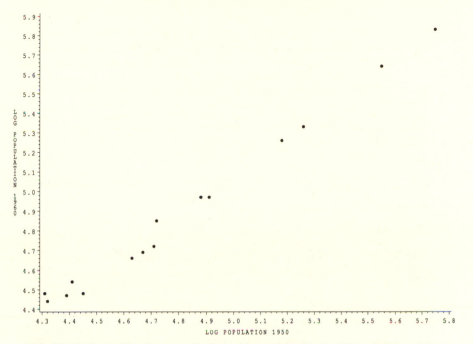

FIG. 6.8. Relationship Between the Logarithms of the National Populations of the Fifteen Largest States in 1950 and the Logarithms of Their National Populations in 1960

(relative to the OLS estimate) in one period to have a larger number of people of child-bearing age in the following periods. For example, states that experience high rates of immigration during a given period are likely to continue to have higher-than-average rates of growth in subsequent intervals, since some of these immigrants will have children during the following period. Alternatively, emigration leads to lower-than-average population growth during the period in which emigration occurs, and reduces the number of people of child-bearing age in the state from which they emigrated in subsequent intervals. Thus nations whose populations grow slowly (quickly) relative to other large states in one period have a difficult time changing their relative rates of growth in subsequent periods.

Turning from population to GNP, table 6.3 shows that, *for GNP, there is weak evidence of positive correlation among the residuals.* The regression coefficient is positive in only eight out of thirteen cases, but it is statistically significant in six of these eight instances. The tendency for the residuals to be directly related is most pronounced during the period preceding World War I and the period after World War II. This suggests that during periods

TABLE 6.3

Regression Coefficients For the Residual of Each State from Each Period in Table 6.2 Regressed on the Residual for the Same State from Each Subsequent Period, for Population, Military Expenditures, Military Personnel, and Gross National Product, 1820–1980

Dependent Variable	Population	Military Expenditures	Military Personnel	GNP
1830–1840	1.04*	−0.46*	−0.20	—
1840–1850	0.84*	0.33*	−0.29	0.77*
1850–1860	1.42*	−0.18	−0.38	0.45*
1860–1870	0.40	−0.39	0.02	0.53
1870–1880	0.52*	−0.29*	−0.14	0.43
1880–1890	0.26*	−0.27	0.39	0.46*
1890–1900	0.87*	0.56	0.74*	−0.07
1900–1913	1.71*	−0.30	0.12	0.97*
1913–1925	1.00	−0.91	1.28	−0.69
1925–1937	−0.12	−1.77*	−0.44*	−0.69*
1937–1950	0.37	−0.35	0.41	−0.11
1950–1960	0.32	−0.11	−0.36	−0.24
1960–1970	0.44*	0.29	0.20	0.64*
1970–1980	0.27	−0.57	0.00	0.37*

* Significant at the .05 level.

that did not surround systemic wars, large increases in total factor productivity, capital formation, and technological progress that produced high rates of growth in one period (relative to the OLS estimate) created the economic infrastructure that sustained relatively high growth rates in subsequent periods. And states that did not develop the infrastructure necessary for high growth in one period continued to experience lagging growth in subsequent intervals.

Turning next to military expenditures, table 6.3 shows that *there is evidence of negative correlation among the residuals for military expenditures* in eleven out of fourteen cases, although the regression coefficient is negative and statistically significant in only three instances. This suggests that there is weak evidence of an inverse relationship between a state's rate of military spending in one interval (relative to the OLS estimate) and its rate of military spending in the subsequent interval.

This finding may reflect the fact that while (as the results in table 6.2 indicate), on average, strategic interdependence (and hence Gibrat's law) guides military spending, in the short run (within each ten-year interval), states are not always able to offset increases in military expenditures made by potential antagonists. Over the longer run, however, states tend to compensate for (what appear to be slight) imbalances that occur in the rate of military spending. In other words, states that increase their military expenditures by less than the mean amount among the largest states in one period may feel compelled to respond by increasing their military spending by more than the mean amount during the subsequent period.[12] But if military expenditures grow more quickly than average in one period and there is little subsequent evidence of an immediate, external threat, there may be domestic pressure brought to bear on policymakers to reduce the rate of growth in the following interval, because (unless fiscal and monetary policies are adjusted accordingly) increases in expenditures can lead to inflationary pressures, higher interest rates, and crowding out of private investment.

The negative correlation among the residuals for military expenditures may also reflect the tendency for states preparing for war to increase their military spending more quickly than states that are not preparing for war. But since states rarely fight wars in consecutive (ten-year) intervals, those states that spend at rates in excess of the OLS estimate in one interval usually decrease their rates of spending in the subsequent interval. This is particularly likely to be the case for the vanquished: they are often forced to reduce their expenditures at a rate disproportionate to that of the victors, which leads to less-than-average growth on their part during the next time period. However, states compelled to maintain artificially low growth of expenditures in one period often allocate resources to the military at a more rapid rate than other states in the following period (Waltz 1979:178; Organski and Kugler 1980, chap. 3).

Finally, *for military personnel, there is little evidence that the assumption of independence among the residuals is violated.* The regression coefficients demonstrate no pronounced pattern and are rarely statistically significant. This may be due to the fact that states find it easier to respond to the growth in a potential adversary's military capabilities by increasing their military expenditures than by enhancing their military personnel. Increases in military expenditures that enhance the productivity of existing personnel may be a more effective and efficient response to a potential

---

[12] Indeed this is the underlying dynamic that drives action-reaction models of arms racing and military spending (Richardson 1960b; Nicholson 1989:147–66).

belligerent's growth than merely outfitting a larger standing army. It may also be politically preferable to vary the growth rate of expenditures more than personnel because increases in personnel often entail conscription and decreases may lead to domestic unemployment (particularly if the economy is operating at well below full capacity).

In sum, there is considerable evidence of positive correlation among the residuals for population, weak evidence of positive correlation among the residuals for GNP, and weak evidence of negative correlation among the residuals for military expenditures. This suggests that, while the probability distribution of the percent change in a state's capabilities from one time period to the next may be independent of its present size, the dynamics of this process may not conform to the expectations of the strongest form of Gibrat's law. However, as Yuji Ijiri and Herbert Simon (1964) have shown, a weaker form of Gibrat's law, which incorporates intertemporal correlation among the residuals, may still prove useful in modeling growth rates over time.

HETEROSKEDASTICITY AMONG THE RESIDUALS

If the dynamics of the change in capabilities over time are in accord with the strongest form of Gibrat's law, it should also be the case that, for all the observations in each interval, the residuals have a common variance. Like autocorrelation, violation of this assumption will produce inefficient OLS estimates and, hence, will bias the tests of statistical significance.

Because the samples of nations are small (twelve or fifteen observations), Goldfeld-Quandt tests for heteroskedasticity were conducted (Goldfeld and Quandt 1972, chap. 3; Maddala 1988:164–65). For each capability in every interval, the states in the sample were divided into halves, according to the "size" of the states in the first year of each interval.[13] Separate OLS regressions were then fit for the larger and smaller half of every sample. The residual sum of squares for each half was estimated and divided by the degrees of freedom for the subsample. An F-test was then conducted to determine if the estimates differed.

The results of these tests (presented in table 6.4) indicate that *there is relatively little evidence of heteroskedasticity*: the F-statistic is statistically significant in only nine of the fifty-nine cases. Further, the nine instances of heteroskedasticity are almost uniformly distributed across the four capabilities. The F-statistic is significant in three cases for population and in

---

[13] Goldfeld and Quandt suggest that this test be conducted after removing some intermediate-sized observations, so as to enhance the ability of the test to distinguish between the error variance of the largest and smallest observations (see also Maddala 1988:164). However, due to the small number of observations for each year (particularly in the period from 1820 to 1913), all observations were used in the following tests.

TABLE 6.4
Results of F-Tests to Determine if a Difference Exists Between the Residual Sum of Squares (Divided by the Degrees of Freedom) of the Largest and Smallest of the Twelve Largest States Until 1913 and the Largest Fifteen Thereafter, in Each Period, for Population, Military Expenditures, Military Personnel, and Gross National Product, 1820–1980

Period	Population	Military Expenditures	Military Personnel	GNP
1820–1830	4.39	7.31	2.24	—
1830–1840	1.50	1.93	1.39	4.25
1840–1850	4.21	3.75	2.57	1.11
1850–1860	10.18*	9.66*	3.92	2.08
1860–1870	17.75*	3.10	1.64	1.45
1870–1880	3.51	1.82	1.01	8.33
1880–1890	4.04	1.43	1.42	12.21*
1890–1900	1.41	1.03	2.59	2.91
1900–1913	3.00	1.27	1.93	1.61
1913–1925	11.68*	12.83*	11.06*	35.94*
1925–1937	5.88	1.57	6.55*	2.74
1937–1950	5.32	3.16	5.06	4.57
1950–1960	5.30	1.15	3.68	2.20
1960–1970	1.72	1.77	2.00	2.52
1970–1980	1.93	2.40	1.37	1.76

* Significant at the .05 level.

two instances for each of the other capabilities. It is also interesting to note that there is no clear relationship between the size of the residual sum of squares based on these regressions and whether the larger or the smaller half of the sample of states is considered.

One of the intervals (1913 to 1925) accounts for four of the nine instances of heteroskedasticity. This is largely due to the changes in capabilities that World War I brought on, and the effects of the war's aftermath and the terms of the peace settlement on Austria-Hungary, Germany, and Russia. Since this war introduced such profound and varied changes (and differences) in the rates of growth among the world's largest states, it is not surprising that this interval is one in which the variances of the error terms are relatively large among these states.

However, aside from this interval, there are only five cases in which the *F*-statistic is statistically significant. And, by chance alone, we would expect this to be the case in about three instances (out of fifty-five). Apparently, except for this interval, this assumption of the strongest form of Gibrat's law is not violated in any serious way.

RESULTS FOR MAJOR POWERS AND FOR NON-MAJOR POWERS

Structural explanations, including neorealist theories, focus primarily on the distribution of capabilities among the major powers, rather than among the twelve or fifteen largest states. Since this strategy was also adopted throughout earlier chapters of this book, it is important to determine whether, in addition to the twelve or fifteen largest states, the rate of change among the major powers also conforms to Gibrat's law.

To this end, the rates of capability growth among those states classified as major powers by Singer and Small (1972), Small and Singer (1982), and Levy (1983) were analyzed,[14] using the same procedure as in the earlier test of Gibrat's law. For each capability, the logarithm of each country at the beginning of each decade was regressed on the logarithm for that state one decade earlier.[15] The results of this analysis are mixed. Table 6.5 shows that *for GNP, Gibrat's law again holds remarkably well*: in no case is the null hypothesis rejected. On the other hand, *the rates of growth of population, military expenditures, and military personnel often do not conform to Gibrat's law*. For many of the regression coefficients, the null hypothesis that the slope equals 1.00 is rejected (at the .05 level). Further, a number of the regression coefficients are much different from 1.00, but the null hypothesis is not rejected because their standard errors are quite large. For each of the component indices, figures 6.9, 6.10, 6.11, and 6.12 show the relationship between the beginning-of-period and end-of-period logarithms for the case where the regression coefficient is closest to its mean value.

Though the probability distribution of the percentage change in a nation's capabilities is independent of its present capabilities for the largest twelve or fifteen states, this is apparently not the case for the major powers, except for GNP. On the one hand, this result may reflect the tendency for

[14] For the purposes of this analysis, states are considered major powers for any time period during which *either* Singer and Small or Levy listed them as major powers.

[15] In this analysis, only those nations that are major powers during the *entire* interval are considered. For example, Austria-Hungary is not included for the interval from 1913 to 1925 because it ceased to be a major power in 1919. Likewise, China is not included from 1937 to 1950 because it was not a major power until 1949.

TABLE 6.5

Regression Coefficients for the Logarithm of Population, Military Personnel, Military Expenditures, and GNP for Each Major Power in the Final Year of Each Ten-Year Period Regressed on the Logarithm of Each Capability and Major Power in the First Year of Each Ten-Year Period, 1820–1980

Period	Population	Military Expenditures	Military Personnel	GNP
1820–1830	0.96	1.03	1.08	—
1830–1840	0.94	0.78	1.21	0.84
1840–1850	0.99	1.11	0.87	0.92
1850–1860	1.00	0.69	0.98	1.22
1860–1870	0.72	0.78	0.12	1.26
1870–1880	1.04	1.12	0.57*	1.04
1880–1890	1.09*	0.76*	0.83	0.99
1890–1900	1.06	0.86	1.23	1.11
1900–1913	1.15*	0.98	0.36*	1.07
1913–1925	0.87	0.15*	0.57	0.87
1925–1937	1.07	0.41	−0.29*	0.87
1937–1950	1.02	0.85	1.16	1.25
1950–1960	1.06*	0.61	1.06	0.88
1960–1970	1.04*	1.04	1.05	0.98
1970–1980	1.05*	1.01	0.67	1.06
Mean slope	1.00	0.81	0.76	1.03
Standard error of the mean slope	0.02	0.07	0.12	0.04

* Significant at the .05 level.

states in the larger sample to grow, on average, at a proportionate rate because those states that are not major powers conform to this rate of growth, but the major powers depart from it so slightly that, in the aggregate, the null hypothesis is not rejected. On the other hand, it may be that neither major powers nor non-major powers conform to the law of proportionate effect, but their respective departures from this law offset one another when they are pooled. To resolve this issue, for each interval, those states in the original group of twelve or fifteen states that were not major

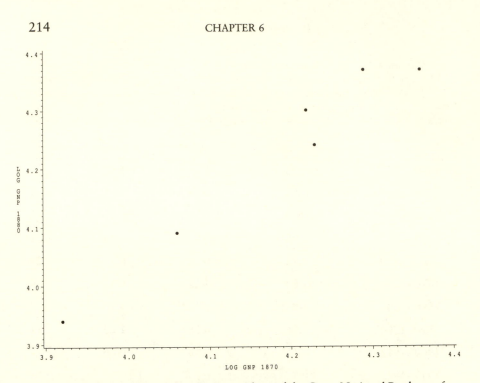

FIG. 6.9. Relationship Between the Logarithms of the Gross National Products of the Major Powers in 1870 and the Logarithms of Their Gross National Products in 1880

powers throughout the entire time period were examined to determine if the law of proportionate effect held for them. The results (shown in table 6.6) provide tentative support for the position that *Gibrat's law holds well for the non-major powers*. There are only five cases in which the null hypothesis that the regression coefficient equals 1.00 is rejected; and two of those cases (military expenditures and GNP from 1913 to 1925) are due solely to the dismemberment of Austria-Hungary after World War I. By chance alone we would expect to reject the null hypothesis three times. For each of the component indices, figures 6.13, 6.14, 6.15, and 6.16 show the relationship between the beginning-of-period and end-of-period logarithms for the case where the regression coefficient is closest to its mean value. These results clearly indicate that the change in capabilities among non-major powers more closely conforms to Gibrat's law than does the change in capabilities among major powers.

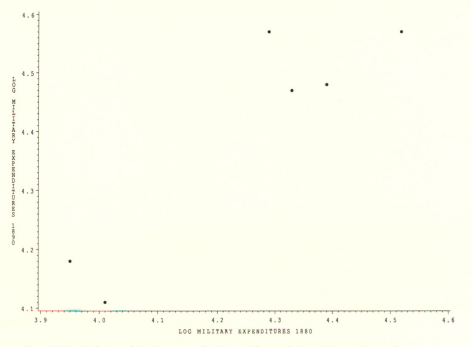

FIG. 6.10. Relationship Between the Logarithms of the Military Expenditures of the Major Powers in 1880 and the Logarithms of Their Military Expenditures in 1890

WHY DO THE MAJOR POWERS DEPART FROM GIBRAT'S LAW?

It is important to determine why the major powers depart from Gibrat's law for every capability except GNP, while non-major powers apparently conform to this law. Among the major powers, the rate of growth of gross national product seems to adhere to the law of proportionate effect. This may reflect the fact that technological advances contribute substantially to growth in national output, and technology tends to diffuse rather quickly among these states. It may also be due to the tendency for international economic conditions to exert relatively uniform effects among the largest economies in the system.

Although the regression coefficients for population are quite close to 1.00, there are two sets of intervals during which growth in national population on the part of major powers departs from the law of proportionate

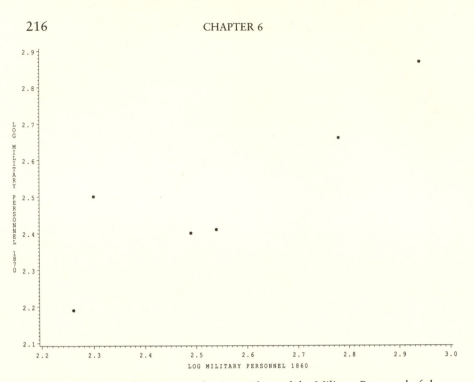

FIG. 6.11. Relationship Between the Logarithms of the Military Personnel of the Major Powers in 1860 and the Logarithms of Their Military Personnel in 1870

effect: from 1950 to 1980 and from 1880 to 1913. To the extent that governments exert only limited control over birth and death rates and because medical technology has probably been much the same among the major powers, it is not very surprising that the regression coefficients are close to 1.00. But the standard errors of the regression coefficients are quite small (reflecting limited divergences of population growth among the major powers from the mean), and hence relatively minor departures from the hypothesized slope of 1.00 result in the rejection of the null hypothesis. These minor divergences are due to two phenomena. First, China became a major power in 1949; and growth in population departs from Gibrat's law during the period from 1950 to 1980 because of China's abnormally rapid rate of population growth. Second, the period from 1880 to 1913 was characterized by large-scale emigration from Europe to the United States. This, and the introduction of new states into the union, contributed to a faster rate of population growth in the United States than among the remaining major powers. Further, the rate of emigration was not uniform among European major powers, which also contributed to uneven growth rates among these states (Thomson 1981:326).

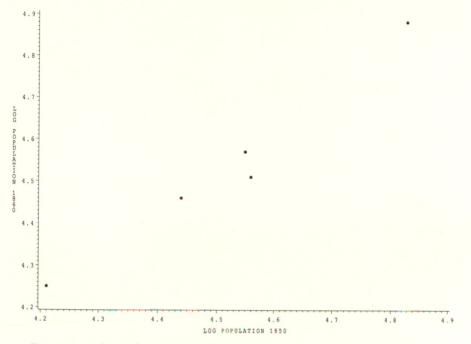

FIG. 6.12. Relationship Between the Logarithms of the National Populations of the Major Powers in 1850 and the Logarithms of Their National Populations in 1860

Both military expenditures and military personnel for major powers also fail to conform to Gibrat's law. The most marked departures for both capabilities occur from 1900 to 1937—that is, during the buildup for, and onset of, World War I; the postwar demobilization; and the subsequent buildup for World War II. Because these events affected different major powers to different degrees, it would be surprising if the law of proportionate effect held. And neorealists generally agree that war may lead to a rate of growth of capabilities that departs from Gibrat's law. Table 6.5 shows that from 1900 to 1913 smaller major powers increased their military spending far more rapidly than their larger counterparts. This appears to be due to Japan's (the smallest major power in terms of expenditures) increase in its expenditures during the Russo-Japanese War and its active efforts to build an Asian empire during this time. Further, Italy's preparation for the Italo-Turkish War (1911), and its and Austria-Hungary's (the next smallest states) preparations for World War I help to account for this result.

The departure of military personnel from Gibrat's law during the period

TABLE 6.6

Regression Coefficients for the Logarithm of Population, Military Personnel,
Military Expenditures, and GNP for Each Non-Major Power in the Final Year of
Each Ten-Year Period Regressed on the Logarithm of the Same Capability and
Non-Major Power in the First Year of Each Ten-Year Period, 1820–1980

Period	Population	Military Personnel	Military Expenditures	GNP
1820–1830	0.99	0.78	0.77	—
1830–1840	1.03	1.04	0.80	1.02
1840–1850	1.02	1.06	0.99	1.04
1850–1860	0.93	0.84	1.11	1.01
1860–1870	0.97	0.90	1.15	1.04
1870–1880	0.99	0.96	0.88	1.14
1880–1890	0.98	0.78	0.97	1.06
1890–1900	0.98	0.88	1.58	1.05
1900–1913	0.98	0.95	1.45	0.76*
1913–1925	1.00	0.83	−0.48*	−0.15*
1925–1937	0.94*	1.02	0.46	0.95
1937–1950	1.00	0.54*	0.34	0.88
1950–1960	0.97	0.55	0.89	1.08
1960–1970	1.02	1.59	0.85	1.04
1970–1980	0.94	0.87	1.12	1.00
Mean slope	0.98	0.91	0.86	0.92
Standard error of the mean slope	0.03	0.12	0.09	0.04

* Significant at the .05 level.

from 1913 to 1925 seems to reflect the much quicker pace of postwar
demobilization among larger than smaller major powers. While all major
powers underwent a reduction in their armed forces after the conclusion of
the war, Russia's quick and extensive demobilization after the Bolshevik
Revolution and the Russian Civil War, and German disarmament under
the terms of the Treaty of Versailles, led to the disproportionate reduction

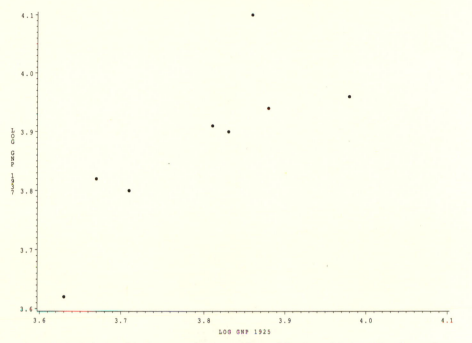

FIG. 6.13. Relationship Between the Logarithms of the Gross National Products of the Non-Major Powers in 1925 and the Logarithms of Their Gross National Products in 1937

of what were the two largest standing armies in 1913. Thus the regression coefficients for both military personnel and expenditures during the interval from 1913 to 1925 are far below 1.00.

As noted earlier, many studies have found that war is one of the most salient determinants of structural change. One leading view is that after the conclusion of the largest major-power wars, the level of concentration is likely to increase. But the results in this chapter indicate that, in the case of military personnel, smaller major powers tend to grow more quickly than larger major powers after wars. This suggests that concentration may decrease after wars between major powers. To determine whether this is the case, for each five-year period from 1820 to 1960 the change in concentration (based on Singer, Bremer, and Stuckey's data) during the period was regressed on the frequency of the conclusion of wars between major powers (based on Levy's data) during the previous period. The results indicate that the regression coefficient of war is negative and statistically significant ($t =$

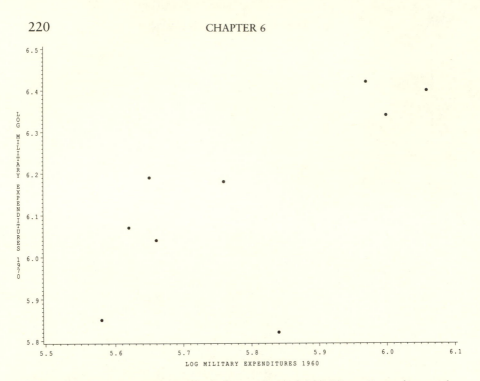

FIG. 6.14. Relationship Between the Logarithms of the Military Expenditures of the Non-Major Powers in 1960 and the Logarithms of Their Military Expenditures in 1970

−2.61), and that the model explains about 15 percent of the variation in the change in concentration.[16]

This may help to explain why such a marked increase occurred in concentration after World War II, while virtually no trend existed in concen-

[16] The OLS model is:

(a)
$$delta\ CON_{t+1} = 0.002 - 0.044\ (War_t),$$
$$(0.88)\quad (-2.61)$$

where $delta\ CON_{t+1}$ is the average annual change in the level of concentration between each consecutive five-year period (see Singer, Bremer, and Stuckey 1972) and War_t is the mean number of wars between major powers ending during the five-year (t) period prior to the period ($t + 1$) during which the change in concentration is measured. T-statistics for the intercept and War_t are presented in parentheses below the respective estimates.

Because the disturbances in the regression presented above were characterized by an AR(1) process (Durbin-Watson = 3.26), the parameters were also estimated using a GLS model. This procedure yields the following equation:

(b)
$$delta\ CON_{t+1} = 0.001 - 0.037\ (War_t).$$
$$(1.34)\quad (-3.28)$$

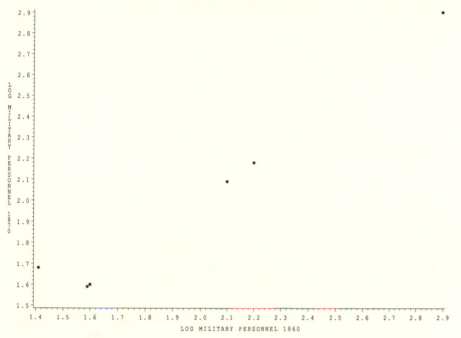

F<small>IG</small>. 6.15. Relationship Between the Logarithms of the Military Personnel of the Non-Major Powers in 1860 and the Logarithms of Their Military Personnel in 1870

tration prior to 1946. Based on Levy's data, only one war between major powers (the Korean War) has been conducted since 1946, and the absence of such wars seems to be associated with increases in concentration. It should be noted, however, that although the conclusion of wars between major powers appears to be inversely, rather than directly, related to the change in concentration, the magnitude of this effect is relatively small. The conclusion of one such war in a five-year period, for example, reduces the level of concentration in the subsequent period by only about .009.

For the period from 1925 to 1937, the regression coefficients for both military indicators remain far below 1.00. However, whereas in the previous period this was the product of the massive demobilization of the largest major powers, during this interval smaller states were rapidly building up. This finding seems to reflect what A.F.K. Organski and Jacek Kugler (1980) refer to as "the phoenix factor"—that is, the tendency for states that suffer the heaviest losses in war to grow disproportionately quickly after the conclusion of war (see also Waltz 1979:178). In fact, both Germany and the Soviet Union (which had become small major powers in

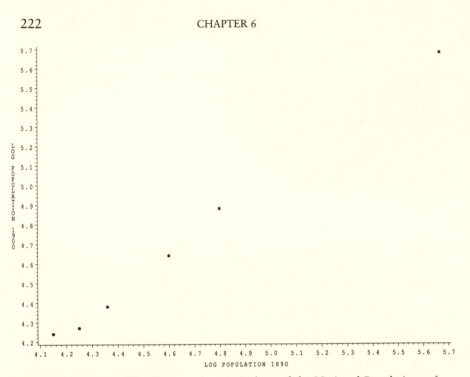

FIG. 6.16. Relationship Between the Logarithms of the National Populations of the Non-Major Powers in 1890 and the Logarithms of Their National Populations in 1900

terms of military capabilities by 1925) were rearming at much quicker rates than their European counterparts as World War II approached.

Clearly, the buildup for, and the fighting and aftermath of, war exerts enormous influence on the rate of change in a state's military capabilities. The fact that wars involving all major powers exert differential pressures on the participants goes a long way toward explaining why Gibrat's law does not hold from 1900 to 1937. When the mean regression coefficients are recomputed for both military indicators without the intervals from 1900 to 1937, the average slopes are much closer to 1.00 than in table 6.5 (0.89 for military personnel and 0.90 for military expenditures). This suggests that, as many neorealists predict, the growth in military capabilities among the major powers is a random process, except for those periods clustered around systemic wars.[17]

It should be noted that, even though the growth of capabilities among

---

[17] It is interesting, however, that this does not appear to be the case for the period immediately following the conclusion of World War II (1950 to 1960).

non-major powers tends to conform more closely to Gibrat's law than does the growth in capabilities among the major powers, those cases in which the growth of the former group of states depart from the law of proportionate effect (in table 6.6) are also clustered around World Wars I and II. Since many non-major powers participated in these wars, this result is not surprising.

IMPLICATIONS OF GIBRAT'S LAW FOR FUTURE RESEARCH

The results of this chapter suggest that stochastic models may prove fruitful in studying the dynamics of concentration. Previous studies have used probabilistic models to examine the formation of alliances, the causes of war, and other related topics.[18] Many of these models build on Gibrat's law; thus these results concerning the law of proportionate effect may be important for research of this type and potentially useful for developing a fully articulated dynamic model of concentration.

The findings of Herbert Simon and Charles Bonini (1958) imply that, if Gibrat's law holds, the distribution of nations by a particular capability index may be either log-normal, Yule, or Pareto, depending on what assumptions are made concerning the "birth rate" of new nations into the system. These distributions are "based on the same assumption[s as] . . . the law of proportionate effect, [but make different assumptions regarding the] rate at which new members are entering the smallest size class" (Zinnes 1976:254). Further research should be conducted to determine if these distributions can be used to model the dynamics of concentration.

If this can be accomplished, it may be possible to analyze more rigorously the relationship between the concentration of capabilities and global outcomes. For example, the results of Simon and Bonini imply that if Gibrat's law holds and there is a "steady introduction of new [states] from below, we obtain the Yule distribution"; and that if the distribution of nations by a particular capability index has the Yule distribution, the Pareto distribution will provide a good approximation in the upper tail (Simon and Bonini 1958:610–11). While it is not clear that this distribution will hold, efforts to use the Pareto distribution (or other probability distributions) may prove fruitful in studying concentration and its effects on international relations.

There may also be computer models built on Gibrat's law which can be used to study the effects of concentration. For example, Ijiri and Simon (1977) used numerical simulation to incorporate additional assumptions

[18] See, for example, Horvath and Foster (1963), McGowan and Rood (1975), Li and Thompson (1978), Richardson (1960a), and Midlarsky (1988). Zinnes (1976, chap. 12) provides an excellent overview of much of this literature.

about the growth rates of business firms in a particular industry and found that the simulation also generates the Yule distribution. Similar techniques may prove useful in studying the factors underlying the concentration of capabilities.

Finally, a number of studies argue that, within industries, technological factors influence the stochastic process that underlies Gibrat's law (Mansfield 1962; Nelson and Winter 1978; Davies and Lyons 1982; Waterson 1984, chap. 9). Some scholars of international relations conclude that differences in the rates of technological development among states are one of the leading sources of structural change (Gilpin 1981). It therefore would be useful to extend the model developed in this chapter by analyzing the effects of technological change on structural change in the global arena.

Conclusions

The preceding four chapters of this book have demonstrated that both static and dynamic aspects of the system's structure are associated with patterns of war and trade. Moreover, aspects of the concentration of capabilities are particularly important in this regard. In this chapter I have therefore analyzed the factors that determine the level of concentration and have modeled the rate of growth of gross national product, military expenditures, military personnel, and national population among the leading states in the system. These results have a number of implications for structural analyses of international relations.

First, one of the primary criticisms of neorealist theories of international relations is their inability to explain structural change. The findings in this chapter indicate that Gibrat's law holds remarkably well for GNP, military expenditures, military personnel, and population for the *dozen* (or so) largest states from 1820 to 1980. This suggests that, on average, larger states do not grow more or less quickly than smaller states. It is clear that the mechanisms underlying the fit of Gibrat's law are likely to vary across these capabilities. But, particularly in the cases of military personnel and military expenditures, these findings are consistent with the neorealist position that strategic interdependence leads states to react (roughly proportionately) to changes in one another's capabilities, because the anarchic nature of the international system compels them to attend to the relative power of their counterparts. These results differ from the neorealist hypothesis, however, to the extent that neorealists expect the rate of growth during periods surrounding systemic wars to depart from the law of proportionate effect.

Second, the strongest form of Gibrat's law assumes that there is no intertemporal correlation or heteroskedasticity among the residuals. Tests conducted in this chapter confirm that there is relatively little evidence that the variation in the rate of growth is related to the size of states, except during the period in which World War I was waged. However, there is evidence of correlation among the residuals for population, gross national product, and (to a lesser degree) military expenditures. While the latter finding suggests that the strongest form of Gibrat's law may not hold, Ijiri and Simon (1964) have shown that a weaker form of Gibrat's law may still prove useful in modeling structural changes over time in the international system.

Third, although Gibrat's law appears to hold for the largest twelve to fifteen states, it does not hold as well for the *major powers*. In large measure, this is a reflection of the fact that changes in the military capabilities of major powers differ during the preparation for, the waging of, and the aftermath of systemic wars. More specifically, smaller powers tend to grow more quickly than their larger counterparts prior to those wars that involve all the major powers. Further, when these wars are concluded, the terms imposed on the vanquished often dictate that they demobilize much more quickly and extensively than the victors. As a result, during periods clustered around wars of this type, Gibrat's law does not hold for the major powers. Even among non-major powers, whose rates of growth are generally more in keeping with Gibrat's law than those of the major powers, these periods are associated with departures from the law of proportionate effect. These findings are in accord with the neorealist hypothesis that systemic wars contribute to systematic variations in the rates of growth among the major powers.

However, the poor fit of Gibrat's law for the rate of population growth among the major powers is at odds with the neorealist hypothesis. So too is the finding that the growth of GNP conforms to Gibrat's law even during periods clustered around systemic wars. These results are not surprising, since states are unlikely to be able to control population growth and the growth of GNP to the extent that they can influence growth in military spending and personnel.

In sum, the results in this chapter indicate that, in certain cases, dynamic models based on Gibrat's law may help to explain and predict the level of, and changes in, the concentration of capabilities. As such, models of this sort may prove fruitful in explaining structural change. Further research should be conducted to develop a more fully articulated dynamic model of concentration and to determine whether such a model can be employed to more accurately predict and more fully explain international outcomes, such as patterns of war and trade.

Chapter 7

CONCLUSIONS

THE PRIMARY PURPOSE of this book has been to further our understanding of the relationships among power, trade, and war. In chapter 1, a series of questions were raised concerning these relationships. First, what effects do the distribution of power and international trade exert on the incidence of war? Second, what influences do the distribution of power, the incidence of war, and economic factors exert on the level of international trade? Third, what factors determine the structure of, and structural change in, the international system? In this chapter, the evidence that has been accumulated throughout this book is summarized and the ways in which these findings help to answer these questions are discussed.

I argued at the outset of this study that the answers to these questions bear on a series of fundamental theoretical issues in the field of international relations. This chapter therefore highlights the implications of these results for a number of leading theories of international relations. Further, I consider how these findings shed light on a number of more general conceptual issues: the usefulness of a systemic approach to the study of international relations; the relative importance of structure and process in explaining global outcomes; and the need to more fully integrate conflict and security studies, on the one hand, and the study of the international political economy, on the other. Finally, some of the limits of this analysis are discussed, and some policy implications of these findings are considered.

THE EFFECTS OF THE DISTRIBUTION OF POWER ON THE ONSET OF MAJOR-POWER WAR

One of the central empirical questions that motivated this study was the extent to which systemic factors influence the onset of war. It was noted in chapter 1 that one of the most important and long-standing sources of friction among scholars of war stems from debates over the strength and nature of the distribution of power's effects on the outbreak of war. Some analysts conclude that the distribution of power exerts little influence on the incidence of war. Others argue that the distribution of power does shape the conditions under which wars begin most frequently. Disagreements among these analysts typically center on whether a balance of power or a preponderance of power reduces the incidence of war.

Many balance-of-power theorists maintain that systems characterized by an (approximately) uniform distribution of capabilities among the major powers are less prone to the onset of major-power war than systems characterized by a more skewed distribution of capabilities. They argue that when the system is balanced, deterrence is enhanced by the variety of potential blocking coalitions that can form to thwart aggression on the part of any state (or small group of states). War becomes more likely as the distribution of capabilities becomes increasingly imbalanced, since disproportionate growth on the part of one (or a few) state(s) is likely to be met forcibly by a blocking coalition comprised of some set of the remaining powers, rather than allow the imbalance to persist (or widen). Indeed, under these circumstances, war is one instrument that can be used to restore a systemic balance.

Power preponderance theorists counter that the incidence of major-power war is likely to be highest when power is (relatively) equally distributed among the major powers, since "[p]arity . . . tempt[s] both sides to believe that they have a good chance of winning, whereas under conditions of preponderance war is unnecessary for the stronger and too risky for the weaker" (Levy 1989:232). Systems characterized by a preponderance of power may also experience a lower incidence of wars between weaker states than balanced systems if potential combatants fear that the preponderant state(s) will intervene in order to avert the possibility that the scope of the war will widen, thereby threatening its (their) relative position(s) in the system.

Many previous *systemic* analyses of these hypotheses have focused on one of two aspects of the distribution of power: polarity and concentration. But these variables rarely have been examined in conjunction with one another. Since they measure different features of the distribution of power and therefore may be related to war in various ways, I analyzed and compared the effects of both polarity and concentration on the incidence of major-power war.

Polarity and Major-Power War

Tests of the effects of polarity on major-power wars did not bear out either the balance-of-power or the power preponderance position. Bivariate tests (conducted in chapter 2) provided some weak support for the power preponderance hypothesis. Major-power wars tend to begin less frequently in bipolar than in multipolar systems, although there is no overall tendency for either hegemonic or nonhegemonic periods to be disproportionately prone to the onset of major-power wars. But multivariate tests (in chapters 3 and 4) yielded *no evidence that either hegemony or polarity is related to the frequency of major-power war.*

Many balance-of-power and (particularly) power preponderance theories of war emphasize the effects of dynamic features of the distribution of capabilities. Certain power preponderance theorists argue that power transitions leading to a more balanced system often create status inconsistencies and other effects that help to account for the outbreak of the most important major-power wars. A number of balance-of-power theorists, on the other hand, suggest that shifts away from balanced systems may induce states whose positions are threatened by the resulting imbalance to initiate hostilities in order to reimpose systemic equilibrium. Preliminary results in chapter 2 did not bear out either of these arguments: there was little evidence that periods during the breakdown or emergence of hegemonic systems are any more or less war-prone than periods during which these dynamics are absent.

Indeed the fact that polarity explains little about the frequency of major-power wars is not entirely surprising, since many structural theories seek to explain only the onset of those wars between major powers that fundamentally alter the structure of the system, and wars of this sort were not examined separately. It is clear that if, for example, the period after World War II was the only instance of bipolarity in modern times, no wars between bipolar powers have occurred; and that many wars occurred among polar powers during the multipolar era that many analysts argue preceded this period. It is also clear that, as pointed out in chapter 5, certain scholars define hegemony in terms of naval and commercial capabilities and maintain that nineteenth-century British political hegemony did not extend to Europe. Since many wars involving major powers were land wars fought among European states, it is not surprising that those classifications of hegemony that emphasize the importance of sea power yielded little evidence that hegemony was related to the incidence of major-power war.

But many scholars argue that polarity is associated with the onset of a wide variety of major-power wars: the results in this book are clearly at odds with their predictions. There is little statistical evidence that the existence or absence of hegemony, bipolarity, or multipolarity is related to the frequency of wars involving major powers. Hence, if the traditional tack is taken of measuring the structure of the system by counting the number of poles, structural explanations seem to provide little insight into the conditions under which major-power wars begin.

Concentration and Major-Power War

Whereas polarity does not seem to be related to the incidence of wars involving major powers, *concentration is strongly related to the incidence of wars of this sort*. As I argued in chapters 1 and 3, concentration is a measure of both the number of major powers in the system and the relative inequality of power among them. These features of the distribution of power are emphasized by a wide variety of scholars, balance-of-power theorists and power preponderance theorists alike, in both their definitions of structure and their explanations of international relations. To the extent that the factors that these analysts highlight influence patterns of war, concentration should have a marked impact on the onset of war.

Polarity, however, provides no information regarding relative inequality in the system, except for that between the poles and the remaining states in the system. If the structure of the system is defined solely in terms of polarity, it is not possible to account for the effects of inequalities among the poles or the effects of nonpolar major powers on global outcomes, such as the onset of war. Relying on polarity therefore poses a problem if we wish to evaluate, for example, those arguments that view the disproportionate growth of one (or a few) state(s) as an important determinant of major-power war. These explanations often highlight the level of inequality *among the poles*. Polarity provides no insight into this aspect of the distribution of power; concentration does measure these factors.

Since many balance-of-power and power preponderance theorists emphasize the effects of inequalities of power among the major powers in their competing explanations of war, concentration should be analyzed in systemic tests of these explanations. In chapter 3, I argued that the importance of concentration has been underappreciated in this regard. I also argued, however, that the *nature* of the relationship between concentration and the incidence of major-power war is considerably different from that which either the balance-of-power or the power preponderance hypothesis leads us to expect.

An Inverted U-Shaped Relationship Between Concentration and Major-Power War

Balance-of-power theory suggests that the relationship between the concentration of capabilities and war is monotonic and direct; power preponderance theory implies that this relationship is monotonic and inverse. However, the analyses in chapters 3 and 4 indicated that *an inverted U-shaped relationship exists between concentration and the frequency of wars involving major powers*.

In conjunction with the findings in this book concerning the effects of polarity on the outbreak of major-power war, these results indicate that *neither balance-of-power theory nor power preponderance theory completely describes the structural conditions under which major-power wars begin most frequently*. This helps to explain why a variety of studies have concluded that the distribution of power exerts little influence on the incidence of major-power war. By virtue of their tendency to focus on whether a balance of power or a preponderance of power is associated with the onset of war, they have ignored the possibility that the relationship between the distribution of power and war is quadratic, and that *both* explanations may *partially* explain when wars are likely to occur. Those balance-of-power theorists who have argued that approximately uniform distributions of power deter war seem to be correct. So too are those power preponderance theorists who have maintained that highly skewed distributions of power lead to few major-power wars. The findings in this study indicate, however, that both of these leading explanations have failed to appreciate the extent to which *moderate imbalances* among the major powers disproportionately encourage the outbreak of wars involving these states.

The existence of an inverted U-shaped relationship is consistent with the hypothesis that major-power wars begin when a potential initiator calculates that the expected costs of waging war will be more than offset by the expected improvement in its relative position in the international system. When concentration is low, successfully waging war against another major power or important minor power is likely to improve substantially the standing of any major power. However, the expected costs of doing so are likely to be prohibitive, since many potential coalitions can form to defeat the initiator.

As in systems that are "balanced," when the level of concentration is particularly high, deterrence is also enhanced. Under these circumstances, smaller states are likely to be reluctant to attack the leading state(s), since the expected costs of doing so are likely to be prohibitive. And the dominant state(s) may try to manage and limit conflicts with smaller states, since wars of this sort can impose substantial costs and offer few prospects for noticeably improving their relative position(s). Large major powers are also expected to refrain from attacking one another. The relatively small disparity of capabilities between them, and thus the expected costs of waging war, are quite high compared to the expected benefits of doing so.

But when concentration is at an intermediate level, fewer potential blocking coalitions exist, which (all other things being equal) is expected to weaken deterrence. Indeed this situation may lead a large major power to determine that war against a smaller state is worth undertaking if victory will improve its position relative to the other large major powers and is likely to be completed before any of the few potential blocking coalitions are able to form and assist the smaller state. Further, the threat posed by a large major power may lead weaker states to band together and launch a preventive war against it, since, left unchecked, the disparity between it and the smaller states may further widen. Under these circumstances, smaller states may conclude that the expected costs of waging war are outweighed by the likely consequences of inaction.

Variations in the Effects of Polarity and Concentration
on Major-Power War

The results of this book clearly indicate that polarity and concentration exert very different types of effects on the incidence of wars involving major powers. One reason for this finding is that systems characterized by both low and intermediate levels of concentration are likely to be multipolar and nonhegemonic. But the frequency of major-power war is greatest when intermediate levels of concentration obtain and is lowest during periods of low (and high) levels of concentration.

This helps to explain the weakness of the relationships between features of polarity and major-power war. Since dichotomous variables were used to measure polarity, they were unable to capture the inverted U-shaped relationship that exists between the distribution of capabilities and war. Hence, in addition to the conceptual problems associated with using polarity, the distinctions between bipolar and multipolar systems and hegemonic and nonhegemonic systems are simply too crude to capture much of the relationship between the distribution of capabilities and the frequency of major-power war.

Moreover, the problems inherent in polarity cannot be redressed merely by describing more precisely the polarity of the system (for example, by distinguishing among tripolar, quadpolar, etc. systems). As I argued in chapter 3, analyses of polarity assume that all poles possess the same levels of capabilities and that nonpolar major powers have no effect on patterns of outcomes in international relations. Distinguishing among systems more precisely in terms of their polarity will not alleviate the problems engendered by making these assumptions, since many theories—and the argument I advance—emphasize the importance of both the relative inequality among all major (not just polar) powers and the number of (polar as well as nonpolar) major powers in explaining the onset of major-power war.

As noted above, in addition to static features of the distribution of capabilities, there has been considerable interest in whether dynamic aspects of this distribution are associated with the incidence of major-power war. Though there is little evidence that dynamic features of polarity are related to war, both increases in concentration and (to a lesser extent) greater movement in the shares of capabilities among the major powers tend to precipitate periods during which major-power wars begin most frequently. Thus, like static features of the distribution of capabilities, the extent to which dynamic features of this distribution are related to the incidence of war depends in large part on which structural variable is considered. Changes between hegemonic and nonhegemonic systems provide little insight into the conditions under which major-power wars occur; however, marginal changes in the distribution of capabilities that are measured by concentration—but not by polarity—are often strongly related to the incidence of wars involving major powers.

The Effects of International Trade on the Onset of Major-Power War

It was pointed out in chapter 1 that, in addition to the effects of the distribution of power, there has been considerable interest in the influence of the international economy on war. I argued that while this topic is important in its own right, analyses of the impacts of both the distribution of power and economic factors on war also provide insights into the relative importance of structural and process-level effects on war and into the relationships between international economics and international security.

Structural theories attribute patterns of war (as well as other phenomena) to the anarchic character of the international system and variations in the distribution of power. As a result, these explanations attach little importance to process-level factors. Throughout this study, I have argued that, in order to adequately test structural theories, it is necessary to hold constant the effects of process-level factors; and that, in order to adequately test process-level explanations, it is necessary to hold constant the effects of structural factors. The analysis in chapter 4 indicated that although structural approaches offer considerable insights into the conditions under which wars involving major powers begin most frequently, supplementing structural models of war with certain process-level factors improves substantially their explanatory power.

As noted in chapter 1, long-standing debates over whether fluctuations in the international economy are related to war remain unresolved; and central to these debates has been the role of global commerce in contributing to political conflict. Some argue that open trading systems and higher levels of trade are associated with fewer wars because, under these circumstances, the opportunity costs of severing existing commercial relations are likely to be quite high. Others maintain that these types of systems foster vulnerabilities that can lead to conflicts and, ultimately, wars. And some scholars conclude that no systematic relationship exists between international trade and war, since (to the extent that they exist at all) relationships between features of the global economy and war are likely to be by-products of the effects of the distribution of capabilities on both international economic conditions and war.

Despite the interest that this topic has engendered, virtually no quantitative research has been conducted on the relationship between trade and war at the level of the international system. A preliminary analysis (in chapter 2) indicated that open international trading systems might be more war-prone than systems that are closed. However, like the features of the distribution of capabilities discussed above, trade's effect on war can only be assessed in the context of a more fully specified model: failing to examine the relationship between trade and war in conjunction with structural variables would clearly produce biased estimates of this relationship.

Tests of the impact of both power and trade on war (in chapter 4) indicated that *the level of international trade is inversely related to the frequency of major-power war, independent of the influence on war exerted by any aspect of the distribution of power.* Moreover, the effect of global trade on war is quantitatively large, as well as statistically significant.

Circumstantial evidence suggests a number of reasons why the relationship between trade and war is inverse. First, all other things being equal, states appear to go to war when the opportunity costs of forgone trade are lowest; and this condition is most likely to obtain during periods when relatively little trade is conducted. In this sense, trade and war may serve as substitutes for one another. Second, it may be that competition over global market share has played a role in creating conditions that are likely to foster the onset of war. Particularly when nations depend on trade for their economic development and national security, a smaller global market may lead to new, and exacerbate existing, tensions.

An Interdependence Approach to the Study of Major-Power War

At first glance, the inverse relationship between trade and war seems consistent with the commercial liberal thesis. However, commercial liberals often suggest that trade exerts a stronger influence on war than the distribution of capabilities, and my results do not support this position. In addition to the level of global trade, the concentration of capabilities (but not hegemony or polarity) is also related strongly to the incidence of major-power war. Rather than supporting the commercial liberal position, *the findings of this study (in chapter 4) point in the direction predicted by interdependence theorists, who suggest that both the distribution of capabilities and trade help to explain the outbreak of war, and that the relationship between trade and the frequency of major-power war is inverse.*

But while the level of global trade is strongly related to the frequency of wars involving major powers, the same is not true for all features of the international economy. First, there is no evidence (in chapter 4) that whether the trading system is open or closed helps to account for variations in the outbreak of war. Second, scholars have long debated whether downturns in the business cycle contribute to increases or decreases in the incidence of war. This study's findings (in chapter 4) do not bear out either position: there is virtually no evidence that either the Kondratieff cycle or short-term fluctuations in the business cycle are related to the incidence of major-power wars.

In sum, the evidence concerning the effects of the international economy on the frequency of major-power war is mixed. *The level of international trade (as a percentage of total output) is strongly related to the outbreak of major-power war; openness and closure and the business cycle are not.* Indeed this is interesting because most empirical research on the relationship between the international economy and war has focused on the business cycle, rather than trade.

The fact that both the distribution of capabilities and international trade are related to the incidence of major-power war is at odds with the predictions of structural theories: the effect of commerce on war is neither due to the impact of the distribution of capabilities on both variables nor is it unsystematic. Hence, by focusing solely on the effects of the system's structure, neorealist and other structural theories are by themselves unlikely to fully explain patterns in the incidence of wars. Alternatively, an "interdependence approach" to the study of war appears promising, since explanations of this sort emphasize the importance of both the distribution of capabilities and (among other process-level factors) trade flows. However, the lack of a unified deductive framework that incorporates features of both the distribution of power and trade continues to hamper theories of this sort (Keohane and Nye 1987:752–53). Further research on this topic may go a long way toward improving our understanding of the systemic conditions under which major-power wars begin.

THE EFFECTS OF POWER AND TRADE ON ALL INTERSTATE WARS

Thus far, the findings of this book concerning the effects of systemic aspects of power and trade on major-power wars have been reviewed. It was noted earlier that, because the prevailing wisdom among systemic theorists is that systemic explanations are primarily applicable to major-power wars (and, in many cases, only to wars between major powers or certain types of wars between major powers), it is important to pay particular attention to the determinants and effects of these events. However, central to the study of war has been the question of whether all wars have similar causes or whether, in order to understand their origins, it is necessary to differentiate among various types of wars. It is therefore interesting that few studies have analyzed whether systemic factors impact the incidence of all interstate wars or interstate wars that do not involve major powers.[1] One purpose of this book was to examine this issue.

Initially, the distinction was made among all wars, all interstate wars,

---

[1] See Maoz (1982) and Bueno de Mesquita and Lalman (1992) for some exceptions.

and wars involving major powers. The results of preliminary tests (in chapter 2) indicated that features of the distribution of power and the global economy are associated with the onset of all wars, but that the nature of their effects varies depending on the type of war in question. Periods of hegemony, openness, and upswings in the business cycle (respectively) were associated with a higher incidence of all wars than periods of nonhegemony, closure, and downswings. However, none of these features had a consistent effect on major-power wars.

Further analysis (in chapters 3 and 4) yielded some evidence that the same systemic variables that influence the frequency of major-power wars also affect the incidence of all interstate wars. For example, changes in concentration appear to be directly related to the frequency of all interstate wars; and there is weak evidence of an inverted U-shaped relationship between concentration and all interstate wars. These results are surprising, since systemic theories lead us to believe that features of the international distribution of capabilities should be largely unrelated to wars of this sort. Particularly striking is the strength of the inverse relationship between the level of global trade and the incidence of all interstate wars.

The Effects of Power and Trade on Interstate Wars That Do Not Involve Major Powers

Since systemic theorists generally focus on explaining major-power wars, it is not clear why both structural and process-level variables also influence the frequency of all interstate wars. I argued in chapter 3 that one reason for this finding concerns the manner in which all interstate wars are defined and operationalized. In particular, because data sets for all interstate wars include both major-power wars and interstate wars that do not involve major powers, the effects of concentration and international trade on all interstate wars may reflect their influences on those interstate wars that involve major powers.

There is considerable evidence to support this argument when the focus is on the effects of *structural* variables: aspects of the distribution of power exert markedly different types of influences on major-power wars than on non-major-power wars. For example, the results in chapter 4 indicated that the concentration of capabilities is associated with the frequency of interstate wars that do not involve a major power. But rather than the inverted U-shaped relationship that exists between concentration and major-powers wars, *the relationship between concentration and non-major-power interstate wars is U-shaped*. Further, there is evidence of this relationship based on results derived using both Gilpin's and Wallerstein's classifications of hegemony, although the results are stronger based on the latter data.

As I argued in chapter 4, this suggests that the *stability-instability para-*

dox may be at work: wars that do not involve major powers tend to begin most frequently when structural conditions deter major powers from going to war. Under these circumstances, smaller states can initiate wars with less fear that a major power will intervene directly to assist their opponents, since doing so may lead to the onset of a major-power war.

There is also evidence (in chapter 4) that polarity is associated with the frequency of non-major-power wars (when Gilpin's—but not when Wallerstein's—classifications of hegemony are used). In particular, analyses of hegemony indicated that *interstate wars that do not involve a major power begin most frequently during periods of hegemony*; and analyses of bipolarity and multipolarity indicated that *such wars begin most frequently during periods of multipolarity*. Hence, unlike the results for major-power wars, both polarity and concentration seem to influence the incidence of non-major-power wars. But like the analyses of both major-power wars and international trade, the *nature* of the effects of polarity and concentration vary markedly.

While structural variables are related in different ways to major-power wars and interstate wars that do not involve major powers, the impacts of *process-level* variables on major-power wars are quite similar to their effects on non-major-power wars. *As in the case of major-power wars, the relationship between the level of international trade and war is inverse; and there is also no evidence that either openness and closure or the business cycle is related to war.* The fact that the level of international trade is related to minor-power wars is not altogether surprising. Smaller states are likely to be more dependent than larger states on fluctuations in the level of international commerce. As such, trade may have an even more pronounced effect on the security of minor states than on major powers.

In sum, various types of wars do seem to have different structural causes. On the one hand, concentration influences each type of war that is considered in this book, although the nature of this relationship differs across major-power wars, all interstate wars, and non-major-power wars. On the other hand, polarity seems to influence non-major-power wars, but it has little effect on wars that involve major powers. Various types of wars, however, do not have different process-level causes. The level of trade, openness and closure, and the business cycle exert much the same effect, regardless of which type of war is analyzed. This suggests that a number of the same factors that give rise to major-power wars also contribute to the onset of other types of wars, and that systemic explanations of war may therefore be more broadly applicable than is commonly believed.

THE EFFECTS OF THE DISTRIBUTION OF POWER
ON INTERNATIONAL TRADE

A second set of empirical issues that form the basis of this book concerns the influence of systemic factors on the level of international trade. Within the field of international relations, there is a long and rich tradition of studies concerning the effects of power relations on war. However, interest in the impact of the distribution of power has not been limited to scholars of war. Indeed studies of the effects of power relations have come to occupy an increasingly prominent position in the field of international political economy. And, as mentioned in chapter 1, one topic that has attracted particular attention is the relationship between the distribution of power and international trade. Since this relationship is clearly central to any study of the relationships among power, trade, and war, it was analyzed at length in chapter 5.

Fundamental to many analyses of the international political economy is the issue of whether hegemony accounts for fluctuations in international trade. Hegemonic stability theorists argue that the existence of a hegemon is a necessary condition for the creation and maintenance of a liberal international economic order. But during the past decade, hegemonic stability theory has come under increasing attack. Many scholars conclude that hegemony (and, more generally, the distribution of power) has little effect on international trade, since free(r) trade does not meet the criteria of a collective good. And even if it does so, other analysts argue that small, in addition to privileged, groups are often able to provide collective goods. Another response to hegemonic stability theory centers on the incentives for hegemons to behave in a predatory fashion. Analysts who pursue this line of argument imply that hegemony is related to trade, but that hegemonic systems are likely to be less open, and to be characterized by less trade, than nonhegemonic systems. Because hegemons possess sufficient market power to render the imposition of an optimal tariff a welfare-improving policy, they have an economic incentive to erect barriers that are likely to reduce commerce.

Hegemony and Trade

In chapter 5 the impact on trade of hegemony (as well as concentration) was examined. As in the analysis of war, various features of the distribution of capabilities exert markedly different effects on international trade. *The effect of hegemony on the level of global trade is ambiguous: the strength of this relationship depends markedly on how hegemony is defined, measured, and operationalized.* The substantial divergence between the findings derived using Gilpin's data (which support the hegemonic stability hypothesis) and Wallerstein's data (which indicate that no relationship exists between hegemony and trade) is troubling and illustrates one reason why hegemonic stability theorists and their critics have arrived at such different conclusions.

I noted in chapter 5 that the observed variations in the relationship between hegemony and trade can be traced to disagreements regarding the dating of the conclusion of British hegemony. And, as discussed further below, these disagreements are not restricted to analyses of trade. Gilpin considers the period from 1874 to 1914 to be hegemonic, while Wallerstein does not. Given these differences, it is not surprising that these results vary considerably depending on whose data are used. Based on the aspects of national power on which Gilpin focuses in his analysis of British hegemony, there is evidence that Great Britain was a declining hegemon during the period in dispute. On these grounds, the results in this book provide some support for the hegemonic stability thesis. But until analysts of international relations arrive at some consensus regarding the requisite conditions for hegemony to obtain, it will be extremely difficult to establish the strength and nature of its effect on trade (and war), and hence the usefulness of hegemonic stability theory.

Concentration and Trade

While much research has been conducted on the effects of hegemony on trade, the influence of concentration has been largely ignored in studies of the international political economy. The dearth of analyses on the impact of concentration is surprising, since it possesses properties that are particularly well-suited for addressing certain issues that both hegemonic stability theorists and their critics have emphasized. The findings in chapter 5 indicated that concentration is often associated more strongly than hegemony with the level of global commerce. These results are indicative of the conceptual advantages of using concentration in studies of this sort.

For example, because analysts generally distinguish only between hegemonic and nonhegemonic systems, they imply that relationships between hegemony and outcomes such as global trade, market power in the global trading system, and the provision of collective goods can be viewed as step functions. Further, analyses of market power and trade that are based solely on hegemony cannot examine whether the level of international trade is anything other than a monotonic function of aggregate market power. In addition, because the theory of collective action forms the bedrock of many variants of hegemonic stability theory, it is important to consider both group size and relative inequality in studies of this sort. But hegemony describes only the most extreme inequalities of power and fails to address the issue of group size. Small-group theorists fall into the opposite trap: they examine only group size and virtually ignore the influence of relative inequality on outcomes in the international political economy. I demonstrated in chapter 3 that concentration, unlike hegemony or group size, reflects both the number of major powers (N) and the relative inequality among them (V). As such, concentration can be used to evaluate the claims of both hegemonic stability theorists and many of their critics.

It was found in chapter 5 that both the number of major powers and the relative inequality among them are strongly related to the level of trade, though not in a manner predicted by either hegemonic stability theorists or many of their critics. *The total effect of the number of major powers on trade (both via concentration and other channels) is direct:* larger numbers of major powers are associated with higher levels of commerce. This result is clearly at odds with the predictions of small-group theorists, who argue that group size is inversely related to the degree of coordination in the international political economy.

The fact that a direct relationship exists between the number of major powers and trade sheds doubt on the assumption (that is relied on by some variants of hegemonic stability theory and by some small-group theories) that a relatively liberal international trading system is a collective good. Instead the market power of each major power may decline as the number of major powers increases. And as the market power of each major power declines, so too does its ability to impose an optimal tariff. Further, as the number of major powers declines, the relative self-sufficiency of each major power is likely to increase. Since states have an incentive to minimize their dependence on one another in an anarchic international system, trade relations under these circumstances are likely to be curtailed. Finally, the direct relationship between the number of major powers and the level of global commerce may reflect the tendency for states to worry about how the gains from trade will be distributed, but for the salience of these concerns to diminish as the number of major powers increases.

A U-Shaped Relationship Between Concentration and International Trade

The results in chapter 5 also indicated that *the total effect of the level of relative inequality among the major powers on trade (both via concentration and other channels) is U-shaped. The relationship between concentration and trade is also U-shaped.* Hence, like concentration's influence on war, *the impacts of relative inequality among the major powers and concentration on trade do not seem to conform to most leading views on this topic.*

In conjunction with disagreements over how hegemony should be defined and measured and which feature of the distribution of power should be emphasized in studies of the international political economy, this finding may go a long way toward accounting for many of the empirical debates among hegemonic stability theorists and their critics. Hegemonic stability theorists seem to be correct in pointing to the advantages of a highly concentrated system: indeed trade appears to flourish under these structural conditions. However, certain critics of this approach also seem to be correct in positing that relatively uniform distributions of power reduce the likelihood that the flow of international trade will be stemmed.

As I argued in chapter 5, the relationships between both relative inequality and concentration, on the one hand, and trade, on the other hand, may reflect the fact that when relative inequality and concentration approach their minimum values, no state is able to alter its terms of trade through the use of predatory commercial policies. Under these conditions, trade barriers tend to be relatively low, and trade levels tend to be relatively high. When relative inequality and concentration approach intermediate levels, states may be tempted to exploit their market power. But when these variables approach their maximum values, states that have the ability to improve their terms of trade by imposing an optimal tariff may choose to forgo this option for both political and economic reasons. Behaving in a predatory manner may be counterproductive for a relatively large state if this strategy creates a demand on the part of smaller states for new global leaders or adversely affects the economies of political allies.

These results suggest that one reason why hegemony is not related more strongly to trade is that the distinction between hegemony and nonhegemony masks the differential effects on trade of various nonhegemonic distributions of capabilities. As noted above, using hegemony to measure the distribution of power assumes that all nonhegemonic systems are structurally equivalent. But this does not appear to be the case. Instead low (as well as high) levels of concentration are associated with the highest volumes of trade, while intermediate levels of concentration are associated with little trade. Both types of systems are likely to be nonhegemonic, but major powers in various types of nonhegemonic systems are likely to be vested with very different amounts of market power. In sum, viewing the structure of the system as a dichotomous variable and therefore ignoring the possibility that the relationship between the distribution of power and international trade may be quadratic has led many scholars of the international political economy to underemphasize the importance of concentration and to misspecify the relationship between the distribution of power and trade.

The Effects of Major-Power War on International Trade

It was pointed out in chapter 1 that, in addition to the distribution of power, it is useful to examine the effects of war and economic factors on international trade. The importance of these influences has been emphasized in a number of studies, but few empirical analyses of the international political economy have explicitly considered their effects. Moreover, as in the case of analyses of war, this research strategy facilitates the comparison of the effects of both structural and process-level variables, and political and economic factors, on the level of global commerce. As a result, these results provide further evidence bearing on the usefulness of structural and process-level approaches, as well as on the relationship between economics and security.

The findings in chapter 5 indicated that *during major-power wars, the amount of global commerce that is conducted tends to decline*. Under these circumstances, combatants are likely to be more inclined toward autarky because of the increased costs of depending on foreign markets. Further, control over trade is also likely to be used as an instrument of statecraft; and the imposition of embargoes, blockades, and sanctions during wars is likely to reduce the level of international trade.

These results indicate that *the relationship between trade and wars involving major powers is multidirectional:* not only do low levels of trade seem to increase the incidence of wars involving major powers, but a high (contemporaneous) incidence of wars involving major powers (as well as wars between major powers) tends to reduce the level of global commerce (see also the appendix to chapter 5). The salience of commercial liberal and interdependence theories of war rests, in part, on the argument that the opportunity costs of trade that is forgone during wars are substantial. Though it was not possible in this study to estimate empirically the magnitude of these opportunity costs, the fact that trade levels decline during wars is consistent with the spirit of these positions. If states are both aware of this tendency and dependent on trade for their economic well-being, they may (as the results in chapter 4 indicated) hesitate to engage in warfare soon after periods when trade levels are relatively high.

THE EFFECTS OF GLOBAL INCOME ON INTERNATIONAL TRADE

In addition to war, there is evidence (in chapter 5) that the level of global income is related to the level of trade. As expected, *higher levels of global income are associated with higher levels of global trade*. This suggests that many critics have been justified in taking strictly political theories of trade—including hegemonic stability theory—to task for failing to account for the effects of economic variables on international economic outcomes. While this study's analysis of the economic correlates of global trade is obviously quite crude, these results suggest that international commerce cannot be understood in either an economic or a political vacuum. Instead both security-related and economic factors influence global trade volumes.

Just as political scientists have tended to downplay the importance of economic variables in explaining commerce, economists have tended to ignore the effects of international politics on trade. The findings in this book suggest that neither strategy is adequate. If political scientists wish to evaluate the effects of politics on economic outcomes, it is necessary to take account of the relevant economic variables as well. Indeed this is the only way to establish clearly the importance of political (and security-related) effects on international economic relations. Less widely recognized is the fact that economists could benefit from adopting a similar tack. Interdisciplinary discussions of these issues have been lacking but offer the best hope for fully explaining variations in international trade.

In sum, certain process-level variables are substantially more important influences on international commerce than structural explanations usually acknowledge. Further, both economic and political variables of this sort need to be examined if we wish to fully account for variations in the level of global commerce. But it is important to reiterate that, in addition to process-level variables, structural theorists are correct in arguing that features of the distribution of capabilities provide important insights into patterns of international trade.

EXPLAINING STRUCTURAL CHANGE

The fact that certain aspects of the distribution of power exert a substantial impact on both war and trade points to the need for an explanation of the determinants and dynamics of the system's structure. The particular importance of concentration in this respect and the widespread criticism of neorealists for failing to provide an adequate explanation of structural change suggested a third set of empirical issues that formed the basis of this study: what determines the level of, and changes in, concentration? As Bruce Russett points out, "If it is conceded that there is something relevant, for policy as well as for theory, in the structure of the international system, it behooves us to devote some effort to description—to get some sense of the *current* distribution of nations by size—and to test some hypotheses about what that distribution *has been* in the past so as to be able to offer some further hypotheses, however speculative, about what the distribution may *be becoming*" (1968b:305; emphasis in original). But as noted earlier, despite calls for further research on this topic, little work of this sort has been conducted. In chapter 6, I therefore sought to help fill this gap.

Since neorealist analyses of international relations draw heavily on microeconomic analyses of market and industry structure, I argued that economic models of structural change might prove useful in this regard. Gibrat's law, which is one leading explanation of the dynamics underlying market and industry structure, posits that growth among firms in a given industry can be viewed as a stochastic process; and in particular, that the rate of growth among firms during a given period of time is independent of their original "sizes" at the outset of the period. Some neorealists suggest that, except for periods clustered around systemic wars, this process also characterizes the rate of growth of capabilities among the largest states in the international system.

The results in chapter 6 indicated that *whether or not Gibrat's law holds depends in large measure on how many of the largest states are used to model structural change. When the largest twelve to fifteen nations are analyzed, it holds remarkably well.* In fact, contrary to the neorealist hypothesis, the rate of growth of capabilities seems to follow this stochastic process even during those periods surrounding systemic wars. Strategic interaction among the members of the international system may help to explain these results: each state has an incentive to keep pace with the growth of other states in order to minimize the possibility that power imbalances will form, thereby undermining its relative position. These findings suggest that for larger and more inclusive samples, modeling structural change as a stochastic process may prove useful in future attempts to explain the effect of concentration on international outcomes.

It was also pointed out in chapter 6 that because neorealists (as well as many other scholars) are concerned primarily with the major powers, rather than the largest twelve to fifteen nations, and because the analyses of the distribution of power in this study centered on the major powers, it is important to consider separately this subset of states. *The results of this study are more in keeping with the expectations of neorealist theories when only the major powers are examined.* During certain periods throughout the nineteenth and twentieth centuries, the rates of growth of military expenditures, military personnel, and gross national product among these states have departed from Gibrat's law.

Some of these instances, such as China's abnormally high population growth, have been unintended; others, such as Germany's and the Soviet Union's military buildups during the interwar period, were the products of policy objectives. Most of these departures occurred during periods in which states were preparing for, waging, and concluding the most serious major-power wars. This suggests that models of this sort may be useful in predicting the onset of systemic wars. Further, to the extent that these models explain patterns of concentration and the change in concentration, they may provide insights into the conditions under which wars begin most frequently and trade levels vary.

War and Structural Change

Much of what systemic research has been conducted on structural change[2] has centered on the rise and decline of hegemonic powers. It is often argued

[2] This topic has also been studied at the level of the nation-state. See, for example, North (1981) and Olson (1982).

that shifts in the distribution of power between (among) a hegemon and a "challenger" (or group of challengers) are likely to give rise to systemic wars and the emergence of a new global leader. Indeed, even among analysts who do not adhere to this explanation or who do not focus on hegemony, the importance of systemic war in accounting for structural change is widely accepted (Keohane and Nye 1977:42; Waltz 1979:177; Levy 1985b; Thompson and Rasler 1988). However, as Jack Levy points out, analyses of the effects of hegemonic and "general" war on the distribution of power have encountered a number of problems. One of the most important limitations is that

> general war is [often] . . . defined in terms of the systemic consequences of the war. . . . [T]he definition of general war in terms of its systemic consequences means that one of the key propositions of . . . [theories of general war]—that the constitution or authority structure of the system is determined by general war—is established by definition and becomes impossible to investigate empirically. . . . This is too important a proposition to simply accept by definition and to leave immune to empirical investigation. (1985b:359, 360)

The model of the growth of national capabilities that was utilized in chapter 6 provides a potential means of helping to resolve this problem. It is often argued that, during the nineteenth and twentieth centuries, World Wars I and II were the only systemic wars that occurred. If it is granted that those periods in which capability growth among the major powers departs from Gibrat's law are ones in which structural changes occur, it can then be determined whether structural changes were clustered around systemic wars, without defining these wars in terms of their systemic consequences. And as noted above, there is substantial evidence that, so long as attention is focused on the major powers, this hypothesis is confirmed.

However, one cautionary note is in order concerning this finding. The fact that, in the absence of systemic war, the growth of capabilities is often characterized by this stochastic process does not imply that states actually grow at the same rate or that power imbalances caused by differential rates of growth will not materialize. What it does imply is that there is little evidence of a systematic relationship between the level of capabilities that states possess at the outset of a given period and the rate at which their capabilities grow during that interval. Thus, *on average*, larger states do not grow any more rapidly or slowly than smaller states (except for periods surrounding systemic wars).

A Systemic Approach to the Study of International Relations

Thus far, I have reviewed my findings and discussed some of their implications for a variety of leading theories of international relations. At this point, it is useful to outline some of the broader implications of this book.

One implication concerns the merits of systemic theories. The results in this book clearly point to the usefulness of a systemic approach to the study of international relations. Relying solely on systemic factors, it has been possible to explain much about why and when wars begin, trade levels vary, and structural change occurs. It is clear that a purely systemic approach can only identify the contextual factors that shape patterns of international relations. As such, systemic approaches are inherently limited in the types of questions that they can be used to answer. But their ability to answer those questions to which they are well-suited has been underestimated by some analysts. One central implication of this book is therefore that a systemic approach is substantially more useful than many critics acknowledge.

In addition, the results in this book bear on a series of controversies among systemic theorists. In the remainder of this section, these controversies are addressed.

Structure and Process in International Relations

It was pointed out in chapter 1 that disagreements concerning the usefulness of neorealist and other structural approaches have been at the forefront of much research on international relations. The results in this book indicate that certain aspects of the distribution of power shape patterns of both the frequency of war and the level of international trade. While polarity appears to have an indeterminate impact on both major-power war and trade, there is considerable evidence that concentration is strongly related to patterns of both outcomes. As a result, critics of neorealist explanations of war and the international political economy have been too quick to dismiss this approach.

The empirical evidence that has been accumulated also demonstrates, however, that despite the importance of neorealist approaches to the study of war and trade, many leading theories of this sort need to be refined. As mentioned above, *their preoccupation with polarity has led many scholars to neglect the influence of concentration, as well as other features of the distribution of power*.

I argued in chapters 1 and 3 that there are a variety of conceptual reasons to examine concentration more carefully in studies of the distribution of power. For example, the microeconomic bases of neorealism suggest that both the number of major powers and the relative inequality among them are important aspects of the system's structure. In this sense, polarity is simply too crude a measure of the distribution of power. In addition, scholars who focus on polarity assume (1) that either no power inequalities exist among the polar powers or that those inequalities that do exist are unimportant features of the international distribution of power; and (2) that nonpolar major powers need not be included in structural analyses of international relations. Each of these assumptions is conceptually trouble-some, since many theories of war and the international political economy highlight the effects of these structural factors.[3]

The empirical results in this study bear out the importance of focusing on both polarity and concentration in studies of war and trade. While both variables provide insights into the conditions under which wars begin most frequently and trade levels vary, concentration is often more strongly re-lated to these outcomes than polarity. Moreover, the nature of their effects often differs markedly. As a result, analyses that rely *exclusively* on polarity are likely to underestimate the importance of the distribution of power and fail to capture the nature of its influence on the frequency of war and the level of international trade. And the fact that many neorealist analyses focus solely on the effects of polarity has, in turn, contributed to the belief on the part of many scholars that neorealist approaches to war and the international political economy are inadequate. In this sense, one underly-ing problem with neorealist and other structural theories is not, as some critics charge, their emphasis on power; rather it is the overly restrictive manner in which they typically define the *distribution* of power.

Existing neorealist theories also have specified too restrictively the rela-tionships between the distribution of power and war and trade, respec-tively. Leading explanations of this sort generally posit that these relation-ships are monotonic. But *both the incidence of war and the level of international trade are quadratic functions of concentration.* Because few previous analyses have considered the possibility that these relationships might be nonmonotonic, there has been much confusion over the strength and nature of the effects of the system's structure on international trade and the onset of war.

Finally, neorealists discount heavily the importance of process-level fac-tors in their analyses of international relations. This research strategy im-poses considerable limits on neorealist approaches to the study of war and trade, since *certain process-level variables are strongly related to both the frequency of war and the level of international trade.*

Neorealists and other structural theorists would be likely to object to supplementing structural models with process-level variables on the grounds that this approach compromises the parsimony and elegance of their framework. This is true. But the price we pay for adopting a purely structural approach is the loss of a considerable amount of explanatory power. Contrary to the assertions of neorealists, *both* structural variables

---

[3] These drawbacks associated with using polarity, as it is conventionally measured, are not limited to studies of war and trade. In addition, the assumptions outlined above also pose potential problems for analyses of balancing behavior that focus solely on polarity (Mansfield 1993a).

and certain process-level variables often exert strong and systematic impacts on the incidence of war and the level of global trade. Aspects of both the distribution of power and international trade influence the frequency of war; and features of the distribution of power, war, and the global economy affect international trade. This suggests that it will be necessary to integrate more fully structural and process-level factors in any comprehensive explanation of international relations. Since process-level influences are both strongly related to the incidence of war and the level of global trade and explain a considerable amount of the variation in these phenomena, it seems undesirable to dispense with them in the name of theoretical elegance. On the contrary, we need to develop theories that include them and their effects.

International Security and the International Political Economy

It was also pointed out in the introduction to this book that scholars of international relations continue to debate the importance and the nature of the relationship between security and economics. The findings of this study demonstrate that *both* security-related factors and economic factors influence patterns of war and trade. As noted above, both power and economic factors influence war; and power, war, and economic factors influence trade. Hence, it is likely that integrating more fully the study of war and the study of the international political economy will foster a more complete understanding of the systemic causes and effects of war and trade.

This conclusion may strike some readers as self-evident. But while scholars of international relations have demonstrated an increasing interest in accomplishing this task, the fields of conflict studies and international political economy continue to be separated from one another. For example, trade (and other economic factors) has been analyzed sparingly in recent studies of war; and virtually no empirical research has been conducted on this topic at the systemic level of analysis. Because trade seems to exert a considerable impact on the frequency of war, scholars of war need to devote more attention to the conditions that shape patterns of international trade.

In addition, it is clear that the benefits of a fuller dialogue between scholars of war and the international political economy will not accrue solely to analysts of war. In particular, since major-power wars are an important determinant of global trade flows, many studies of the international political economy need to consider more explicitly the conditions under which these wars begin. And since both subfields have displayed much interest in the role of power, it is likely that building bridges between them will benefit both of them.

MEASUREMENT ISSUES IN INTERNATIONAL RELATIONS

A final implication of this book that should be emphasized concerns the extent to which data limitations and measurement problems hamper the ability of scholars to conduct empirical research on international relations.

The Reliability and Limits of Existing Data on War

At the outset of this study, I argued that the reliability of empirical studies of international relations depends in large measure on the reliability of the data that are utilized. Some of the initial results in this study suggested that problems of this sort might be especially acute in analyses of war. In particular, the results in chapter 2 indicated that surprisingly little correlation exists between the number of wars beginning in a year according to different data sets.

This suggests that analysts should be careful in choosing which data set they utilize in empirical studies of this sort. Until scholars of war arrive at some consensus regarding how to define and operationalize war, there is likely to be limited convergence in the conclusions at which they arrive. I am not implying that any of the data sets that were used in this book are flawed. I am implying, however, that these data sets should not be viewed as interchangeable; and that scholars should be cautious in picking the appropriate data set for the task at hand.

The extent to which this study's empirical results concerning war differ across various data sets of war depends on the research question that is posed. In certain cases, different data sets regarding the same type of war elicit different results. The variations in the strength of the relationships (in chapter 4) between hegemony, polarity, concentration, and trade, on the one hand, and all interstate wars, on the other hand, derived using Singer and Small's and Bueno de Mesquita's (adjusted and unadjusted) data illustrate this point. (See table 4.3.) This lack of internal validity indicates that there are good reasons to conduct research on war using a variety of data sets and to determine whether and why important deviations exist in the findings.

However, in other cases, there is often much regularity in the results of tests of leading hypotheses concerning war's onset. For example, the directions of the relationships between these variables and the incidence of a given type of war are very much the same, regardless of the data that are used. Indeed many of these results are considerably more robust than would be expected, given the low correlation between different compilations. Particularly if different types of wars are analyzed separately, there is often relatively little difference in my empirical results.

Measuring and Operationalizing the International Distribution of Power

Differences also exist in the operationalization of indices that have been used to measure structural features. I have reviewed at length many of the conceptual drawbacks with using polarity to measure the distribution of capabilities. Leaving these limitations aside, pronounced disagreements persist regarding how to distinguish systems according to their polarity. The long-standing debates that, for example, mark discussions of how many poles existed during the nineteenth century and the post–World War II era suggest that scholars who rely on this variable to measure the distribution of capabilities need to address this issue more fully.

Perhaps the clearest example of this dispute concerns hegemony. Particularly problematic in this respect is the ambiguity surrounding what is meant by hegemony. Unfortunately, operationalizing hegemony usually amounts to the functional equivalent of "you'll know a hegemon when you see one." But since it is not always clear what we should expect to "see" when looking at a hegemon, it is difficult to distinguish in a rigorous manner hegemonic from nonhegemonic systems. This issue is brought into sharp relief by the considerable variations in the empirical relationships that exist between different classifications of hegemony and outcomes such as non-major-power interstate wars and the level of global trade. Indeed, as pointed out earlier, various classifications influence not only the relationship between hegemony and the incidence of non-major-power wars, they also impact the relationships between other features of polarity and concentration and the frequency of war.

In contrast to polarity, there is considerable uniformity regarding how to measure concentration: few studies (that I am aware of) have failed to use the Ray and Singer index. However, this is not to imply that the measurement of concentration has been straightforward. For example, scholars do not agree on *which capabilities* should be used to measure concentration. Singer, Bremer, and Stuckey (1972) and Bueno de Mesquita and Lalman (1988) use demographic, economic, and military capabilities to measure concentration, while Thompson (1983b; 1988) and Modelski and Thompson (1988) rely on naval (and air) capabilities. Bueno de Mesquita (1981a) does not utilize capabilities at all; instead he assigns nations to one of five ranks, based on their aggregate capabilities. Further, differences over *which countries* should be used to measure concentration mark studies of this sort. Singer, Bremer, and Stuckey's criteria for inclusion in the major-power subsystem are quite different from Thompson's which, in turn, vary from those of Bueno de Mesquita and Bueno de Mesquita and Lalman. This would be unimportant if these differences had little influence on the results of tests of concentration; however, the markedly different conclusions at which these studies (and the present study) arrive strongly suggest that, as in the case of hegemony, this is not the case.[4]

Though these data limitations are important, they do not preclude conducting useful empirical research on international relations. Rather, until some consensus emerges on which data are most reliable and appropriate for particular purposes, they indicate that a comparative approach should be taken to determine when and why results are sensitive to various data on international relations.

LIMITS OF THE ANALYSIS

Before concluding, the limitations of the present study should be reviewed. First, this study has focused on testing and refining a number of systemic theories. However, the strength of these results has not been compared with findings derived from explanations that operate at other levels of analysis. Various studies have highlighted the importance of (among other things) dyadic power relations; military-strategic considerations; domestic politics, economics, culture, and history; crisis management; and decision-making processes in accounting for the onset of war and aspects of commerce. As noted at the outset, the systemic focus of this book was a matter of research strategy, since one of the basic purposes of this study was to determine the extent to which particular systemic variables explain patterns of international relations. But further research needs to be conducted comparing the merits of systemic and competing approaches.

Second, an explicitly neorealist typology of structure has been adopted in this study. Yet neorealists have been criticized for defining structure in an overly restrictive manner. Much of the burgeoning literature on international regimes, for example, argues that these phenomena are also structural. The fact that I was primarily interested in examining neorealist theories of international relations led me to define the system's structure solely in terms of the distribution of power. But it is clear that before we can adequately evaluate the claims made by various (neorealist and other) structural theories, we will need to utilize a number of different typologies of structure.

Third, a limited range of process-level factors has been examined in this

---

[4] Of course, as noted earlier, much of the disagreement among these studies may also be traced to differences in what feature of war they seek to explain. Even features of war that appear on the surface to be similar are often different. For example, while both Singer, Bremer, and Stuckey and Thompson analyze the magnitude of major-power war, the fact that they define the members of the major-power subsystem differently produces variations in the value that the dependent variable takes on for any given period of time.

study. Of course, it is not possible to examine all such influences in any single study. But it would, for example, be particularly useful to consider the effects of international institutions and regimes in a study of this sort, since a variety of studies (including those that emphasize the usefulness of interdependence theory) conclude that they are important determinants of many types of global outcomes (Keohane and Nye 1977, 1987; Krasner 1983; Keohane 1984, 1986; Snidal 1985b; Nye 1988; Martin 1992). Although data limitations precluded such an analysis for the time period covered in this book, further research of this sort would be useful.

Fourth, throughout this study, a basic-force model of power has been used. Because they are easier to construct than models that include important intangible aspects of power, basic-force models have dominated empirical studies of the distribution of power in international relations. However, national power is clearly a function of more than just the capabilities that a state possesses. Similarly, the distribution of power cannot be measured precisely using only a capability-based index. However, scholars have been unable to operationalize better proxies for, and measures of, power; and many of them believe that those that were used in this study are the best that are presently available.

Finally, this study is largely a statistical analysis of power, trade, and war. The basic rationale for this research strategy stemmed from my interest in examining long-term patterns in international relations and assessing the influence of a wide variety of factors while holding constant the effects of others. But it is clear that this study has only scratched the surface of the historical record, and that further research is necessary to compare the patterns uncovered in this study with the detailed historical record during the nineteenth and twentieth centuries.[5]

---

[5] Given the previous discussion of the limitations of the present study, a number of avenues for future research seem promising. First, it was noted above that this study's efforts to examine structural effects on international relations have been hampered by an inadequate analysis of both power and the structure of the international system. In particular, a more sophisticated analysis of networks of international relations may be useful in determining the importance of the structure of the international system in shaping global outcomes. By relying on capabilities to measure power, many analysts treat power as attributional, rather than relational: a state's power is determined by various capabilities at its disposal. But to the extent that we define power as the ability of A to get B to do something that B would not otherwise do (Dahl 1976), attributional measures of power may not be adequate. Though political scientists have conducted little research in this area (Frey 1986), one potential solution to this problem may be the development of network-related models of the distribution of power.

Second, additional facets of the international system should be addressed in subsequent analyses of this sort. Further, more attention should be devoted to the interaction between various political and economic features of the international system. Third, it would be useful to compare the relative merits of the explanations that have been analyzed in this study with competing theories of international relations. Regional and domestic political, historical, and

IMPLICATIONS FOR PUBLIC POLICY

Shelley once wrote that "[w]ar is the statesman's game, the priest's delight, the lawyer's jest, the hired assassin's trade." It is clear, however, that the stakes of this "game" have risen dramatically over time and that statesmen are keenly aware of this development. While it is obvious that no simple, deterministic relationships exist, certain systemic conditions tend to be related to variations in both the frequency of war and the level of international trade. In conclusion, it is useful to consider some of the ways that this study's findings concerning these relationships might be of use to policymakers.

There is some evidence that upward shifts in concentration and movement in the shares of capabilities on the parts of major powers tend to precipitate major-power wars. And those periods in which the growth in major-power capabilities departs from Gibrat's law tend to be clustered around the occurrence of systemic wars. To a certain extent, this may reflect the disproportionate buildup of major powers that are preparing for war in the near future. However, it may also be the case that high rates of growth on the part of one (or a number of) major power(s) with benign intentions are perceived by other leading states as a threat. As such, policymakers should consider carefully the implications of policies that lead to large shifts in relative capabilities, and that may exacerbate the security dilemma (Herz 1950; Jervis 1978).

There is also considerable evidence that intermediate levels of concentration tend to precipitate major-power wars. While the advent of the nuclear revolution has done much to mitigate the effects of the distribution of capabilities on major-power war (Jervis 1989), at least one recent study concludes that the emergence of such a distribution is distinctly possible in the near future, and that this bodes poorly for the avoidance of war in Europe (Mearsheimer 1990). Even if such a structural condition is emerging, I am clearly not suggesting that a major-power war is imminent if statesmen do not coordinate their actions in such a way as to promote

---

economic factors are of obvious importance in explaining why and when wars begin and trade levels vary. Cohen argues that studies of the international political economy need to consider "domestic- and systemic-level variables simultaneously, rather than sequentially and [to specify] whatever interactions there may be among all relevant variables in a rigorous manner" (1990:269). Indeed not only is this admonition useful, it applies equally well to studies of war.

Finally, more research needs to be conducted on both the relative importance of structural and process-level variables and the relative impacts of economic factors and security-related factors on patterns of global outcomes. The findings of this study indicate that each of these types of influences is centrally important. But it is clear that this study has offered only a preliminary analysis of these issues.

either a more uniform or highly skewed distribution of capabilities. But the fact that similar structural conditions historically have been vested with dangerous characteristics should induce caution on the part of, and should not be overlooked by, decision makers.

In addition, the continued expansion of international trade offers an avenue for improving political relations while, at the same time, increasing global welfare. The findings of this study suggest that the prescriptions offered by interdependence theorists may have more merit than many scholars and policymakers have come to believe. Aside from economic welfare considerations, freer trade seems to produce security externalities that warrant the attention of statesmen (Gowa 1989b; Gowa and Mansfield 1993).

The extent to which trade flourishes may depend on the relative power positions of the leading states in the international system, as well as international economic conditions. Much has been made about the importance of a hegemon for the coordination of the global economy. But while many observers lament the economic decline of the United States and attribute rising levels of protectionism to the decline of American hegemony, the decline or absence of a hegemon need not augur poorly for the future of the international trading system. If we have entered into a period marked by an intermediate level of concentration, the prospects for regional trading blocs and enhanced protectionism (Gilpin 1987; Bhagwati 1988, 1991; Mansfield 1993b) (and of major-power war) are likely to increase.[6] However, if, for example, Germany and Japan gain military strength commensurate with their economic strength and thereby join the ranks of the major powers, the effect may be to depress concentration. The advent of a system characterized by a relatively low level of concentration may actually enhance the prospects for international economic stability. And lower levels of concentration and higher levels of trade may, in turn, reduce the likelihood of major-power war.

While this section illustrates some of the potential policy implications of this study's findings, it is also obvious that much additional research needs to be conducted before the importance of these results for policymakers is clear. Toward this end, further interdisciplinary research between political scientists and economists needs to be conducted, and is likely to foster a fuller understanding of the relationships among power, trade, and war.

[6] For an analysis of the potentially liberalizing forces of economic regionalism, see Oye (1992).

BIBLIOGRAPHY

Alcock, Norman Z., and Alan G. Newcombe. 1970. "The Perception of National Power." *Journal of Conflict Resolution* 14: 335–43.

Allison, Graham T. 1971. *Essence of Decision: Explaining the Cuban Missile Crisis*. Boston: Little, Brown.

Aron, Raymond. 1981. *Peace and War: A Theory of International Relations*. Malabar: Robert E. Krieger Publishing.

Axelrod, Robert, and Robert O. Keohane. 1985. "Achieving Cooperation Under Anarchy: Strategies and Institutions." *World Politics* 38: 226–54.

Bairoch, Paul. 1976. "Europe's Gross National Product, 1800–1975." *Journal of European Economic History* 5: 273–340.

Baldwin, David A. 1979. "Power Analysis and World Politics: New Trends versus Old Tendencies." *World Politics* 31: 161–94.

———. 1980. "Interdependence and Power: A Conceptual Analysis." *International Organization* 34: 471–506.

———. 1985. *Economic Statecraft*. Princeton: Princeton University Press.

———, ed. 1993. *Neorealism and Neoliberalism: The Contemporary Debate*. New York: Columbia University Press.

Berry, William D. 1984. *Nonrecursive Causal Models*. Beverly Hills: Sage.

Bhagwati, Jagdish. 1988. *Protectionism*. Cambridge: MIT Press.

———. 1991. *The World Trading System at Risk*. Princeton: Princeton University Press.

Blainey, Geoffrey. 1973. *The Causes of War*. New York: Free Press.

Boswell, Terry, and Mike Sweat. 1991. "Hegemony, Long Waves, and Major Wars: A Time Series Analysis of Systemic Dynamics, 1496–1967." *International Studies Quarterly* 35: 123–49.

Bueno de Mesquita, Bruce. 1975. "Measuring Systemic Polarity." *Journal of Conflict Resolution* 19: 187–216.

———. 1981a. "Risk, Power Distributions, and the Likelihood of War." *International Studies Quarterly* 25: 541–68.

———. 1981b. *The War Trap*. New Haven: Yale University Press.

———. 1985. "Toward a Scientific Understanding of International Conflict: A Personal View." *International Studies Quarterly* 29: 121–36.

Bueno de Mesquita, Bruce, and David Lalman. 1988. "Empirical Support for Systemic and Dyadic Explanations of International Conflict." *World Politics* 41: 1–20.

———. 1992. *War and Reason: Domestic and International Imperatives*. New Haven: Yale University Press.

Bull, Hedley. 1977. *The Anarchical Society: A Study of Order in World Politics*. New York: Columbia University Press.

Buzan, Barry. 1984. "Economic Structure and International Security: The Limits of the Liberal Case." *International Organization* 38: 597–624.

Cannizzo, Cynthia. 1978. "Capability Distribution and Major-Power War Experience, 1816–1965." *Orbis* 21: 947–57.

Cassing, James, Timothy J. McKeown, and Jack Ochs. 1986. "The Political Economy of the Tariff Cycle." *American Political Science Review* 80: 843–62.

Choucri, Nazli, and Robert C. North. 1975. *Nations in Conflict*. San Francisco: Freeman.

Chow, Gregory C. 1960. "Tests of Equality Between Subsets of Coefficients in Two Linear Regression Models." *Econometrica* 28: 591–605.

Christensen, Thomas J., and Jack Snyder. 1990. "Chain Gangs and Passed Bucks: Predicting Alliance Patterns in Multipolarity." *International Organization* 44: 137–68.

Claude, Inis L. 1962. *Power and International Relations*. New York: Random House.

Cohen, Benjamin J. 1990. "The Political Economy of International Trade." *International Organization* 44: 261–81.

Conybeare, John A. C. 1983. "Tariff Protection in Developed and Developing Countries: A Cross-Sectional and Longitudinal Analysis." *International Organization* 37: 441–67.

———. 1984. "Public Goods, Prisoners' Dilemma and the International Political Economy." *International Studies Quarterly* 28: 5–22.

———. 1985. "Trade Wars: A Comparative Study of Anglo-Hanse, Franco-Italian, and Hawley-Smoot Conflicts." *World Politics* 38: 147–72.

———. 1987. *Trade Wars: The Theory and Practice of International Commercial Rivalry*. New York: Columbia University Press.

Correlates of War Project. 1991. "National Material Capabilities Data." Ann Arbor: University of Michigan.

Cowhey, Peter, and Edward Long. 1983. "Testing Theories of Regime Change: Hegemonic Decline or Surplus Capacity?" *International Organization* 37: 157–83.

Craig, Gordon A., and Alexander L. George. 1983. *Force and Statecraft: Diplomatic Problems of Our Time*. New York: Oxford University Press.

Dahl, Robert A. 1976. *Modern Political Analysis*. 3d ed. Englewood Cliffs, N.J.: Prentice-Hall.

Davies, S., and B. R. Lyons. 1982. "Seller Concentration: The Technological Explanation and Demand Uncertainty." *Economic Journal* 92: 903–19.

Davis, Kingsley. 1954. "The Demographic Foundations of National Power." In Morrow Berger, Theodore Abel, Charles H. Page, eds., *Freedom and Control in Modern Society*. New York: Farrar, Straus and Giroux.

Davis, William W., George T. Duncan, and Randolph M. Siverson. 1978. "The Dynamics of Warfare, 1816–1965." *American Journal of Political Science* 22: 772–92.

Deardorff, Alan V., and Robert M. Stern. 1987. "Current Issues in Trade Policy: An Overview." In Robert M. Stern, ed., *U.S. Trade Policies in a Changing World Economy*. Cambridge: MIT Press.

Deutsch, Karl W., and J. David Singer. 1964. "Multipolar Power Systems and International Stability." *World Politics* 16: 390–406.

Domke, William K. 1988. *War and the Changing Global System*. New Haven: Yale University Press.

Doran, Charles F. 1991. *Systems in Crisis: New Imperatives of High Politics at Century's End*. New York: Cambridge University Press.

Doran, Charles F., and Wes Parsons. 1980. "War and the Cycle of Relative Power." *American Political Science Review* 74: 947–65.

Duvall, Raymond. 1976. "An Appraisal of the Methodological and Statistical Foundations in the Correlates of War Project." In Francis Hoole and Dina Zinnes, eds., *Quantitative International Politics*. New York: Praeger.

Earle, Edward Meade. 1986. "Adam Smith, Alexander Hamilton, Friedrich List: The Economic Foundations of Military Power." In Peter Paret, ed., *Makers of Modern Strategy: From Machiavelli to the Nuclear Age*. Princeton: Princeton University Press.

Ethier, Wilfred. 1983. *Modern International Economics*. New York: W. W. Norton.

Frey, Frederick W. 1971. "Comment: On Issues and Nonissues in the Study of Power." *American Political Science Review* 65: 1081–1104.

———. 1986. "The Distribution of Power in Political Systems." Paper presented at the annual meeting of the American Political Science Association, Washington, D.C., August 28–31.

Friedberg, Aaron L. 1988. *The Weary Titan: Britain and the Experience of Relative Decline, 1895–1905*. Princeton: Princeton University Press.

Gaddis, John Lewis. 1986. "The Long Peace: Elements of Stability in the Postwar International System." *International Security* 10: 99–142.

Gallant, Ronald, and J. Jeffery Goebel. 1976. "Nonlinear Regression with Autocorrelated Errors." *Journal of the American Statistical Association* 71: 961–67.

Gallarotti, Giulio M. 1985. "Toward a Business Cycle Model of Tariffs." *International Organization* 39: 155–88.

Garnham, David. 1985. "The Causes of War: Systemic Findings." In Alan Ned Sabrosky, ed., *Polarity and War: The Changing Structure of International Conflict*. Boulder, Colo.: Westview.

Gasiorowski, Mark. 1986. "Economic Interdependence and International Conflict: Some Cross-National Evidence." *International Studies Quarterly* 30: 23–38.

Gasiorowski, Mark, and Solomon W. Polachek. 1982. "Conflict and Interdependence." *Journal of Conflict Resolution* 26: 709–29.

Gilpin, Robert. 1975. *U.S. Power and the Multinational Corporation: The Political Economy of Foreign Direct Investment*. New York: Basic Books.

———. 1977. "Economic Interdependence and National Security in Historical Perspective." In Klaus Knorr and Frank N. Trager, eds., *Economic Issues and National Security*. Lawrence: University Press of Kansas.

———. 1981. *War and Change in World Politics*. New York: Cambridge University Press.

———. 1986. "The Richness of the Tradition of Political Realism." In Robert O. Keohane, ed., *Neorealism and Its Critics*. New York: Columbia University Press.

———. 1987. *The Political Economy of International Relations*. Princeton: Princeton University Press.

———. 1989. "The Theory of Hegemonic War." In Robert I. Rotberg and Theodore K. Rabb, eds., *The Origin and Prevention of Major Wars*. New York: Cambridge University Press.

Gochman, Charles S., and Zeev Maoz. 1984. "Militarized Interstate Disputes, 1816–1976: Procedures, Patterns, and Insights." *Journal of Conflict Resolution* 28: 585–616.

Goldfeld, S. M., and R. E. Quandt. 1972. *Nonlinear Methods in Econometrics*. Amsterdam: North-Holland.

Goldstein, Joshua S. 1985. "Kondratieff Waves as War Cycles." *International Studies Quarterly* 29: 411–44.

——. 1988. *Long Cycles: Prosperity and War in the Modern Age*. New Haven: Yale University Press.

Goldstein, Morris, and Mohsin S. Khan. 1984. "Income and Price Effects in Foreign Trade." In R. W. Jones and P. B. Kenen, eds., *Handbook of International Economics*. Amsterdam: North-Holland.

Gowa, Joanne. 1984. "IOs, Hegemons, and Markets: The Case of the Substitution Account." *International Organization* 38: 661–84.

——. 1989a. "Rational Hegemons, Excludable Goods, and Small Groups: An Epitaph for Hegemonic Stability Theory?" *World Politics* 41: 307–24.

——. 1989b. "Bipolarity, Multipolarity, and Free Trade." *American Political Science Review* 83: 1245–56.

Gowa, Joanne, and Edward D. Mansfield. 1993. "Power Politics and International Trade." *American Political Science Review* 87: 408–20.

Green, Robert T., and James M. Lutz. 1978. *The United States and World Trade*. New York: Praeger.

Grieco, Joseph M. 1988. "Anarchy and the Limits of Cooperation: A Realist Critique of the Newest Liberal Institutionalism." *International Organization* 42: 485–507.

——. 1990. *Cooperation Among Nations: Europe, America, and Non-Tariff Barriers to Trade*. Ithaca: Cornell University Press.

Gulick, Edward Vose. 1955. *Europe's Classical Balance of Power*. New York: W. W. Norton.

Haas, Michael. 1970. "International Subsystems: Stability and Polarity." *American Political Science Review* 64: 98–123.

Haggard, Stephan, and Beth A. Simmons. 1987. "Theories of International Regimes." *International Organization* 41: 491–517.

Hannah, Leslie, and J. A. Kay. 1977. *Concentration in Modern Industry: Theory, Measurement and the U.K. Experience*. London: Macmillan.

Hanushek, Eric A., and John E. Jackson. 1977. *Statistical Methods for Social Scientists*. 3d ed. New York: Academic Press.

Hardin, Russell. 1982. *Collective Action*. Baltimore: Johns Hopkins University Press.

Hart, Jefferey A. 1985. "Power and Polarity in the International System." In Alan Ned Sabrosky, ed., *Polarity and War: The Changing Structure of International Conflict*. Boulder, Colo.: Westview.

——. 1986. "Polarity, Hegemony and the Distribution of Power." Paper presented at the annual meeting of the American Political Science Association, Washington, D.C., August 28–31.

Hart, P. E., and S. J. Prais. 1956. "The Analysis of Business Concentration." *Journal of the Royal Statistical Society* 119: 15–81.

Harvey, A. C. 1981. *The Econometric Analysis of Time Series*. New York: John Wiley.

Herz, John H. 1950. "Idealist Internationalism and the Security Dilemma." *World Politics* 2: 157–80.

———. 1951. *Political Realism and Political Idealism*. Chicago: University of Chicago Press.

———. 1959. *International Politics in the Atomic Age*. New York: Columbia University Press.

Hibbs, Douglas A. 1974. "Problems of Statistical Estimation and Causal Inference in Time-Series Regression Models." In Herbert L. Costner, ed., *Sociological Methodology, 1973–1974*. San Francisco: Jossey-Bass.

Hinsley, F. H. 1963. *Power and the Pursuit of Peace*. London: Cambridge University Press.

Hirschman, Albert O. [1945] 1980. *National Power and the Structure of Foreign Trade*. Berkeley: University of California Press.

Hitch, Charles J., and D. McKean. 1965. *The Economics of Defense in the Nuclear Age*. Cambridge: Harvard University Press.

Hopf, Ted. 1991. "Polarity, the Offense-Defense Balance, and War." *American Political Science Review* 85: 475–93.

Horvath, William J., and Caxton C. Foster. 1963. "Stochastic Models of War Alliances." *Journal of Conflict Resolution* 7: 110–16.

Houweling, H. W., and J. B. Kune. 1984. "Do the Outbreaks of War Follow a Poisson Process?" *Journal of Conflict Resolution* 28: 51–61.

Ijiri, Yuji, and Herbert A. Simon. 1964. "Business Firm Growth and Size." *American Economic Review* 41: 77–89.

———. 1977. *Skew Distributions and the Sizes of Business Firms*. New York: North-Holland.

Ikenberry, G. John, and Charles A. Kupchan. 1990. "Socialization and Hegemonic Power." *International Organization* 44: 283–316.

Jackson, William D. 1977. "Polarity in International Systems: A Conceptual Note." *International Interactions* 4: 87–96.

Jacquemin, Alexis. 1987. *The New Industrial Organization: Market Forces and Strategic Behavior*. Cambridge: MIT Press.

Jervis, Robert. 1978. "Cooperation Under the Security Dilemma." *World Politics* 30: 167–214.

———. 1984. *The Illogic of American Nuclear Strategy*. Ithaca: Cornell University Press.

———. 1989. *The Meaning of the Nuclear Revolution: Statecraft and the Prospect of Armageddon*. Ithaca: Cornell University Press.

———. 1991–92. "The Future of World Politics: Will it Resemble the Past?" *International Security* 16: 39–73.

Johnson, Harry G. 1953–54. "Optimum Tariffs and Retaliation." *Review of Economic Studies* 22: 142–53.

Johnston, J. 1972. *Econometric Methods*. 2d ed. New York: McGraw-Hill.

Jovanovic, Boyan, and Saul Lach. 1990. "The Diffusion of Technology and Inequality Among Nations." New York: C. V. Starr Center for Applied Economic Research.

Kahler, Miles. 1979–80. "Rumors of War: The 1914 Analogy." *Foreign Affairs* 58: 374–96.

Kaysen, Carl. 1990. "Is War Obsolete? A Review Essay." *International Security* 14: 42–64.

Kelejian, Harry H., and Wallace E. Oates. 1989. *Introduction to Econometrics*. 3d ed. New York: Harper and Row.

Kennedy, Paul M. 1983. *The Rise and Fall of British Naval Mastery*. Atlantic Highlands, N.J.: Ashfield Press.

———. 1987. *The Rise and Fall of the Great Powers: Economic Change and Military Conflict from 1500 to 2000*. New York: Random House.

Keohane, Robert O. 1980. "The Theory of Hegemonic Stability and Changes in International Economic Regimes, 1967–1977." In Ole R. Holsti, Randolph M. Siverson, and Alexander L. George, eds., *Change in the International System*. Boulder, Colo.: Westview.

———. 1984. *After Hegemony: Cooperation and Discord in the World Political Economy*. Princeton: Princeton University Press.

———. 1986. "Theory of World Politics: Structural Realism and Beyond." In Robert O. Keohane, ed., *Neorealism and Its Critics*. New York: Columbia University Press.

Keohane, Robert O., and Joseph S. Nye Jr. 1977. *Power and Interdependence: World Politics in Transition*. Boston: Little, Brown.

———. 1987. "*Power and Interdependence* Revisited." *International Organization* 41: 725–53.

Keynes, John Maynard. [1935] 1964. *The General Theory of Employment, Interest, and Money*. New York: Harcourt Brace Jovanovich.

Kindleberger, Charles P. 1966. *Foreign Trade and the National Economy*. New Haven: Yale University Press.

———. 1973. *The World in Depression, 1929–1939*. Berkeley: University of California Press.

———. 1981. "Dominance and Leadership in the International Economy: Exploitation, Public Goods, and Free Riders." *International Studies Quarterly* 25: 242–54.

King, Gary. 1988. "Statistical Models for Political Science Event Counts: Bias in Conventional Procedures and Evidence for the Exponential Poisson Regression Model." *American Journal of Political Science* 32: 838–63.

———. 1989. "Event Count Models for International Relations: Generalizations and Applications." *International Studies Quarterly* 33: 123–47.

Kissinger, Henry A. 1964. *A World Restored: Metternich, Castlereagh and the Problems of Peace, 1812–1822*. New York: Grosset and Dunlap.

Kmenta, Jan. 1986. *Elements of Econometrics*. 2d ed. New York: Macmillan.

Knorr, Klaus. 1966. *On the Uses of Military Power in the Nuclear Age*. Princeton: Princeton University Press.

Kondratieff, Nikolai D. [1926] 1979. "Long Waves in Economic Life." *Review* 2: 519–62.

Krasner, Stephen D. 1976. "State Power and the Structure of International Trade." *World Politics* 28: 317–47.

———, ed. 1983. *International Regimes*. Ithaca: Cornell University Press.

———. 1985. "Toward Understanding in International Relations." *International Studies Quarterly* 29: 137–44.

Kuczynski, Thomas. 1980. "Have There Been Differences Between the Growth Rates in Different Periods of the Development of the Capitalist World Economy since 1850?" In J. M. Clubb and E. K. Scheuch, eds., *Historical Social Research*. Monograph series, no. 6. Stuttgart: Klett-Cotta.

Kugler, Jacek, and Marina Arbetman. 1989. "Choosing Among Measures of Power: A Review of the Empirical Record." In Richard J. Stoll and Michael D. Ward, eds., *Power in World Politics*. Boulder, Colo.: Lynne Rienner.

Kugler, Jacek, and William Domke. 1986. "Comparing the Strength of Nations." *Comparative Political Studies* 19: 39–69.

Lake, David A. 1983. "International Economic Structure and American Foreign Economic Policy, 1887–1934." *World Politics* 35: 517–43.

———. 1988. *Power, Protection, and Free Trade: International Sources of U.S. Commercial Strategy, 1887–1939*. Ithaca: Cornell University Press.

———. 1991. "The Theory of Hegemonic Stability: An Interim Report." Paper presented at the 15th World Congress of the International Political Science Association, Buenos Aires, July 21–25.

Lasswell, Harold D., and Abraham Kaplan. 1950. *Power and Society: A Framework for Political Inquiry*. New Haven: Yale University Press.

Leamer, Edward E., and Robert M. Stern. 1970. *Quantitative International Economics*. Boston: Allyn and Bacon.

Levy, Jack S. 1983. *War in the Modern Great Power System, 1495–1975*. Lexington: University Press of Kentucky.

———. 1984. "Size and Stability in the Modern Great Power System." *International Interactions* 10: 341–58.

———. 1985a. "The Polarity of the System and International Stability: An Empirical Analysis." In Alan Ned Sabrosky, ed., *Polarity and War: The Changing Structure of International Conflict*. Boulder, Colo.: Westview.

———. 1985b. "Theories of General War." *World Politics* 37: 344–74.

———. 1989. "The Causes of War: A Review of Theories and Evidence." In Philip E. Tetlock, Jo L. Husbands, Robert Jervis, Paul C. Stern, and Charles Tilly, eds., *Behavior, Society, and Nuclear War*. New York: Oxford University Press.

———. 1991. "Long Cycles, Hegemonic Transitions, and the Long Peace." In Charles W. Kegley, ed., *The Long Postwar Peace*. New York: HarperCollins.

Li, Richard P. Y., and William R. Thompson. 1978. "The Stochastic Process of Alliance Formation Behavior." *American Political Science Review* 72: 1288–1303.

Liesner, Thelma. 1984. *Economic Statistics, 1900–1983*. New York: Facts on File.

Lipson, Charles. 1984. "International Cooperation in Economic and Security Affairs." *World Politics* 37: 1–23.

Lucus, Robert. 1973. "Some International Evidence on Output-Inflation Tradeoffs." *American Economic Review* 63: 326–34.

———. 1981. *Studies in Business Cycle Theory*. Cambridge: MIT Press.

McGowan, Patrick J., and Robert M. Rood. 1975. "Alliance Behavior in Balance of Power Systems: Applying a Poisson Model to Nineteenth Century Europe." *American Political Science Review* 69: 859–70.

McKeown, Timothy J. 1983. "Hegemonic Stability Theory and 19th-Century Tariff Levels in Europe." *International Organization* 37: 73–91.

———. 1991. "A Liberal Trade Order? The Long-Run Pattern of Imports to the Advanced Capitalist States." *International Studies Quarterly* 35: 151–72.

Macfie, A. L. 1938. "The Outbreak of War and the Trade Cycle." *Economic History* 2: 89–97.

Maddala, G. S. 1983. *Limited-Dependent and Qualitative Variables in Econometrics.* New York: Cambridge University Press.

———. 1988. *Introduction to Econometrics.* New York: Macmillan.

Maddison, Angus. 1982. *Phases of Capitalist Development.* New York: Oxford University Press.

Mansfield, Edward D. 1988. "The Distribution of Wars Over Time." *World Politics* 41: 21–51.

———. 1989. "International Trade and the Onset of War." Paper presented at the annual meeting of the American Political Science Association, Atlanta, August 31–September 3.

———. 1992a. "The Concentration of Capabilities and International Trade." *International Organization* 46: 731–64.

———. 1992b. "The Concentration of Capabilities and the Onset of War." *Journal of Conflict Resolution* 36: 3–24.

———. 1993a. "Concentration, Polarity, and the Distribution of Power." *International Studies Quarterly* 37: 105–28.

———. 1993b. "The Effects of International Politics on Regionalism in International Trade." In Kym Anderson and Richard Blackhurst, eds., *Regional Integration and the Global Trading System.* London: Harvester Wheatsheaf.

Mansfield, Edwin. 1962. "Entry, Gibrat's Law, Innovation, and the Growth of Firms." *American Economic Review* 52: 1023–51.

Maoz, Zeev. 1982. *Paths to Conflict: International Dispute Initiation, 1816–1976.* Boulder, Colo.: Westview.

March, James G. 1966. "The Power of Power." In David Easton, ed., *Varieties of Political Theory.* Englewood Cliffs, N.J.: Prentice-Hall.

Martin, Lisa L. 1992. *Coercive Cooperation: Explaining Multilateral Economic Sanctions.* Princeton: Princeton University Press.

Mastanduno, Michael. 1985. "Strategies of Economic Containment: U.S. Trade Relations with the Soviet Union." *World Politics* 37: 503–31.

Mearsheimer, John. 1990. "Back to the Future: Instability in Europe After the Cold War." *International Security* 15: 5–56.

Midlarsky, Manus I. 1988. *The Onset of World War.* Boston: Unwin Hyman.

Milner, Helen V. 1991. "The Assumption of Anarchy in International Relations Theory: A Critique." *Review of International Studies* 17: 67–85.

Milward, Alan S. 1977. *War, Economy and Society: 1939–1945.* Berkeley: University of California Press.

Mitchell, Brian R. 1980. *European Historical Statistics, 1750–1975.* London: Butler and Tanner.

———. 1982. *International Historical Statistics: Africa and Asia.* New York: New York University Press.

———. 1983. *International Historical Statistics: The Americas and Australia.* Detroit: Gale Research.

Mitrany, David. 1975. *The Functional Theory of Politics*. London and New York: St. Martin's Press.

Modelski, George. 1978. "The Long Cycle of Global Politics and the Nation-State." *Comparative Studies in Society and History* 20: 214–35.

———. 1981. "Long Cycles, Kondratieffs, and Alternating Innovations: Implications for U.S. Foreign Policy." In Charles W. Kegley and Patrick McGowan, eds., *The Political Economy of Foreign Policy Behavior*. Beverly Hills: Sage.

Modelski, George, and William R. Thompson. 1987. "Testing Cobweb Models of the Long Cycle." In George Modelski, ed., *Exploring Long Cycles*. Boulder, Colo.: Lynne Rienner.

———. 1988. *Sea Power in Global Politics, 1494–1983*. Seattle: University of Washington Press.

Morgenthau, Hans J., and Kenneth W. Thompson. 1985. *Politics Among Nations: The Struggle for Power and Peace*. 6th ed. New York: Knopf.

Most, Benjamin A., and Harvey Starr. 1980. "Diffusion, Reinforcement, Geopolitics, and the Spread of War." *American Political Science Review* 74: 932–46.

———. 1987. "Polarity, Preponderance and Power Parity in the Generation of International Conflict." *International Interactions* 13: 225–62.

———. 1989. *Inquiry, Logic and International Politics*. Columbia: University of South Carolina Press.

Most, Benjamin A., Harvey Starr, and Randolph M. Siverson. 1989. "The Logic and Study of the Diffusion of International Conflict." In Manus I. Midlarsky, ed., *Handbook of War Studies*. London: Unwin Hyman.

Moul, William B. 1989. "Measuring the 'Balance of Power': A Look at Some Numbers." *Review of International Studies* 15: 101–21.

Moyal, J. E. 1949. "The Distribution of Wars in Time." *Journal of the Royal Statistical Society* 112: 446–49.

Mueller, John. 1989. *Retreat from Doomsday: The Obsolescence of Major War*. New York: Basic Books.

Nagel, Jack H. 1975. *The Descriptive Analysis of Power*. New Haven: Yale University Press.

Nelson, Richard R., and Sidney G. Winter. 1978. "Forces Generating and Limiting Competition Under Schumpeterian Competition." *Bell Journal* 9: 524–48.

Nicholson, Michael. 1989. *Formal Theories in International Relations*. Cambridge: Cambridge University Press.

Niou, Emerson M. S., and Peter C. Ordeshook. 1990. "Stability in Anarchic International Systems." *American Political Science Review* 84: 1207–34.

Niou, Emerson M. S., Peter C. Ordeshook, and Gregory F. Rose. 1989. *The Balance of Power: Stability in International Systems*. New York: Cambridge University Press.

Nogee, Joseph L. 1975. "Polarity: An Ambiguous Concept." *Orbis* 18: 1193–1224.

North, Douglass C. 1981. *Structure and Change in Economic History*. New York: W. W. Norton.

Nye, Joseph S. 1988. "Neorealism and Neoliberalism." *World Politics* 40: 235–51.

———. 1990. *Bound to Lead: The Changing Nature of American Power*. New York: Basic Books.

Odell, John S. 1990. "Understanding International Trade Policies: An Emerging Synthesis." *World Politics* 43: 139–67.

Olson, Mancur. 1971. *The Logic of Collective Action: Public Goods and the Theory of Groups*. Cambridge: Harvard University Press.

———. 1982. *The Rise and Decline of Nations: Economic Growth, Stagflation, and Social Rigidities*. New Haven: Yale University Press.

✓Oneal, John R. 1989. "Measuring the Material Base of the Contemporary East-West Balance." *International Interactions* 15: 177–96.

Organski, A. F. K. 1958. *World Politics*. New York: Knopf.

Organski, A. F. K., and Jacek Kugler. 1980. *The War Ledger*. Chicago: University of Chicago Press.

Ostrom, Charles W., and John H. Aldrich. 1978. "The Relationship Between Size and Stability in the Major Power International System." *American Journal of Political Science* 22: 743–71.

Oye, Kenneth A. 1985. "Explaining Cooperation Under Anarchy: Hypotheses and Strategies." *World Politics* 38: 1–24.

———. 1992. *Economic Discrimination and Political Exchange: World Political Economy in the 1930s and 1980s*. Princeton: Princeton University Press.

Polachek, Solomon W. 1978. "Dyadic Disputes: An Economic Perspective." *Papers of the Peace Science Society* 28: 67–80.

———. 1980. "Conflict and Trade." *Journal of Conflict Resolution* 24: 55–78.

Pollins, Brian M. 1989a. "Does Trade Still Follow the Flag?" *American Political Science Review* 83: 465–80.

———. 1989b. "Conflict, Cooperation, and Commerce: The Effects of International Political Interactions on Bilateral Trade Flows." *American Journal of Political Science* 33: 737–61.

Pomfret, Richard. 1988. *Unequal Trade: The Economics of Discriminatory International Trade Policies*. Oxford: Basil Blackwell.

Posen, Barry R. 1984. *The Sources of Military Doctrine: France, Britain, and Germany Between the World Wars*. Ithaca: Cornell University Press.

Prais, S. J. 1974. "A New Look at the Growth of Industrial Concentration." *Oxford Economic Papers* 26: 273–88.

Rao, Potluri, and Zvi Griliches. 1969. "Small-Sample Properties of Several Two-Stage Regression Methods in the Context of Auto-Correlated Errors." *Journal of the American Statistical Association* 64: 253–72.

Rapkin, David P., and William R. Thompson with Jon A. Christopherson. 1979. "Bipolarity and Bipolarization in the Cold War Era: Conceptualization, Measurement, and Validation." *Journal of Conflict Resolution* 23: 261–95.

Ray, James Lee, and J. David Singer. 1973. "Measuring the Concentration of Power in the International System." *Sociological Methods and Research* 1: 403–37.

Rich, Norman. 1985. *Why the Crimean War? A Cautionary Tale*. Hanover, N.H.: University Press of New England.

Richardson, Lewis F. 1944. "The Distribution of Wars in Time." *Journal of the Royal Statistical Society* 107: 242–50.

———. 1960a. *Statistics of Deadly Quarrels*. Pittsburgh: Boxwood Press.

———. 1960b. *Arms and Insecurity*. Pittsburgh: Boxwood Press.

Roemer, John E. 1977. "The Effect of Sphere of Influence and Economic Distance on the Commodity Composition of Trade in Manufactures." *Review of Economics and Statistics* 59: 318–27.

Rosecrance, Richard. 1963. *Action and Reaction in World Politics*. Boston: Little, Brown.

———. 1966. "Bipolarity, Multipolarity, and the Future." *Journal of Conflict Resolution* 10: 314–27.

———. 1986. *The Rise of the Trading State: Commerce and Conquest in the Modern World*. New York: Basic Books.

Ruggie, John Gerard. 1983. "Continuity and Transformation in the World Polity: Toward a Neorealist Synthesis." *World Politics* 35: 261–85.

Russett, Bruce M., ed. 1968a. *Economic Theories of International Politics*. Chicago: Markham.

———. 1968b. "Is There a Long-Run Trend Toward Concentration in the International System?" In Bruce M. Russett, ed., *Economic Theories of International Politics*. Chicago: Markham.

———. 1968c. "Components of an Operational Theory of International Alliance Formation." *Journal of Conflict Resolution* 12: 285–301.

———. 1985. "The Mysterious Case of Vanishing Hegemony." *International Organization* 39: 207–32.

Russett, Bruce M., and John D. Sullivan. 1971. "Collective Goods and International Organization." *International Organization* 25: 845–65.

Schelling, Thomas C. 1978. *Micromotives and Macrobehavior*. New York: W. W. Norton.

Scherer, F. M. 1979. *Industrial Market Structure and Economic Performance*. 2d ed. Chicago: Rand McNally.

Schroeder, Paul W. 1977. *Austria, Great Britain, and the Crimean War: The Destruction of the European Concert*. Ithaca: Cornell University Press.

———. 1986. "The 19th Century International System: Changes in the Structure." *World Politics* 39: 1–26.

Schweller, Randall L. 1993. "Tripolarity and the Second World War." *International Studies Quarterly* 37: 73–103.

Simon, Herbert A., and Charles P. Bonini. 1958. "The Size Distribution of Business Firms." *American Economic Review* 48: 607–17.

Singer, J. David, Stuart Bremer, and John Stuckey. 1972. "Capability Distribution, Uncertainty, and Major Power Wars, 1820–1965." In Bruce M. Russett, ed., *Peace, War, and Numbers*. Beverly Hills: Sage.

Singer, J. David, and Melvin Small. 1968. "Alliance Aggregation and the Onset of War, 1816–1945." In J. David Singer, ed., *Quantitative International Politics*. New York: Free Press.

———. 1972. *The Wages of War, 1816–1965: A Statistical Handbook*. New York: John Wiley.

Siverson, Randolph M., and Harvey Starr. 1990. "Opportunity, Willingness, and the Diffusion of War." *American Political Science Review* 84: 47–67.

Siverson, Randolph M., and Joel King. 1979. "Alliances and the Expansion of War, 1815–1965." In J. David Singer and Michael Wallace, eds., *To Augur Well: The Design and Use of Early Warning Indicators in Inter-state Conflict*. Beverly Hills: Sage.

Siverson, Randolph M., and Michael P. Sullivan. 1983. "The Distribution of Power and the Onset of War." *Journal of Conflict Resolution* 27: 473–94.

Small, Melvin, and J. David Singer. 1979. "Conflict in the International System, 1816–1977: Historical Trends and Policy Futures." In J. David Singer, ed., *Explaining War*. Beverly Hills: Sage.

———. 1982. *Resort to Arms: International and Civil Wars, 1816–1980*. Beverly Hills: Sage.

Snidal, Duncan. 1985a. "The Limitations of Hegemonic Stability Theory." *International Organization* 39: 579–614.

———. 1985b. "Coordination versus Prisoners' Dilemma: Implications for International Cooperation and Regimes." *American Political Science Review* 79: 923–42.

———. 1991. "Relative Gains and the Pattern of Cooperation." *American Political Science Review* 85: 701–26.

Snyder, Glenn H. 1965. "The Balance of Power and the Balance of Terror." In Paul Seabury, ed., *The Balance of Power*. San Francisco: Chandler.

———. 1984. "The Security Dilemma in Alliance Politics." *World Politics* 36: 461–95.

Snyder, Glenn H., and Paul Diesing. 1977. *Conflict Among Nations: Bargaining, Decision Making, and System Structure in International Crises*. Princeton: Princeton University Press.

Spiezio, K. Edward. 1990. "British Hegemony and Major Power War, 1815–1939: An Empirical Test of Gilpin's Model of Hegemonic Governance." *International Studies Quarterly* 34: 165–81.

Spiro, David E. [Forthcoming.] *Hegemony Unbound: The International Political Economy of Recycling Petrodollars*. Ithaca: Cornell University Press.

Sprout, Harold, and Margaret Sprout. 1965. *The Ecological Perspective on Human Affairs with Special Reference to International Politics*. Princeton: Princeton University Press.

Starr, Harvey, and Benjamin A. Most. 1976. "The Substance and Study of Borders in International Relations Research." *International Studies Quarterly* 20: 581–620.

Stein, Arthur A. 1984. "The Hegemon's Dilemma: Great Britain, the United States, and the International Economic Order." *International Organization* 38: 355–86.

Stoll, Richard J., and Michael Champion. 1985. "Capability Concentration, Alliance Bonding, and Conflict Among the Major Powers." In Alan Ned Sabrosky, ed., *Polarity and War: The Changing Structure of International Conflict*. Boulder, Colo.: Westview.

Strange, Susan. 1987. "The Persistent Myth of Lost Hegemony." *International Organization* 41: 551–74.

———. 1988. *States and Markets*. New York: Basil Blackwell.

Summers, Robert, and Alan Heston. 1984. "Improved International Comparisons of Real Product and Its Composition." *Review of Income and Wealth* 30: 207–62.

Taagepera, Rein, and James Lee Ray. 1977. "A Generalized Index of Concentration." *Sociological Methods and Research* 5: 367–84.

Taylor, A. J. P. 1971. *The Struggle for Mastery in Europe: 1848–1918*. London: Oxford University Press.

Theil, H. 1967. *Economics and Information Theory*. Amsterdam: North-Holland.

Thompson, E. 1979. "An Economic Basis for the 'National Defense Argument' for Aiding Certain Industries." *Journal of Political Economy* 87: 1–36.

Thompson, William R. 1983a. "Cycles, Capabilities, and War: An Ecumenical View." In William R. Thompson, ed., *Contending Approaches to World System Analysis*. Beverly Hills: Sage.

———. 1983b. "Uneven Economic Growth, Systemic Challenges, and Global Wars." *International Studies Quarterly* 27: 341–55.

———. 1988. *On Global War: Historical-Structural Approaches to World Politics*. Columbia: University of South Carolina Press.

Thompson, William R., and Karen A. Rasler. 1988. "War and Systemic Capability Reconcentration." *Journal of Conflict Resolution* 32: 335–66.

Thompson, William R., and L. Gary Zuk. 1982. "War, Inflation, and the Kondratieff Long Wave." *Journal of Conflict Resolution* 26: 621–44.

Thomson, David. 1981. *Europe Since Napoleon*. 2d ed. New York: Alfred A. Knopf.

Thucydides. 1954. *The Peloponnesian War*. Translated by R. Warner. New York: Penguin.

Tobin, James. 1958. "Estimation of Relationships for Limited Dependent Variables." *Econometrica* 26: 24–36.

Toynbee, Arnold J. 1954. *A Study of History*, vol. 9. New York: Oxford University Press.

Vagts, Alfred. 1956. *Defense and Diplomacy: The Soldier and the Conduct of Foreign Relations*. New York: King's Crown.

Vasquez, John A. 1986. "Capability, Types of War, Peace." *Western Political Quarterly* 38: 313–27.

———. 1987. "The Steps to War: Toward a Scientific Understanding of the Correlates of War Findings." *World Politics* 40: 108–45.

Väyrynen, Raimo. 1983. "Economic Cycles, Power Transitions, Political Management and Wars Between Major Powers." *International Studies Quarterly* 27: 389–418.

Viner, Jacob. 1948. "Power versus Plenty as Objectives of Foreign Policy in the Seventeenth and Eighteenth Centuries." *World Politics* 1: 1–29.

———. 1951. "Peace as an Economic Problem." In Jacob Viner, ed., *International Economics*. Glencoe, Ill.: Free Press.

Wagner, R. Harrison. 1986. "The Theory of Games and the Balance of Power." *World Politics* 38: 546–76.

———. 1993. "What Was Bipolarity?" *International Organization* 47: 77–106.

Wallace, Michael D. 1973. "Alliance Polarization, Cross-Cutting, and International War, 1815–1964: A Measurement Procedure and Some Preliminary Evidence." *Journal of Conflict Resolution* 17: 575–604.

Wallerstein, Immanuel. 1974. *The Modern World System: Capitalist Agriculture and the Origins of the European World-Economy in the Sixteenth Century*. New York: Academic Press.

———. 1983. "The Three Instances of Hegemony in the History of the Capitalist

World-Economy." *International Journal of Comparative Sociology* 24: 100–108.

Walt, Stephen M. 1987. *The Origins of Alliances*. Ithaca: Cornell University Press.

Waltz, Kenneth N. 1959. *Man, the State, and War*. New York: Columbia University Press.

———. 1964. "The Stability of a Bipolar World." *Daedalus* 93: 881–909.

———. 1970. "The Myth of National Interdependence." In Charles P. Kindleberger, ed., *The Multinational Corporation*. Cambridge: MIT Press.

———. 1979. *Theory of International Politics*. Reading: Addison-Wesley.

———. 1986. "Reflections on *Theory of International Politics*: A Response to My Critics." In Robert O. Keohane, ed., *Neorealism and Its Critics*. New York: Columbia University Press.

———. 1989. "The Origins of War in Neorealist Theory." In Robert I. Rotberg and Theodore K. Rabb, eds., *The Origin and Prevention of Major Wars*. New York: Cambridge University Press.

Waterson, Michael. 1984. *Economic Theory of the Industry*. Cambridge: Cambridge University Press.

Wayman, Frank Whelon. 1984. "Bipolarity and War: The Role of Capability Concentration and Alliance Patterns Among Major Powers, 1816–1965." *Journal of Peace Research* 21: 61–78.

Wayman, Frank Whelon, and T. Clifton Morgan. 1990. "Measuring Polarity in the International System." In J. David Singer and Paul F. Diehl, eds., *Measuring the Correlates of War*. Ann Arbor: University of Michigan Press.

Wendt, Alexander. 1992. "Anarchy Is What States Make of It: The Social Construction of Power Politics." *International Organization* 46: 391–425.

White, Halbert. 1980. "A Heteroskedasticity-Consistent Covariance Matrix Estimator and a Direct Test for Heteroskedasticity." *Econometrica* 48: 817–38.

Wilkinson, David. 1980. *Deadly Quarrels: Lewis F. Richardson and the Statistical Study of War*. Berkeley: University of California Press.

Wolfers, Arnold. 1962. *Discord and Collaboration: Essays on International Politics*. Baltimore: Johns Hopkins University Press.

Wolfson, Murray, Anil Puri, and Mario Martelli. 1992. "The Nonlinear Dynamics of International Conflict." *Journal of Conflict Resolution* 36: 119–49.

World Bank. 1983. *China: Socialist Economic Development*, vol. 1. Washington, D.C.: World Bank.

Wright, Quincy. 1965. *A Study of War*. 2d ed. Chicago: University of Chicago Press.

Zarnowitz, Victor. 1985. "Recent Work on Business Cycles in Historical Perspective: A Review of Theories and Evidence." *Journal of Economic Literature* 23: 523–80.

Zinnes, Dina A. 1970. "Coalition Theories and the Balance of Power." In S. Groennings, E. W. Kelly, and M. Leiserson, eds., *The Study of Coalition Behavior: Theoretical Perspectives and Cases from Four Continents*. New York: Holt, Rinehart and Winston.

———. 1976. *Contemporary Research in International Relations*. New York: Free Press.

———. 1980. "Why War? Evidence on the Outbreak of International Conflict." In Ted Robert Gurr, ed., *Handbook of Political Conflict: Theory and Research*. New York: Free Press.

INDEX